100
HIKES in™ the

INLAND
NORTHWEST
SECOND EDITION

100
HIKES in™ the

INLAND
NORTHWEST
Eastern Washington • Northern Rockies • Wallowas

SECOND EDITION

Rich Landers
and the Spokane Mountaineers

THE MOUNTAINEERS BOOKS

Published by
The Mountaineers Books
1001 SW Klickitat Way, Suite 201
Seattle, WA 98134

First edition, 1987; second edition 2003

No part of this book may be reproduced in any form, or by any electronic, mechanical, or other means, without permission in writing from the publisher.

Published simultaneously in Great Britain by Cordee, 3a DeMontfort Street, Leicester, England, LE1 7HD

Manufactured in Canada

Project Editor: Laura Slavik
Editor: Paula Thurman
Cover and Book Design: The Mountaineers Books
Layout: Jennifer LaRock Shontz
Mapmaker: Marge Mueller, Gray Mouse Graphics
Photographer: All photographs by Rich Landers unless otherwise noted

Cover photograph: *Hub Lake in the Bitterroot Mountains of Montana*
Frontispiece: *Glacier lilies at Chimney Rock in the Idaho Selkirk Mountains*

Library of Congress Cataloging-in-Publication Data
Landers, Rich, 1953-
  100 Hikes in the Inland Northwest : Eastern Washington-Northern
Rockies-Wallowas / By Rich Landers and the Spokane Mountaineers.— 2nd ed.
    p. cm.
Includes bibliographical references and index.
  ISBN 0-89886-908-0 (pbk.)
1. Hiking—Washington (State)—Spokane Region—Guidebooks.
2. Hiking—Northwest, Pacific—Guidebooks. 3. Spokane Region
(Wash.)—Guidebooks. 4. Northwest, Pacific—Guidebooks. I. Title: One
hundred hikes in the Inland Northwest. II. Spokane Mountaineers (Club)
III. Title.
  GV199.42.W22S64 2003
  917.97'37—dc21
                          2002155240

 Printed on recycled paper

DEDICATION

In memory of John Carter, Suzie McDonald, and Don Hutchings,

who were as helpful to people as they were to trails and the completion

of this book; in reverence to Tom Rogers, father of the Dishman Hills;

in appreciation to Ida Rowe Dolphin, always the teacher and model of

loveliness; in veneration of The Lands Council founder John Osborn

and his commitment to conservation; in honor of Ken Mondal, the first

person to hike all 100 of the original hikes as well as Judy Waring and

the "Amazon Women" who were hot on his heels; and with fondness to

hiking families, without whom we'd be walking through life alone.

CONTENTS

COLUMBIA RIVER BASIN

Columbia River

Grand Coulee

Crab Creek

COLVILLE NATIONAL FOREST

Kettle River Range

Pend Oreille River

Sullivan Lake

Salmo River

AROUND SPOKANE/COEUR D'ALENE

Spokane River

LOLO NATIONAL FOREST

Thompson River

IDAHO PANHANDLE NATIONAL FORESTS

COEUR D'ALENE RIVER DISTRICT

PRIEST LAKE DISTRICT

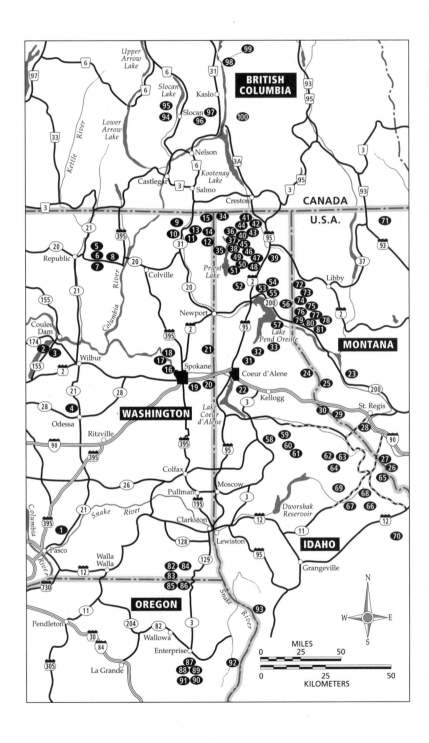

KEY TO MAP SYMBOLS

═══════ freeway	ⓟ parking
++++++++++ railroad	ⓣⓗ trailhead
▬▬▬▬ paved road	♦ ranger station
══════ gravel or dirt road	⌂ building
========= primitive (walking) road	⁚⁚ buildings in town
············· trail described in text	▲ campground
- - - - - - trail not described in text	开 picnic area
················ cross-country route described in text	◼ backcountry shelter
················ cross-country route not described in text	⌂ backcountry campsite
·—··—· boundary (park or wilderness area)	🛈 lookout
	✕ mine
	)(pass
·—··—· state line	][bridge
··—·—· powerline	•—• gate
•—•—• ski lift	ρ spring
(84) interstate highway	river or stream
(97) US highway	waterfall
(291) state highway	lake
[26] county highway	marsh
[3060] National Forest road	glacier
/643/ trail number	

KOOTENAI NATIONAL FOREST

Tobbaco River

UMATILLA NATIONAL FOREST

Blue Mountains

WALLOWA-WHITMAN NATIONAL FOREST

Wallowa Mountains

HELLS CANYON NATIONAL RECREATION AREA

Snake River

BRITISH COLUMBIA

PREFACE

This guidebook, massively revised in this edition, originated in 1984 as a project of the Spokane Mountaineers, a club based in Spokane, Washington, for people who are active in the outdoors. Although the Spokane Mountaineers is a separate organization from the publisher of this book, The Mountaineers based in Seattle, the two groups have much in common, including a love for Northwest wild places.

The by-laws of the Spokane Mountaineers express broad and noble goals:

> "To encourage a spirit of good fellowship among lovers of outdoor life; to maintain a program of mountaineering trips, including mountain climbing, scrambling, backpacking, hiking, skiing, ski touring, snowshoeing and bicycling, and provide capable and experienced leadership for all trips; to educate aspiring mountaineers in the skills of mountaincraft; to endorse the principles of mountain safety as prescribed by the climbing code and, when called upon, to provide all possible aid to mountain accident victims; to create greater public awareness of the intrinsic value of our wilderness, forests, waters, primitive parks, and monument lands and to seek the preservation of the natural beauty and scenic value of this national heritage; to preserve by the encouragement of protective legislation or otherwise the natural beauty of our great out-of-doors."

This guidebook was compiled with the assistance of many helpers, young and old, over the years. They provided legwork, advice, verification, and good company. The author offers special thanks for assistance from dedicated professionals within British Columbia Parks, the U.S. Forest Service, and the U.S. Bureau of Land Management, plus the dedicated conservationists who are working with them and watching over them.

Feedback Welcomed
Comments and suggestions for future updates to this book are encouraged. Contact author Rich Landers through The Mountaineers Books, 1001 SW Klickitat Way, Suite 201, Seattle, WA 98134; email *mbooks@mountaineers.org*.

Eagle Cap Peak from Moccasin Lake

INTRODUCTION

The Inland Northwest defies boundaries that make for neat, tidy, marketable guidebook titles. This book did not focus on becoming *100 Hikes in Idaho* because such a book would have to ignore too many choice destinations at the north end of the state. It is not *100 Hikes in the Cabinet Mountains Wilderness* because 10 detailed trip reports are enough to pique a hiker's interest in that exceptional area and still leave a little room to discover. This guide was not designed for maximum retail profits. It is tailored for people lucky enough to live in this wonderful inland refuge from big-city life, as well as for hikers savvy enough to come here for a backcountry getaway.

WHERE IN THE WORLD IS THE INLAND NORTHWEST?
The Inland Northwest is the real estate roughly bordered on the west by the Okanogan and Columbia Rivers and on the east by the rugged Montana mountains jamming up to form the Continental Divide. The imaginary boundary slips south slightly into Oregon and north a smidgen into the glaciered mountains of Canada.

The Inland Northwest includes the population centers of Libby in Montana, of Nelson in British Columbia, of Enterprise in Oregon, of Coeur d'Alene, Sandpoint, Moscow, and Lewiston in Idaho, and of Spokane, Pullman, and Walla Walla in Washington. It also includes hundreds of thousands of acres, from sagebrush country to alpine meadows, populated only by wildlife and occasional human visitors. This book is designed to introduce hikers to some of the best routes in these diverse wild areas.

Roughly half of the Inland Northwest is public land, free of no trespassing signs and open for hunting, fishing, backpacking, and other uses. Within the imaginary boundaries are 16 million acres of national forests, 2 million acres of national parks and recreation areas, and portions of more than 6 million acres of officially designated or proposed wilderness areas. To put it simply, there's plenty of breathing room in the Inland Northwest and there probably always will be: The region is blessed with just enough glaciers, grizzly bears, and rattlesnakes to keep immigration to a trickle. It's a splendid area to explore on foot.

Times and Trails Are Changing
Much has transpired in the Inland Northwest backcountry since the original version of this guidebook went to print in 1987. Conservation programs have restored or protected thousands of acres from Eastern Washington's channeled scablands to the natural area along the Little Spokane River in Spokane. More than 15,000 acres were annexed and protected on the flanks of Kokanee Glacier Provincial Park in British Columbia in 1995.

Improvements have been made to many trails. For instance, the loop routes created around Sherman Peak and Columbia Mountain in the Kettle River Mountains are the work of recreation planners who know what hikers like.

Natural forces are at work, of course, such as the forest fires that changed the look of the Kettle Crest Trail near Sherman Peak and the decomposition of trapper cabins from bygone eras. The marvelous trip to Kokanee Glacier's Joker Lakes has been deleted from this book revision as park managers are letting vegetation overtake the trail to discourage increasing numbers of hikers from a grizzly bear haven. The "Giant White Pine" that was the centerpiece for a hike in the original book is no longer standing. The tree was a seedling when Columbus made his first voyage in 1492, but with its base rotting more than five centuries later, the 200 footer was felled for the safety of the area's many visitors.

Unfortunately, the bulk of the changes are not so natural. Private land-owners have posed issues with access to public lands at areas such as the Juniper Dunes Wilderness and the east end of Bee Top Ridge north of Lake Pend Oreille. Tools and items from the early 1900s that were left and remarkably well preserved at the Silver Spray Mine in Kokanee Glacier Park have been pilfered a few at a time by people who couldn't leave them be. Father Peter DeSmet tells us that people weren't always that way. The Jesuit missionary who named some of the prominent destinations found in this book wrote this observation in the 1800s of the Kootenai Indians, the region's original models of trust:

"Their honesty is so great and so well known, that the trader leaves his storehouse entirely, the door remaining unlocked often during his absences of weeks. The Indians go in and out and help themselves to what they need, and settle with the trader in his return.... In doing business with them in this style he never lost the value of a pin."

More recently, development and logging continue to whittle away at wild areas. A proposed copper and silver mine threatens the integrity not only of the Cabinet Mountains Wilderness but also of the water quality so important to the people and wildlife around Lake Pend Oreille. Where Indian paintbrush once dominated the roadsides in the Bitterroot Mountains south of Hoodoo Pass, spotted knapweed now proliferates. Some land managers say the invasion of noxious weeds is the most serious threat unfolding for native flora and fauna in the backcountry.

But that brings us to the most blatant and obnoxious modern change to the landscape.

The Invasion of Off-Road Vehicles

Motorized vehicles, and all the noise, pollution, weed spreading, and erosion that comes along for the ride, are pounding at the door of the wilderness experience. Some land management agencies have drawn the line, saying motorcycles, four-wheel all-terrain vehicles (ATVs), and other off-road vehicles (ORVs) are fine, but not beyond a certain point.

Silver Spray Cabin outhouse, Kokanee Glacier Provincial Park

However, the machines come anyway, sometimes with official blessing. ORVs are big business, and their sales started soaring in the 1990s. The motorized industry hires full-time lobbyists to make in-roads, and they've been terribly effective. The most shocking examples are on the Idaho Panhandle National Forests and especially on the Clearwater National Forest, where motorized vehicles have been allowed in areas the Forest Service has proposed as the Great Burn Wilderness. Even motorcyclists are annoyed at how ATVs have been transforming interesting single-track trails into road-width raceways.

Hikers cannot afford to ignore this issue. Other groups should be wary too, including anglers, horse riders, and especially hunters, since research has clearly shown that mature bull elk and mule deer bucks disappear quickly in heavily roaded or trailed forests where motorized vehicles are allowed. Two trips have been added to this book in the proposed Great Burn Wilderness (see Hikes 26 and 65) primarily because they are premier hiking destinations, but also to bring the non-motorized public closer to Fish Lake and the threats to wildlands that are manifested there.

The Cause for Conservation

Most of the region's choice wildlife viewing and walking areas are threatened by some form of intrusion. Hikers would do themselves a favor by tuning in to the ongoing debates over maintaining the integrity of national forest roadless areas. For perspective, consider that the 1951 United States Geological Survey (USGS) Mount Pend Oreille quadrangle showed only about 18 miles of roads. The 1974 Idaho Panhandle National Forests travel plan showed more than 140 miles of roads in that area. The road system continued to grow until the 1990s, when conservationists finally started getting through to taxpayers that their money was being wasted on subsidized roads that the national forests could no longer afford to maintain. At the turn of the millennium, the Idaho Panhandle National Forests had 11,400 miles of inventoried roads. Even foresters admit that's a senselessly high mileage that's had a serious impact on water quality and fisheries. The tide is turning, and the Panhandle Forests have been obliterating more roads than they've been building in recent years. In many cases, hikes start on closed logging roads that once gave vehicle access higher into the mountains. But there's a vocal contingent of motorized users who want those roads back, and more.

While islands of protected wilderness are found within the boundaries of the Inland Northwest, it is sobering to realize that most of our favorite retreats have little or no official protection from development. The wide open spaces might always be here, but what good will they be if the trees become stumps and the trails become roads and the trout streams become silt-choked funnels for erosion? Local conservationists are fighting gallant battles that deserve much more support, from urban issues at Tubbs Hill in Coeur d'Alene to the watch to make sure that Long Canyon remains one of the last unroaded drainages in the Idaho Selkirk Mountains.

Will Rogers clearly spelled out why people must stand up for what's left of our natural landscape. As he put it, when it comes to land, "They ain't makin' it no more."

Disappearing Trails

Hundreds of miles of trails in this region are being destroyed or neglected. It's a national trend. In 1944, the Forest Service was maintaining about 150,000 miles of trails and about 107,000 miles of roads. By 1983, trails had decreased 34 percent to about 98,800 miles while roads had increased more than 200 percent to about 321,000 miles. Many additional trails have been abandoned since aircraft have replaced lookouts and fire crews in fighting forest fires. Many other trails have simply been gobbled up by roads and clearcuts.

Trails aren't always a major consideration in the Forest Service's "services" anymore. For example, the Idaho Panhandle's St. Joe River District might have only four staffers to maintain 800 miles of trail. This explains why hundreds of miles of trails that look inviting on a map turn out to be disappointing, if not totally eliminated by neglect. This book can't do anything about the trend other than to alert its readers and hope they protest with constructive comments to the proper politicians and agencies. (See Appendix C for a list of agencies.) Volunteer trail maintenance and conservation opportunities also are available. (See Appendix E for a list of organizations.)

Keep in mind that within the Forest Service are many dedicated workers who love the land and believe in trails. Some of them get great pleasure in milking dimes out of sparse budgets and muscling into the hard work of making trails friendly to our feet. They deserve our thanks, over and over again.

Trails Need Friends

People have blasted guidebooks as evil works that encourage crowds to get out and trample the wildflowers. Please study the section "Heading Out on Foot" and learn the techniques for treading lightly on these places. Pack out your garbage and sack up some that's been left behind by less considerate people. Camp as far as possible from the fragile shores of lakes and streams and keep their waters pure by going far away to use soap or latrines. Avoid campfires when possible and never cut or scar a living tree.

That said, there should be no remorse in selling this guidebook or in buying it. First, it's one of the few guidebooks of its kind that earmarks profits for trail-related projects. Significant contributions have been made to projects such as restoring the Little Snowy Top Lookout in the Salmo-Priest Wilderness, as well as to building the Snow Peak Cabin in the Kettle River Range, West Fork Cabin in the Selkirks, and the new cabin that replaces the Slocan Chief Cabin in Kokanee Glacier National Park. Thousands of dollars have been donated to support volunteers who rerouted trails and restored meadows in the Selkirk Mountains at Pyramid and Ball Lakes and for trail signage at Mount Spokane State Park.

The book makes a more significant contribution, however. Everyone who follows these routes is likely to be another friend of Inland Northwest hiking trails. People who see the peaks, meadows, and lakes along these routes can't help but become advocates who will help protect them against interests that see no good in wildlands because they selfishly can see no profit in letting them be wild. So read on, hike on, and be a good friend to the trails.

Little Snowy Top Lookout was restored by volunteers and by funds from the first edition of this guidebook.

How to Use This Guidebook

This book does not seek to tell everything about the trails and areas it describes. A hiker who doesn't want to put any effort into exploring a trail and its surrounding area needs a guide, not a guidebook.

This book purposely leaves out some detail for two major reasons. First, all surprises shouldn't be ruined. Hikers should be looking and discovering with every step down a trail. Second, since people and nature never quit tinkering with the land, detailed information has a way of being out-of-date before it's out in print. New roads, clearcuts, and other man-made alterations are constantly being made and nature never stops its doodling with wind, fire, flood, drought, and other modes of change.

The trips are organized by region and management authority. The following information is summarized for each of the featured 100 hikes:

Distance: Usually a round-trip distance for the hike, although variations can occur according to the possibilities described in the text.

Hiking time: Figures allow time for the average steady walker to take a few breaks and snap a few photos; "overnight" identifies hikes suitable for camping.

Difficulty: A subjective evaluation to give hikers a quick reference to skills required. Generally, the term *easy* means well-defined trails with little elevation gain; *moderate* means rougher trails and more elevation gain and possibly more remoteness; *difficult* means trails could be sketchy in some areas and terrain can be steep, rough, or remote. Distances could be long. The text will elaborate.

Hiking season: Months the trails typically are accessible, reasonably free of snow, and suitable for walking.

Maps: The name of the U.S. Geological Survey (USGS) topographical map or other agencies' maps covering the hike.

Information: Who to contact for up-to-date trail access information, fee requirements, bear activity, and additional maps. (Appendix C has contact details for each source.)

Elevation profiles: Charts help peg the difficulty of each hike by visually displaying a route's elevation gain and loss.

Narrative: Text for each hike discusses directions to the trailhead and gives a brief description of the hike, including information on landmarks, history, possible difficulties that might be encountered, and the availability of additional hiking options and bonus activities such as berry picking and fishing.

Permits and Fees

A trend emerged in the 1990s to charge fees for parking or recreating on public lands, and it's not likely to fade away. This book does not list specific fee requirements because they are so unsettled. The Wallowa-Whitman National Forest (Eagle Cap Wilderness and Hells Canyon National Recreation Area) and the Umatilla National Forest (Wenaha-Tucannon Wilderness) were among the first areas covered in this book to require a trailhead parking pass. Other state and federal areas are likely to follow. Always contact land management agencies before heading into new territory (see "Information" above). Ask for road and trail updates, and whether any fees or permits are required.

Making Way with Maps

This book and the maps it contains are not designed to replace the need for topographical maps produced by the U.S. Geological Survey or Natural Resources Canada. The maps recommended for each hike are as essential as the boots on your feet. Maps of 1:100,000 scale, such as those in popular statewide topo map booklets, are useful for overall planning and road travel, but more detailed maps of 1:24,000 scale are necessary for off-trail travel and scrambling. High-tech companies are producing impressive mapping software that enables users to customize topographic maps for each trip. The weakness in maps produced at home is in the size of the page, the quality of the printing, and the susceptibility of the ink to moisture.

Beyond topos, it's essential to get the big picture, especially when driving forest roads and hiking backcountry trails. Carry additional references, such as appropriate Forest Service road maps.

The hikes in this book are scattered through public lands managed by agencies ranging from state and provincial parks and forestry districts to local government agencies. Forest Service and Bureau of Land Management maps can be purchased from some businesses or they can be ordered directly from land management offices. In some cases, special wilderness maps also have been published. They are highly recommended.

In Canada, the privately produced *Backroad Mapbook* for the Kootenays (Mussio Ventures) is widely available and useful for navigating forest roads. See Appendix D for a list of map sources.

HEADING OUT ON FOOT

All a modern pilgrim needs to explore the wilds on foot is a pack load of equipment (more or less depending on the length of the visit) and some idea of how to use it, a realistic evaluation of physical limitations, and a reasonable level of fitness.

Getting Tuned

As the sunset hours of long mountain walks have approached, the fittest hikers have gasped the Tired Walker's Prayer: "If you pick 'em up, O Lord, I'll put 'em down." Anyone has the right to be tired after a hearty hike, but there's a difference between being pooped out and being knotted in a ball of cramps and blisters. Some sort of pre-trip fitness program should be included in the preparation for a backpacking trip. This book includes hikes with numerous options for length and difficulty. Many of the day hikes are perfect training walks for the longer backpacks.

Day hiking, incidentally, is a dandy way to explore new areas without the trauma a heavy backpack inflicts to the back and knees. Even on multi-day trips, consider car-camping and hiking several different hikes or trails in a weekend, coming back to a cooler full of fresh food and cold beverages, fold-up chairs, and perhaps a water container wrapped in a black plastic bag—solar-heated for a warm shower!

Be Realistic
Backpackers should either prepare their bodies for the trip or modify the trip to the limitations of their bodies. Make sure the same considerations have been made for others in the party. Especially during the heat of the summer, it's often important to get up early so most of the mileage can be logged during the coolest part of the day. This also allows some grace time, should unexpected discoveries or emergencies occur along the trail. In the words of Ben Franklin, "He that riseth late must trot all day."

Hikers have good reason to eat heartily and drink far more water than they think they need. Always carry water. Dress in layers that can be added or peeled off to keep body thermostats working in the comfort range. Avoid any rush that might tempt group members to neglect first aid to the inevitable hot spots on their feet. These are buds ready to bloom into juicy blisters if moleskin or other blister prevention isn't applied immediately. For more reasons than one, it's good to stop occasionally for a snack, a photograph, or a moment of nature observation. As Gandhi said, "There's more to life than increasing its speed."

Hiking with Kids
Years of experience in hiking with children can pretty much be boiled down to a simple formula for success:

Tailor the walk to their abilities. Let them wander and set the pace, but don't be afraid to point out every now and then that a "fairy" has stashed some M&M's for good little hikers in a secret spot just up the trail. Hydration is particularly important for kids. Get them a hydration system so they can suck regularly on their own supply as they hike and they will be far less likely to be grumpy. (Same goes for adults.) And remember, kids don't care about the scenery much beyond stick-poking range. If you don't get to the top of the peak because it took an hour for the inchworm to walk up the kid's arm, no problem. A hike with kids is a journey, not a destination.

Gearing Up
Lightweight equipment such as tents, sleeping pads, and stoves eliminate the need to cut firewood for cooking or tree boughs for insulation and lean-tos. Modern gear makes it easier than ever to travel through the wilderness without leaving a trace of your visit. A list of recommended gear is published in Appendix B, but a few items require elaboration.

The Ten Essentials

First, never go anywhere in the backcountry—not even on the short day hikes covered in this book—without the Ten Essentials:

1. Map
2. Compass
3. Flashlight
4. Knife
5. Matches in waterproof container
6. Firestarter
7. Extra clothing
8. Extra food and water
9. First-aid kit
10. Sun protection (includes sunglasses and sunscreen)

Keep essential items in nylon or plastic bags in your equipment storage area so they can easily be transferred back and forth from day pack to backpack, depending on the trip of the day.

Other Gear

Clothing: Modern synthetic fabrics, fleeces, and breathable waterproof fabrics have revolutionized the way hikers dress. Unlike cotton, the synthetics fight hypothermia by wicking sweat from your skin, drying quickly, and offering warmth even when wet. The synthetics work even better than wool, although the heat from a fire can melt them. Modern nylon long-sleeve shirts and pants are so light, soft, and cool, they can be worn comfortably for protection from dirt, bugs, and sun.

Footwear: For short hikes on established trails, there's no need to spend a fortune on hiking boots. Rugged running or walking shoes are cheaper, more comfortable, and more functional in or out of the mountains. But if you plan a lot of backpacking and scrambling on and off trails, it's wise to consider the rugged but lightweight boots many manufacturers are making. Just be sure to break them in before tackling a substantial hike.

Rainwear: Always carry some sort of raingear. Consider a parka and pants made of a breathable waterproof fabric. While hiking through intermittent rain, it might be more convenient and less sweaty to forgo a rain jacket and simply drape a nylon poncho over your body and pack.

Sleeping bags: Down bags are expensive, but they're still the lightest and most compressible way to a warm night's sleep. Synthetic fills are good investments, though, and getting better all the time. They are a few ounces heavier than down and add a few inches of bulk to the pack, but they cost considerably less. A bag made with synthetic insulation will dry faster and retain warmth better when wet. Climbers have long known that they can carry a smaller, lighter bag by planning to wear their insulating clothing while sleeping.

Tents: Modern tents are a beauty to behold, light and strong and—if properly maintained and pitched—waterproof. Minimalists simply use a tarp to make a lean-to, but many hikers prefer the all-element protection (that includes protection from mosquitoes) of a tent. Consider taking a lightweight tarp in addition to a tent to use as a lean-to for eating in foul weather.

Packs: A huge topic in themselves, backpacks come with external or internal frames. Both have their devotees. Look them over. Talk to dealers, read sales material and reviews, try them on with weight in them to test for comfort, and then buy one. Just be sure it fits.

Organizing a Pack

Organizing a backpack is as personal as the way you arrange underwear in a chest of drawers. Nevertheless, keep frequently used items, such as maps, trail snacks, water container, insect repellent, and sunglasses, handy in the outside pockets of the pack. Organize gear in plastic bags or stuff sacks so it's protected from wetness and easy to find.

Dinners and breakfasts go in one bag buried in the pack. Lunches are packed in another bag near the top of the pack for easy access on the trail. Some items, such as powdered drinks, are ideal for stuffing in pots, helping to take advantage of every square inch of space in the pack. Large items, such as tents and camp shoes, can be strapped to the outside. A rain cover for the pack will keep everything dry. (See Appendix B for an equipment list.)

Wilderness Etiquette

Somewhere between 30 and 50 million Americans every year leave the cities—where people are employed to dispose of our garbage and sewage—to tramp through the wilderness where there is no one to pick up after them. The result in some areas has been devastating. The cumulative effects of all this nature loving has destroyed vegetation, eroded trails, polluted streams, and degraded some areas with human waste. For those who don't want the backcountry to go the way of the cities, here are some tips on wilderness etiquette.

Campsites: Sleep on rock slabs or in places already trampled by other campers rather than packing down another area of vegetation. Avoid camping on fragile shores of lakes and streams, especially when tenting on higher knolls and ridges probably will offer a better view and relief from bugs. Lightweight water bags can be carried empty, filled from a purified water source near camp, and strung up in a tree to provide handy water at dry sites. In the age of tents, tarps, and foam pads, cutting vegetation for shelter is to be done only in an emergency.

Soap: Never use soap near a lake or stream. Hikers who must use even biodegradable soap should lather up and rinse using a pot of water hauled well away from the shore.

Human waste: Dig personal latrines 200 feet from any trail, campsite, or water source. Schedule a short, pleasant walk from camp, perhaps. A personal latrine can be dug with a stick, rock, or boot heel in some soils. It only needs to be about 6 inches deep. Cover the waste with dirt and re-place the duff to hide the digging. Pack out toilet paper in plastic bags or, when fire danger is not an issue, carry a butane lighter to burn toilet paper before burying the waste. Few things are worse than walking into a lovely campsite surrounded by piles of wilting tissue. Scrape away the duff and burn the paper on bare dirt. Then be sure the ashes are cool before scraping them into the latrine for a proper burial.

Horses: When confronted with horse riders, give them the right of way. Walk toward the horses to make sure they see you, then step off the trail to the low side and let them pass. A few friendly words not only is a neigh-borly way to greet the rider, but also soothes the lead horse and alerts fol-lowing stock to your presence so they don't spook.

Party size: Keep groups small to minimize impact to camping areas. In grizzly country, the ideal group size is five or six.

Pets: Dogs can be good companions on hikes, although not everyone will agree, especially if a dog is noisy or aggressive. One hiker might think his dog is cute, but when it poops on the trail, barks at night, jumps on other people and their equipment, chases deer and squirrels, or ruins the fishing by taking a swim in a wilderness lake, anyone should be able to understand why others won't share the sentiments. Dogs that run ahead can trigger attacks by bears as well as by moose, elk, and deer, especially when the females have young. The attack might focus on the dog, but the dog always runs back to deliver the consequences to the accompanying people. If you insist on bringing a dog hiking, tend to it. Bury its droppings and carry a leash.

Garbage: Don't leave foil or waste in a fire pit. Never bury trash be-cause critters will soon dig it up. Pack out all garbage.

Camping with and without Campfires

In most cases, wilderness travelers should avoid campfires unless there's a designated fire pit or an urgent need. Sure, fires are romantic, but so are candles. Consider these good reasons for *not* building a campfire:

1. Campfires can start forest fires.
2. The smoke gets in your eyes and fouls your hair and clothes.
3. Sparks burn holes in expensive coats, tents, and raingear.
4. Light from the fire blots out the surroundings, including many of the stars. This leaves you in a little compartment even while visiting a vast wilderness.
5. Noise from the fire blares over sounds of owls, crickets, and coyotes.
6. Fire chars rocks and earth, leaving unsightly scars for other wilderness lovers to see.
7. Gathering fuel for fires has left many campsites bare of wood, and trees bare of branches as high as a camper can reach.
8. Fires are messier than stoves for cooking. A stove is ready instantly; a fire must burn down to coals before it's ready.

Fly fishing on the Upper Coeur d'Alene River

9. Fires take more time than stoves to extinguish. If there's no water, you must let a fire burn out completely and stir with dirt. Using water to douse the fire, putting it out before its time, leaves unsightly chunks of charred wood and a messy camp.

Hikers who insist on building fires should avoid making a fire ring with rocks. Gather wood from the ground rather than breaking dead branches off standing trees. Scrape away the duff down to bare dirt and build a *small* fire. Let it burn out to ashes so they can be extinguished, cooled, scooped, and scattered away from the campsite. Then replace the duff to hide the scorched ground.

Fishing the Backcountry

Most of the trails described in this book lead to, along, or near a lake or stream that holds fish. That's the nature of the Inland Northwest. Fish are common in the backcountry; so are anglers.

The supply of fish is not endless, however. Native backcountry fisheries, such as that of the west-slope cutthroat trout found in many northern Idaho streams, have evolved in relatively sterile mountain waters by eating virtually every food item they see. Thus, they are fairly easy to catch and are prone to being fished out. Most high mountain lake fisheries are not native, but rather introduced by man. Some of these fish are in lakes with access to inlets or outlets that allow cutthroats and rainbows to reproduce. Most of the high lakes, however, have no reproduction and must be stocked every three years or so.

Mountain fisheries are dynamic. Non-native golden trout are fading out of the stocked lake scene as hatchery egg supplies are disappearing. More grayling are being put in lakes and the Idaho Fish and Game Department is experimenting with sterile rainbows in some lakes and stocking a few bull trout and even tiger muskies in some waters to help thin out stunted brook trout. Incidentally, the limit on brook trout usually is much higher than for other trout because of their propensity to overpopulate. West-slope cutthroats are the most common stocked species in the region's high lakes because they are native to many of the watersheds. Concerns about the impact introduced fish are having on native amphibians is causing fish biologists to study and rethink their high-lake stocking programs. One thing is almost certain: new fisheries are not likely to be created in any of many lakes where stocking is not currently practiced.

Safety Considerations

The Ten Essentials recommended earlier are advised because backcountry hiking entails unavoidable risk. Hikers can minimize risks on the trail by being knowledgeable, prepared, and alert. This book is not designed to fully prepare hikers for exploring the backcountry. Many good general backpacking books are available. Also, backpacking courses are offered through clubs or schools in many communities (see Appendix E).

Look ahead. Leave a trip itinerary with a responsible person who will contact authorities should you not return on schedule. If adverse conditions are stacking up against your skill and conditioning, abandon the trip. Resort to an easier trail. It's better to bag a questionable outing than to be the subject of a mountain rescue.

Remember, cellular phones may not work everywhere in the backcountry, and even if they do, quick assistance may not be possible. The wilderness is a free and exciting place to visit, but it's not a place to be without common sense.

Water in the Wilderness

No one can unconditionally guarantee that a backcountry water source is safe for human consumption, not even from free-flowing streams in our most pristine wilderness. No reference to water sources in this book is a guarantee the water is safe to drink.

Playing it safe means either carrying water from home or treating water obtained in the backcountry to prevent contracting microorganisms that can cause illness. For example, giardiasis is an intestinal disorder caused by a microscopic organism, *Giardia lamblia*. This parasite is found all over the world and even in some treated municipal water systems in the Inland Northwest. *Giardia* are carried in the feces of some animals and humans. Cysts of *Giardia* can contaminate surface water supplies that look clear, feel cold, smell clean, and taste pure. One hiker might drink from a *Giardia*-infested stream and show no symptoms while another could in a couple of

Straight Creek Cascades, proposed Great Burn Wilderness

weeks start suffering diarrhea, loss of appetite, abdominal cramps, gas, and bloating.

With proper diagnosis, the disease is treatable by a physician, but prevention is the sanest route. First, help avoid the spread of *Giardia* by burying human waste far from water sources. Second, treat all water before drinking or even brushing teeth. Just as important, wash hands. A growing body of evidence suggests that fecal-to-mouth and food poisoning issues contribute as much or more than water to backcountry illness.

Boiling water is perhaps the surest method of fighting against the myriad organisms that can go bump in your tummy. If boiling is impossible, many experts say iodine treatments can be effective. The National Park Service, however, points out that while iodine (and less-effective chlorine compounds) work well against most waterborne bacteria and viruses, they are not as effective as heat in killing *Giardia*. They also have a very limited shelf life after being exposed to air. Be sure to carefully follow directions in treating water with chemicals, which are affected by water temperature, turbidity, and the length of treatment. Read the warnings and follow label directions on iodine tablets, and then double or triple the treatment time. When treatment is complete, a vitamin C tablet (citric acid) will neutralize the iodine taste.

Water purifiers have become indispensable to some hikers. Top models are effective and easily produce pure, good-tasting water. The filters should be field maintainable.

Hiking in Bear Country

An old joke explains the two sure ways to tell a grizzly from a black bear. When you see a bear, it is said, climb a tree. If the critter climbs up after you, it's a black bear; if it rips the tree out of the ground and shakes you out, it's a grizzly. However, since several of the hikes suggested in this book lead into grizzly country, hikers should take a little more serious approach to the subject.

All bears deserve respect. Grizzlies in particular are notorious for their infrequent but highly publicized attacks on humans. Check with park or forest rangers regarding bear activity, especially in prime grizzly habitat such as Canada's Purcell Mountains, Kokanee and Valhalla Provincial Parks, Salmo-Priest Country, and the Cabinet Mountains Wilderness. Avoid areas were recent bear problems have occurred.

Always cook, eat, and hang food away from sleeping areas. Properly stored food must be at least 4 feet from a tree trunk or branch that can support the weight of a bear, and 10 feet off the ground (see below). Bring plenty of cord. If a suitable hanging limb cannot be found on a single tree, make a "highline" by tossing a rock with cord attached over a limb and behind the trunk of one tree. Tie off one end and repeat the process with the same rock and cord on a nearby tree. Tie the food bag to this line midway between the two trees, then pull the free end of the highline to raise the bag out of a bear's reach. Pull the line taut between the two trees and tie off.

Be mindful of hikers who will come later. Avoid opening a can of tuna, for instance, and draining the juice near a campsite—yours or anyone else's. Similarly, don't try to burn leftover food in a fire pit. Cabinet Mountains Wilderness rangers have worried that the low rate of grizzly encounters tends to make wilderness travelers drop their guard and get

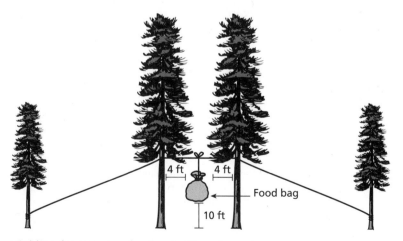

Highline for securing food out of bear's reach

sloppy. Plan meals carefully. If there's any waste, pack it out in a plastic bag. Also, hikers in grizzly country should avoid wiping peanut-buttery knives on their pants and then wearing them into the tent. Anglers who catch fish to eat should puncture the air sack on the entrails and throw them back into the middle of the streams or lakes away from the shores. Better yet, backcountry travelers could catch and release their fish to totally avoid another possible attraction to grizzlies.

Experts warn against wearing perfumes, deodorants, hair sprays, or cosmetics that might have some flowery appeal to bears. Some inconclusive evidence suggests that women should avoid bear country during their menstrual periods.

The surest way to avoid a grizzly encounter is to hike in a close group. Don't hike solo in bear country. Virtually all grizzly attacks on hikers have involved people who were alone or in pairs or in scattered groups. A group of five or six is ideal. Surprise is a common element in many bear attacks, especially in encounters with sows that have cubs. Make noise, especially when hiking around corners and in dense cover such as avalanche slopes. Most experts say that talking, singing, and sometimes yelling are probably more effective deterrents than subtle sounds, such as the tinkling of bells.

Pepper sprays have proved effective in thwarting bear attacks. Three basic tips on using the sprays emerge from interviews with bear attack victims:

- The spray must be on your chest strap or hip belt and accessible in a split second.
- All the hikers in the group should have pepper spray.
- Don't waste money on anything less than the 12-ounce cans.

Hikers traveling north from the United States across the international border must contend with the inconsistency and maddening senselessness of Canada Customs rules regarding pepper spray. Agents have been known to prevent border crossers from bringing pepper spray into Canada even though it can be purchased without question at any Canadian sporting goods store. If the canister label says the product is designed to repel bears, the agents usually will allow it across the border. If the same exact product has a label that indicates it's for self-defense but makes no mention of bears, they may not allow it into the country.

Every bear encounter is a different situation. Hikers must base their response on educated gut feelings. Hikers are routinely warned that they should never run after spotting a grizzly or any other dangerous critter, including dogs. Generally, slow movements are preferred to avoid stimulating a charge or chase. On the other hand, a few hikers have been known to save themselves from injury by climbing out of reach 15 feet up a tree before a grizzly could catch up to them. But don't underestimate a bear's speed. At full charge, a grizzly can hit 30 mph, or 44 feet per second. By comparison, an Olympic sprinter can only manage 34 feet per second. In the rare event that a grizzly charges and pepper spray is not available, play

Rattlesnake in Northrup Canyon

dead by rolling into a fetal position with hands clasped behind your neck to protect your face and vital areas. Most recorded bear attacks are one-swat affairs.

Advice shared above is not intended to scare hikers away from bear country. Use this information to go prepared into our wildlands. Grizzlies are extremely wary and elusive. To even see a silvertip is a rare prize.

At Peace with Rattlesnakes

Perhaps more misconceptions have been spread about rattlesnakes than about any other creature in the West. No, they aren't slimy; they don't hypnotize potential prey; they don't have to coil to strike; and they don't go slithering each day hunting for a human to bite. But they are a potential hazard in some of the areas covered by this book, such as the Columbia Basin of Eastern Washington, portions of the Kettle River Range, Hells Canyon, and the Wenaha-Tucannon Wilderness.

Nationally, about 15 people die each year from poisonous snakebites. To put that in perspective, about 35 people die each year from bee or wasp stings. Furthermore, nearly half of the snakebite victims are people who keep, collect, handle, or attempt to kill the snakes. An even smaller fraction of these victims is struck by Western rattlesnakes, the only poisonous snakes found in the region covered by this book. Generally, rattlers only bite those who are careless, foolish, or ignorant.

Western rattlesnakes get their name from the rattles at the end of their tails. The snakes use the rattles to warn intruders that they are getting too close. Invariably, rattlers would rather retreat than hold their ground or make an advance on anything larger than a ground squirrel.

In the extremely rare instance when a hiker surprises a rattler, the snake might strike. Humans rarely die from rattlesnake bites. About 20 percent of these bites are dry; that is, no venom is injected. The other 80 percent of the time, the victim is most likely to suffer symptoms such as pain, swelling, and nausea. Sometimes permanent damage owes less to the snake's venom and more to improper first aid.

Snakebite suction devices can help, but only if used within seconds after the bite. Making an incision is unnecessary and risks damage to nerves. Cold treatments can increase tissue damage. Generally, experts agree that victims of poisonous snakebites should receive antivenin. Since it is impractical for hikers to carry antivenin, which must be kept cool, there's only one commonly accepted first-aid treatment for snakebite: Calm the victim, gently wash the bite area with soap and water, immobilize the limb, apply a cold wet towel, and get the victim to medical attention as quickly as possible. Do not apply a tourniquet or any bandage that could cut off circulation.

Tricks for Ticks

Ticks can be active and waiting for Inland Northwest hikers, especially in sagebrush country, and most notably in spring. Pride yourself in the nerdy look: tuck pant legs into socks and wear light-colored lightweight long-sleeve shirts. Check for ticks in hair (and other places) during and after a hike. Most ticks will scan your pores for hours before attaching. Too late? Lightly squeeze the head of the tick with tweezers right at the skin line and pull gently until it loosens and pulls out. Then wash and disinfect the wound. Some people save the tick in a film container for analysis should they later develop a rash, fever, or flu-like symptoms that might indicate a tick-borne disease. However, these diseases are rare in the Inland Northwest.

Leaves of Three

Poison ivy infests many dryland areas, especially along river corridors, such as the Snake and Spokane. While most hikers know the "leaves of three, leave it be" adage, some might not recognize the menacing plant in spring, before the leaves have come on. Watch for long or tall woody stems festooned with clumps of white berries, both of which contain the oil that can cause rashes. If you accidentally come in contact with the plant, washing within several minutes can dramatically reduce effects.

Poison ivy along the Spokane River (Photo by Robert J. Shaer)

INTRODUCING THE BACKCOUNTRY AREAS

A library could be filled with books about the wealth of natural beauty, history, and wildlife in the Inland Northwest. Following is but an overview of the diverse landscapes that hikers will experience in some of the special areas covered by this book.

HIKES 16–22   Close to Civilization

Before venturing into the outback, consider for a moment the gems you can find just down a city street. Riverside State Park in Spokane comes to mind. Consider, too, that most of them are here for the masses to enjoy because of the generosity or devotion of a few. Tubbs Hill is a hiker's treasure adjacent to downtown Coeur d'Alene right next to the lavish lakeside Coeur d'Alene Resort. The Little Spokane River Natural Area is one of the most diverse summer spectacles of bird species in the country, but it could just as easily have been a circus of trophy homes and condos if a county parks director hadn't spearheaded an effort to preserve it.

The Dishman Hills Natural Area would surely be off limits to the public had it not been for Tom Rogers, a high-school science teacher, who launched a gentle and successful crusade in 1966 to secure the first parcels of land. In 1986, at the age of 72, he was still working for the hills, leading the winning effort against the odds of raising $154,000 to secure a 140-acre parcel needed to keep the area intact. With the cooperation of Spokane County Parks, the Washington Department of Natural Resources, and The Nature Conservancy, the area now is a condo-proof preserve of at least 530 acres crisscrossed with trails and blessed with wildlife. Spring is particularly pleasurable here as wildflowers splash the pine-studded hills with color. About 300 species of flowering plants have been documented in the meadows and ravines and 73 varieties of mushrooms, many types of lichens and ferns, more than 100 species of birds, and 50 different butterflies. Dedicated volunteers have taken up the cause of preserving the Dishman Hills after Rogers passed away, but while some noteworthy people leave structures as monuments to their greatness, Rogers was a naturalist remembered for devoting his life to The Hills, and to leaving the landscape be.

HIKE I   Juniper Dunes Wilderness

The Juniper Dunes Wilderness, situated about 15 miles northeast of Pasco, Washington, is one of the areas given protection under the 1984 Washington Wilderness Act. But that is about the only similarity it shares with other wilderness in the state. Juniper Dunes is managed by the U.S. Bureau of Land Management (BLM), not the Forest Service. It is desert country rather than alpine. And it doesn't fit the average American's vision of "pretty." The vegetation that has taken hold on the ever-changing dunes is fragile and, lacking dependable water sources, there's no reasonable way to make camping easy or comfortable.

The 7,140-acre wilderness is the last remnant of an ecosystem that once spread over 250,000 acres down to the Snake and Columbia Rivers before agriculture gobbled it up. It was set aside primarily as a natural sanctuary. The ecosystem includes some of the largest sand dunes and the six largest remaining natural groves of western junipers in the state. The dunes, formed by the nearly incessant southwesterly winds, are up to 130 feet high and a quarter-mile wide. The juniper groves are up to 170 years old and represent the northernmost limits of the species.

One of the major complications in managing the wilderness, BLM officials say, is that much of the surrounding area has been a popular off-road vehicle (ORV) playground for decades. BLM has compromised and allowed ORVs along the west side of the wilderness. ORV clubs in the Tri-Cities area have helped educate riders that the rest of the wilderness is off-limits to vehicles, but the tracks of a few renegades have left deep scars in the unstable hillsides. A fence built along the western boundary of the wilderness in the mid-1980s helps control vehicles. BLM is trying to acquire additional land near the wilderness to set aside for ORV use and to secure dependable access for hikers, an issue that's posed another nagging problem.

No fires are allowed and no drinking water is available in the Juniper Dunes. But what a privilege it is to have this gem set aside for the mule deer, coyotes, kangaroo rats, Swainson's hawks—and the few people who will come here to study and soul-search in a sanctuary of the past.

HIKES 1–4 Columbia Basin Channeled Scablands

The Great Floods that scoured the Inland Northwest landscape at the end of the Ice Age have left us a vast masterpiece to explore from Spokane west to the heart of Washington. Steamboat Rock and Northrup Canyon are models of what has transpired in the wake of the world's greatest torrents. Waters that burst from glacial Lake Missoula several times around 15,000 years ago raced over Steamboat Rock at 65 mph—nearly 10 times faster than any flood a modern man might see. The volume of water in one of these floods was roughly equivalent to 10 times the combined flow of all the rivers of the world! Channels were gouged and boulders tumbled like grains of sand and soil was stripped to leave scabs of bare rock. In spring, Martin Falls plunges into a punch bowl beside Highway 155 at Milepost 17. Farther south, however, you must use imagination to comprehend Dry Falls, which once roared with a deafening volume that would have made Niagara Falls look like the proverbial drop in the bucket. Dry Falls was 3.5 miles wide with a drop of 400 feet. That's about three times bigger than Niagara, but the water flow was greater than 100 Niagaras. Nowadays, hawks launch from rimrocks above this Grand Coulee area. Geese waddle in pairs through the sage below. Fish swim in lakes surrounded by a tortured land with surprising pockets of wildlife richness.

The BLM, once the runt of land management agencies in Eastern

Wildflowers on Steamboat Rock (Hike 2)

Washington, has been building its stature since 1990, one section at a time. BLM was the agency that got the region's leftovers of federal lands that weren't homesteaded, purchased, or productive for timber. The agency had a wealth of land, but it was scattered across the state in small parcels that were difficult to manage and mostly useless to the public.

This changed with a program that has allowed BLM to liquidate the small parcels in order to buy ranches and other properties, primarily in the sage scablands, to assemble large blocks of land from willing sellers. The results have been exciting for hikers, as well as for hunters, anglers, and other nature enthusiasts who welcome the recovery of sage and sharp-tailed grouse and other native species. Although the scattered parcels are throughout Eastern Washington, the agency has focused its acquisitions into the scabland country in Adams, Lincoln, and Whitman Counties.

Two BLM hikes are featured in this book (see Hikes 4 and 22), and other scablands hikes are mentioned in Appendix A. Other BLM areas with hiking routes to explore include the 14,000-acre Escure Ranch south of Lamont, which has a day hike, especially appealing in spring (before the cheatgrass dries out), to Rock Creek's Towell Falls.

HIKES 5–8   Kettle River Range

Although Congress deleted the 80,000-acre Kettle River Mountains from the 1984 Washington Wilderness Act, the Kettle Crest itself has all the qualities to qualify as a protected wilderness. Conservationists are still fighting timber sales threatening to encroach on this scenic area, which is blessed with rolling mountains and flowered meadows in the area's only roadless mountain terrain. Few mountain lakes and rocky peaks are found here. Think Great Smokies rather than Rocky Mountains.

The north and south sections of the Kettle Crest National Recreation Trail combine for about 43 miles of ridge trail crossed by only one road, State Highway 20 at Sherman Pass. This is some of the best scenery in Ferry County, but certainly not all of it. Another 14 trails in the Kettle Range account for 80 miles, about 60 of which are proposed by conservationists for inclusion in wilderness or some sort of protective classification. Although it's not one of the featured hikes in this book, a classic Kettle Range route goes through the virgin stand of ponderosa pines in the Thirteenmile drainage southwest of Sherman Pass (see Appendix A).

HIKES 13–15 AND 34–37   Salmo-Priest Country

The mountains and valleys of northeastern Washington and northern Idaho called the Salmo-Priest were hunting grounds of the Kalispel Indians before being invaded by white men surveying the border between the United States and Canada in 1861. The area's history was heavily influenced by Father Peter DeSmet and other Jesuit missionaries, the namesakes for 26,000-acre Priest Lake.

In 1908, the international border survey was completed between the United States and Canada and in 1927 the boundary swath, maintained as a linear clearcut today, was cut through the dense forest. By 1925, a trail had been built from Salmo Mountain and along the South Salmo River, and the Shedroof Mountain Lookout had been constructed. Between 1924 and 1929, the west side of the wilderness was swept by fires from which much of the area has never recovered. From the 1930s into the 1950s, the Forest Service used cabins and lookouts at Ace High Camp near Helmer Mountain and at Crowell Point, Thunder Mountain, Shedroof Mountain, Round Top, Little Snowy Top, and Pass Creek Pass. Salmo Cabin, which is along Hike 15, was staffed until 1951. It has deteriorated, but fire lookouts still exist in one form or another on Salmo, Sullivan, Little Snowy Top, and Round Top Mountains.

A road was built to the head of Deemer Creek in 1938. In 1963 it was extended to the Salmo Mountain Lookout and in 1968 it was reconstructed in preparation for timber sales in the area. In 1968, Ray Kresek, a Spokane firefighter and former Spokane Mountaineers president, began to drum up support to save the Salmo-Priest area. In 1970, the Forest Service backed off its plans to build roads and harvest the timber, and, in 1971, recommended about 21,000 acres for wilderness study in the first Roadless Area

Review and Evaluation (RARE I). Finally, after years of work by conservationists, 41,335 acres of the area were included in the 1984 Washington Wilderness Act. Thousands of adjoining acres in Idaho's Upper Priest Lake area are proposed as an addition to this wilderness, but Idaho wilderness bills have failed to receive Congressional approval. Conservationists are making strong cases for additional acreage in Washington, including the roadless area around Grassy Top Mountain (see Hike 12).

The wilderness and proposed additions offer a variety of trail scenery from the cedars along the Upper Priest River to the treeless Crowell Ridge that leads to Gypsy Peak. The Upper Priest area is known as being the highest precipitation zone in Washington east of the Cascades. Elevations on the Idaho side range from the Upper Priest River at 2,900 feet to Snowy Top Mountain, one of the highest points in the region at 7,548 feet. A few miles away is Gypsy Peak, officially rated at 7,309 feet, but at one time it was considered to be 7,322

Endangeed mountain caribou at Upper Two Mouth Lake

feet. Check the topo and the USGS marker near the summit and judge for yourself. Either way, Gypsy is the highest point in Eastern Washington. The area is rich with dense forests of western hemlock and some of the largest cedars in Eastern Washington and northern Idaho—some up to 10 feet in diameter. Mycologists around the world know the Priest Lake area for its abundance and variety of mushrooms, more than 1,000 documented species.

But it's a wilderness backed into a corner. From the summit of Snowy Top, you can see a road or a powerline or a clearcut in every direction. The Upper Priest drainage seems to be losing the battle to remain a viable spawning area for native bull trout and west-slope cutthroats. Upper Priest Lake is surrounded by Forest Service land, while main Priest Lake has considerable private land that's been developed and subdivided. The main lake has 12 campgrounds and six resorts, give or take a few. More than 200 miles of trails are maintained on the Priest Lake Ranger District, including trails running much of the length of the lake's west side, which is dominated by national forest. (The east side is managed mostly by the Idaho Department of Lands, which is heavy into logging with little interest in recreation.) In 2000, the Pend Oreille Divide Trail (west of Priest Lake) from Kalispell Rock south to North Baldy Peak was reopened after nearly three decades. The trail had been neglected to keep hikers away from the ugly site of massive clearcuts on nearby private timberland. It's a good hike, but check on maintenance. With the whims of weather, politics, and budgets, nothing is certain, not even in paradise.

Big game species, too, are making a last stand here against development. Mountain caribou, found in the United States only in northeastern Washington and northern Idaho, were federally protected as an endangered species in 1983. The grizzly bear, wolf, and bald eagle are other threatened and endangered species found here. This is the only remaining area in Washington and Idaho where the grizzlies are known to live on a regular basis. While many other species of wildlife live in this region—including deer, black bears, elk, mountain goats, bighorn sheep, lynx, wolverines, and a healthy population of cougars—it's the existence of these endangered species that distinguishes this wilderness and the Selkirks mentioned below from any other area in the country.

HIKES 37, 38, AND 40–52   American Selkirk Mountains

On the east side of the Priest River drainage, the Selkirk Mountains of Idaho are a haven for mosquitoes and heaven to hikers who can deal with them. From the mile-long scramble into Hunt Lake to the 35-mile Long Canyon Loop, hikers of all abilities can find suitable scenic routes punctuated with trout-filled lakes and gleaming granite peaks.

With the notable exception of Long Canyon, virtually every major drainage in the Selkirks has been pegged for timber sales and roads. This generally means good road access to some trailheads near the Selkirk Crest, but it also means that roads have gobbled up miles of good trails into timbered drainages. Near the turn of the millennium, however, policies had changed and many logging roads were being blocked off and allowed to become trails again, albeit tangled with vine alder and other vegetation that take advantage of bulldozed earth to haunt the hikers who follow. Many trails in this region were originally constructed by the Civilian Conservation Corps between 1933 and 1942.

The Selkirks, a 250-mile-long mountain range running from Sandpoint, Idaho, well into British Columbia, are studded with distinctive peaks such as Chimney Rock and Harrison Peak. (Note: Some geographers argue that the range extends south into Spokane, Washington, but there's no official designation.) The high point, however, is unceremoniously situated on Fisher Ridge at 7,709 feet. Some of the Selkirk Crest and all of Long Canyon have been recommended for wilderness.

The Selkirk Mountains region averages about 75 lightning fires a year and another 20 caused by man. In 1967, the 16,400-acre Trapper Peak fire and the 55,910-acre Sundance Fire made massive alterations in large areas of the Selkirks covered by this book. Looking down from a rock outcropping on Hunt Peak, you can see two of numerous lakes in basins carved by glaciers that retreated and disappeared roughly 10,000 years ago. But just as dramatic are the vast openness and silvery snags that stand as monuments to the Sundance Burn. On September 1, having been nearly contained at about 2,000 acres, the fire blew up and advanced 16 miles, covering 50,000 acres in 9 hours. Then it suddenly pooped out just short of Bonners Ferry, Idaho. The fire's run killed a bulldozer operator and his spotter at the head of McCormick Creek. The man across the Pack River valley in the Roman Nose Fire lookout saved his life by hunkering through the night in a rockslide. Hunt Peak was near the northwest edge of the flames. The burn was so hot in some spots, the timber has yet to show much sign of recovery. The wildflowers and huckleberries, however, are doing just fine, thank you.

HIKES 9, 10, 22, 24, 25, 30–33, AND 53–57
Coeur d'Alene/Pend Oreille Country

A broad swath of mountains roughly from Sandpoint, Idaho, south to St. Maries and from Spokane, Washington, east to the Idaho-Montana border is dominated by two lowland lakes that are remarkably like those found high in the mountains, only much larger.

Lake Coeur d'Alene extends 23 miles south from the city of Coeur d'Alene. It covers 77 square miles and has 109 miles of shoreline. Major tributaries are the St. Joe and Coeur d'Alene Rivers, both of which are the sources for hikes in this book. Just to the north is Lake Pend Oreille, which dips down to the mind-boggling depth of 1,150 feet, so deep that it was a Navy submarine testing base during World War II. The lake is 43 miles long, 6.5 miles wide, and has 111 miles of shoreline. The Clark Fork River, which originates in Montana, is the lake's main feeder stream. The Pend Oreille River originates from the lake, heading west across the Idaho Panhandle before taking a turn at Newport, Washington, and becoming one of only two major north-flowing rivers in America. Coeur d'Alene (pronounced "core-da-LANE") is of French origin meaning "heart of the awl," or "sharp-hearted." It's not clear whether the term was most commonly used by European fur traders describing the shrewd Indians confronted in this region or by the Indians as they referred to the greedy traders. Pend Oreille (pronounced "pon-der-AY") is another French name meaning "Indians who wear earrings."

Mineral exploration played a major role in the region's history. Mining began in 1881 when gold was discovered in what was later to be called the Silver Valley. The area was acclaimed to be the richest silver, lead, zinc, and antimony mining area in the United States and was once ranked with the 20 richest known mineralized areas in the world. Now that many of the minerals have been taken and market prices have made remaining ore uneconomical to mine, much of the land is left permanently scarred; some of its waterways are still polluted with heavy metals, but Superfund cleanup has begun.

Several of the hikes selected for this book seek out the most pristine and scenic areas remaining in this region. While the word *spectacular* might be used to describe the peaks of the Cabinet and Eagle Cap Wilderness Areas, *picturesque* more accurately describes the Coeur d'Alene and Pend Oreille areas. Most of the mountains are rounded and the valleys are timbered. The highest summit in the area is Stevens Peak, elev. 6,838 feet, and there are no glaciers and few sky-scraping pinnacles.

Wildlife management has had a hand in reviving this country. For instance, the healthy elk herds in the Coeur d'Alene area developed almost entirely from four plants totaling 237 head made between 1925 and 1939. And trout streams are getting some respect after years of abuse from logging and mining.

HIKES 26, 27, 65, 66, 68   Great Burn Wilderness Proposal

Since the 1970s, conservation groups and even the Forest Service have recommended that roughly 250,000 acres along the Montana-Idaho border be designated as the Great Burn Wilderness. Few things are more amazing than this landscape transformed by glaciers and fire, except, perhaps, the inability of Congress to give it official wilderness protection.

The name Great Burn stems from the epic 1910 forest fire "blow-up." Hundreds, perhaps thousands of lightning- and human-caused blazes were burning with relatively modest impacts in a tinder-dry year before they came together on August 20 and exploded into an inferno whipped by hurricane-force winds. When it was over 2 days later, 78 firefighters and 7 civilians were dead. The Idaho towns of Wallace, Kellogg, Osburn, Burke, and Murray were ravaged. The Montana towns of Taft, DeBorgia, Saltese, Haugan, and Tuscor were consumed. And much of a 3-million-acre path 260 miles long and 200 miles wide from the Salmon River north to Canada was charred. Most of the destruction occurred in just 6 hours.

In the following decades, roadless remains of the Great Burn make an extraordinarily diverse and captivating wilderness candidate. The area runs roughly along the state line south of Interstate 90 between Superior and Missoula. The 1910 fires essentially transformed a subalpine environment into an alpine environment that is in a subalpine setting. In other words, two environments exist in one area. Beargrass grows at lower than normal elevations and cedar trees grow at elevations to 6,000 feet, which is higher than normal for the Bitterroots. Species not typically associated are growing in common. Ponderosa pines and western larch are growing among cedars and hemlocks. The 600 inches of snowpack that irrigates portions of this area produce particularly robust Indian paintbrush.

Fireweed grows at almost all elevations in the Great Burn. Insect species are exceptionally diverse here, especially butterflies.

Mountains in the Great Burn are not as high and craggy as in the Bitterroot Range farther south. But Rhodes Peak, the burn's highest at elev. 7,930 feet, is a lofty goal for hikers seeking a view, and the crags at the headwaters of Kelly Creek require climbing skill to scale. The cirque basins along the Stateline National Recreation Trail are settings for jewel-like lakes. Pockets of forest that survived the Great Burn hold 500-year-old Western red cedars flanked by the vast meadows that have evolved from the burn itself. The proposed wilderness ranges in elevation from 3,200 feet to nearly 8,000 feet. That means the Great Burn includes not only summer range for elk but also winter range, which would be an unusual but welcomed combination for official wilderness.

HIKES 58–64   St. Joe River/Mallard-Larkins Area

The 32,331-acre Mallard-Larkins Pioneer Area and the regions surrounding the nearby St. Joe River drainage are an Eden-like refuge for fisheries, big game, and backcountry explorers. The Mallard-Larkins averages more than 60 inches of annual precipitation, compared to only 25 inches in the western reaches of the Idaho Panhandle National Forests' St. Joe River Ranger District. Within this district alone are 560 miles of fishable streams and at least 17 fishable high-mountain lakes. The trail systems are relatively good, servicing the hikers, horsepackers, and large numbers of hunters who flock to the area each fall to pursue elk.

As in most of the forests in this part of the country, the trail systems were largely designed for servicing lookouts and fighting forest fires. The cabin on Mallard Peak is a monument to this era. The structure was built in 1929 from materials that included 3,750 pounds of cement mix packed in on the backs of men and livestock over 43 miles of trails. The cabin was decommissioned in 1957. Now that roads have punched into the area, the trek to the peak is a day's walk. Maintenance of the cabin is left to volunteers.

Use in the St. Joe area is concentrated along the St. Joe River, the upper reaches of which are part of the Wild and Scenic River System. Use in the Mallard-Larkins centers around 12 alpine lakes that are showing the wear and tear. The name Mallard-Larkins is derived from two prominent peaks in the area. The origin of the name Mallard is not clear, but Larkin is the name of a former homesteader in the North Fork of the Clearwater River. The homestead was inundated by Dworshak Reservoir.

HIKES 65–69   Clearwater River/Lewis and Clark Trail

Hikes 65 to 69 in the Clearwater National Forest cover territory explored by Lewis and Clark in their famous expedition of 1804–06. The trailhead for Hike 66 to Goat Lake and Rhodes Peak is situated on the historic Lolo Trail west of the Lochsa River drainage and Lolo Pass. The expedition nearly starved as it followed this Indian trail through the Clearwater country. Today, however, the area is rich with elk and deer and other wildlife. Indeed, it is one of Idaho's most prolific producers of west-slope cutthroat trout. Wolves have been reintroduced.

The Clearwater National Forest has published a descriptive brochure on the expedition's travels in this area. It's called "Lewis and Clark on the Lolo Trail."

HIKES 72–81   Cabinet Mountains Wilderness

The 94,272-acre Cabinet Mountains Wilderness, established in 1964, is a wild island that's routinely stormed by threats of development around its perimeter. The Cabinets slice proudly through the Big Sky of northwestern Montana's Kootenai National Forest near Libby. Remnants of the Ice Age, including one named glacier and several permanent snowfields, still cling to the north slopes of jagged peaks, such as 8,738-foot Snowshoe Peak, the area's tallest. The low point in the wilderness is 2,500 feet, and nearby Troy, Montana, is the lowest-elevation town in Montana. Such a wide elevation range makes the wilderness available to a spectrum of flora, including 125 species of wildflowers and 13 conifers.

Some portions of the Cabinets are soaked by up to 100 inches of annual precipitation. The steep terrain is scenic and wet with cascading waterfalls and about 85 lakes. Cedar forests thrive to a timberline of about 7,000 feet, just about as high as the species goes without an oxygen tent and an IV. The wet area's "brush zone" factors thickly into off-trail exploration. Granite

Mountain goat watching on St. Paul Peak, Cabinet Mountains Wilderness

Lake, for example, is at elev. 4,605 feet and scramblers must labor through a dense brush zone before breaking out into open slopes above. Leigh Lake, being just 500 feet higher in elevation, offers hikers a much easier brush zone to negotiate for higher adventure. Trails indicated on official wilderness maps produced by the Forest Service can be misleading. Routes to Hanging Valley and Little Ibex Lake, for example, have been on the maps even though they were not planned and are not officially maintained. The result is disappointment to some hikers, who don't appreciate the extra work of routefinding, while other hikers realize that a poor trail can be a virtue of sorts that has kept the destinations wild and remarkable. Meanwhile, the wilderness includes some pretty darned good trails that are not even indicated on some maps. Trails on the east side of the wilderness attract far more visitors, although the trail heading to Wanless Lake, the largest lake in the wilderness, gets a good share of traffic from the southwest side.

Mosquitoes thrive in the Cabinets, but the most worrisome vermin are the development interests buzzing around the lowlands. The vast ASARCO tailings on the flats that are visible far below while hiking Cabinet Divide Trail 360 above Cedar Lakes are a reminder that industries are looking into the Cabinets for profit, not a wilderness experience. The proposed Rock Creek mine near Noxon, Montana, would start outside the wilderness and tunnel underneath its borders. Geologists say the mining could have various unsavory affects, such as causing leaks that could drain the charm out of Cliff Lake and flush heavy metals into Lake Pend Oreille. As proposed, the mine's processing facility would be situated near the confluence of the east and west forks of Rock Creek. The copper and silver mining waste, or tailings, would be left forever on 320 acres that would reach to within a third of a mile from Rock Creek and the Clark Fork River.

Hikers and other conservationists should not feel greedy in demanding more protection for this area. The Cabinet Mountains Wilderness is only 34 miles long and ranges from 0.5 to 7 miles wide. The wilderness and the smaller Ten Lakes Scenic Area to the north near Eureka are the only large scenic areas in this region that haven't been laced with logging roads. The wilderness is home for a small population of grizzly bears, countless trout, plenty of elk, some mountain goats, bighorn sheep, black bears, and a variety of other creatures. Hikers can do their part to keep this sanctuary intact by following wilderness rules, such as those limiting groups to no more than eight people, and supporting conservation groups monitoring development in the region. A solid starting point is The Lands Council based in Spokane (see Appendix E).

HIKE 70   Selway-Bitterroot Wilderness

The 1.3-million-acre Selway-Bitterroot Wilderness was among the standout wildlands officially secured by the original 1964 Wilderness Act. It is named after the Selway River, the National Wild and Scenic River that drains its core, and the Bitterroot Range, which provides the backbone. About 1,000 miles of trails enable visitors to enjoy an area ranging from 1,800 feet elevation on the Selway to 10,000 feet along the Bitterroot Divide.

Since the Selway-Bitterroot is on the outer limits of the region this book covers, only one hike within its boundaries has been included. This trip into Cove Lakes penetrates the popular Selway Crags, a dramatic line of glacier-carved peaks 8,000 feet high at the northwest edge of the wilderness. While a good trail system covers this region, the Forest Service, to its credit, also is managing a large portion of the Crags as a pristine area with no maintained trails. Life is fragile here, where plants must survive in the thinnest of soils, endure long winters, and cram a growing season into a short two or three months.

Hikers should look beyond the Crags to other tempting areas for exploration in the Selway. The hiking season begins as early as late May on lowland trails, such as the trail along the Selway River, long before high country trails are open. Most of the wilderness is densely forested with Douglas fir, spruce, and lodgepole pine. It is host to a large population of elk, good numbers of moose, some black bears, wolves, and many other creatures. Virtually all of the deeper lakes and streams hold trout. The wilderness is accessible from U.S. Highway 93 in the Bitterroot Valley south of Missoula and from the Selway River area off U.S. Highway 12 along Idaho's Lochsa River.

HIKES 82–86 Wenaha-Tucannon Wilderness

Established in 1978, the Wenaha-Tucannon Wilderness is composed of 177,412 acres, of which 110,995 are in Washington, the remainder in Oregon. Though its northerly trailheads are only 150 miles south of Spokane, this area of the Blue Mountains is seldom visited by hikers. Except in late October and early November during the elk hunting season, it is common to cover miles of trails without seeing another human.

The area consists of horizontal basalt flows thousands of feet thick that have been deeply and steeply eroded by streams. Trails either follow the broad rolling ridge tops near 6,000 feet or drop down to parallel the streams 2,000 to 3,000 feet below. Scenic vistas are common on all ridge trails and along the good trout-fishing waters of the Wenaha River. Camping areas are determined by water availability. Most high-elevation springs identified on the maps remain flowing even during summer, though some may require a steep descent from the trail (Sheephead and Table Camp Springs near Trail 3113) or they may be only a murky trickle (Rettkowski, Twin, and Clover Springs also near Trail 3113). Springs are not always obvious, but trails used by stock and wildlife usually lead the way. With summer temperatures into the 90s and water sources sometimes 5 miles apart, smart hikers carry more than the usual quart of water.

The area is relatively dry and is sparsely forested on south-facing slopes. The western half receives more precipitation and thus is more heavily forested. River trails are generally snow-free in May, although the higher elevations in the western sections could have snow at the end of June. Aside from the rugged basalt canyons, the characteristic that makes this area unique for Inland Northwest hikers is the Rocky Mountain elk. It is common to see elk, or at least elk sign, on a daily basis here.

The dry climate makes mosquitoes rare, but horseflies can be bothersome. Don't confuse them with the unusually large numbers of hummingbirds that choose these mountains for their breeding grounds. Rattlesnakes are common at lower elevations.

The flora is much as you would expect to find anywhere else in Eastern Washington, although the mountain mahogany is found nowhere else in the state. Grand firs seem to outnumber the Douglas firs, and yew trees grow in profusion along the streams. Beautiful ponderosa pine-grass parklands cover the higher slopes above the Wenaha River in the southeast corner's Smooth Ridge/Moore Flat area. Campgrounds near trailheads are small and primitive. Reaching any trailhead will involve a 10- to 30-mile drive over dusty dirt roads, either south from the Pomeroy, Washington, area or from Dayton, Washington. Oregon approaches are off of Forest Road 62.

HIKES 87–91 Eagle Cap Wilderness

The Eagle Cap Wilderness is a ruggedly captivating collection of glacier-cut valleys, shimmering peaks and waterfalls, and 53 named mountain lakes in the Wallowa Mountains of northeastern Oregon. The centerpiece in the 361,446-acre preserve is 9,572-foot Eagle Cap Peak, although it isn't the highest mountain within the wilderness boundaries. Sacajawea Peak and the Matterhorn, adjacent to each other on a long ridge above Hurricane Creek north of Eagle Cap, both stand about 9,800 feet tall.

The wilderness, situated just west from the rim of Hells Canyon of the Snake River, was established in 1940. It has four main access areas. The most heavily used is the paved highway to Wallowa Lake, which is south of Enterprise, Oregon, and just 1 mile from the wilderness boundary. Other main routes are the Hurricane Creek Road, Imnaha River Road, and Lostine River Road. All the roads pass by developed campgrounds and lead to five main trails heading into the heart of the wilderness and linking to 535 miles of maintained trails. The scenic high country is usually free of snow by early July.

Beginning in mid-September, hunters infiltrate a few areas, primarily the Bear Creek, Imnaha, and Minam drainages, but generally this is the time when crowds subside and snow is always a possibility. Anglers will find fish in more than 37 miles of streams and numerous lakes. Self-sustaining brook trout populate virtually all of the waters that can hold fish life, while rainbows are stocked in about a dozen lakes, including Anaroid, Crater, Duck, Eagle, Fish, Frances, Hawk, Heart, Hobo, Lookingglass, and Prospect. Lake trout are found in a few lakes. Golden trout and cutthroats are all but history.

Oregon's original mountain goat herd was transplanted into the wilderness

Glacier Lake, Eagle Cap Wilderness (Hike 90) (Photo by Chuck Kerkering)

in 1944. Since then, the herd has increased slowly. Goats are most often seen at Ice and Frances Lakes, the Matterhorn, Sacajawea Peak, and Chief Joseph Mountain. (The area is rich with history of the Nez Perce tribe and its leader, Chief Joseph.) Elk and mule deer make their home in the wilderness. A bighorn sheep herd introduced to the Lostine area was decimated by a viral disease during the winter of 1986–87, but wild sheep are being reintroduced.

Timberline in the Wallowas varies from about 8,500 to 9,000 feet, from which autumn hikers can look down on a patchwork of golds and greens among the trees struggling for existence in a world of crumbling granite, limestone, and marble. There's a price to pay for country this beautiful. For instance, at a trail junction along Hurricane Creek a Forest Service sign pointing up the seemingly vertical slopes of the canyon once said "Echo Lake 3 miles." Hikers had tried to scratch the 3 into an 8. Somebody else had tried to make the 8 into an 18. The sign had other comments about the last 3 miles to Echo Lake, such as "Pure hell!" and "With Jesus, 4 hours."

The popular Lakes Basin area of the wilderness is heavily used, particularly in August. Most trails near the basin are liberally splattered with horse manure, and hikers abound. To help counter human impact, wilderness rangers have been enforcing regulations printed on the wilderness permits obtained at trailheads. Beware of campfire closures at certain lakes, and note that camping within 100 feet of wilderness lakes is prohibited. The fine for violators is about $50.

HIKES 92, 93   Hells Canyon of the Snake River

The Hells Canyon National Recreation Area is a rugged land of extremes covering 652,500 acres on the Oregon and Idaho sides of the 1,000-mile-long Snake River. The term *Hells Canyon* evolved for the rugged 110-mile stretch of river from around Oxbow Dam downstream to Heller Bar at the mouth of the Grande Ronde River.

Calculated from the 9,393-foot summit of He Devil Peak in the Seven Devils Mountains to the roaring Snake River nearly 8,000 feet below, this is the deepest canyon in North America. Summer temperatures of 100 degrees can bake the lower landscape while the temps might be 20 degrees cooler above. These extremes of elevation create diversity in both plant and wildlife communities. The Forest Service says 24 species of plants at Hells Canyon are found nowhere else on earth. Elk, deer, and bighorn sheep cohabitate in the canyon with rattlesnakes, canyon wrens, and a river holding fish such as salmon, steelhead, smallmouth bass, and sturgeon. These critters have special adaptations to the elements here, a point less-adapted visitors need to keep in mind. The area has 19 developed campgrounds, but drinking water isn't part of the development at all of them. Come prepared.

Within the recreation area is a 215,000-acre wilderness, which includes the excellent Seven Devils Mountains summer hiking destinations and about 360 miles of trails worth exploring. Most of the trails are at higher elevations and blocked by snow until July. This book, however, features two of the canyon's best lowland routes, which are at their prime for hiking in early spring and again in fall. Hikes up the Rapid River during late spring and into the Seven Devils–Sheep Lake area during summer are not in this book but highly recommended.

In all, the Hells Canyon area includes nearly 900 miles of trails along the rims, ridges, and benches, and, of course, along the river itself. But don't expect to be the first person to find out about this place. Scatterings of humans have eked out a living in the canyon for 8,000 years, according to carbon dating of artifacts found at camps and pit houses. Pictographs and petroglyphs are common along the river. The Nez Perce tribe flourished here, fishing the Snake and its tributaries for salmon and gathering roots for sustenance for centuries before being uprooted from their homeland by the U.S. Army in 1877. The first known white people to venture into the canyon were members of the Lewis and Clark Expedition in 1806. Gold miners followed in the 1860s. Then came a sparse but particularly hardy stock of homesteaders and ranchers.

As the Hells Canyon National Recreation Area was declared in 1975, about 67 miles of the Snake within it was included in the National Wild and Scenic Rivers System. The corridor is revered by rafters for the eight sets of Class III–V rapids, which, combined with the remoteness, make it one of the country's great rafting attractions. Jet boats run portions of the river year-round.

Conflicts between the canyon user groups, such as power boaters and rafters, ecologists and livestock grazers, and hikers and motorized vehicle enthusiasts, are decades old. Some say the place should be declared a national park while others say multiple-use opportunities should be expanded. The debate isn't likely to end soon.

HIKES 94–97   Kokanee Glacier/Valhalla Provincial Parks

Of all the hiking areas covered in this book, none is more spectacular than these two provincial parks preserved as wilderness in southeastern British Columbia near Nelson and Slocan.

Kokanee Glacier Provincial Park is an 80,000-acre wilderness encompassing three glaciers in the Slocan Range of the Canadian Selkirks. Established in 1922, it is one of the oldest jewels in British Columbia's provincial park system. It is named for the glacier that clings to the north slopes of 9,154-foot Kokanee Peak and the area's highest mountain, 9,200-foot Cond Peak, in the center of the park. From this hub of scenery and the human activity it attracts, glacier-cut valleys branch out like spokes from a wheel. Clockwise from the south, Kokanee, Lemon, Enterprise, Keen, Woodbury, Lendrum, and Coffee Creeks drain the park's waters to Kootenay Lake to the east and Slocan Lake to the west. Major access trails run up five of these drainages.

The Slocan Chief Cabin, built near Kokanee Glacier in 1896 as a bunkhouse for miners, had also sheltered thousands of summer hikers and winter skiers for decades before being transformed into a historical site in 2002. A new cabin for wilderness visitors was built nearby. Two other trails, Woodbury and Silver Spray, also have cabins for users.

Most of Kokanee Park lies at elevations above 6,000 feet, with half of it above 6,900 feet. That leaves a short summer hiking season to explore assets that include more than 30 lakes. Traces of early mining activity still can be found here, since much of the 50-some-mile trail system was originally built by miners. Incidentally, the word *kokanee* means "red fish," a Kootenay Indian word referring to the landlocked sockeye salmon of Kootenay Lake.

Valhalla Provincial Park was designated in 1983 as a 122,560-acre preserve in the West Kootenays to protect an extraordinarily scenic mountain area from the encroachment of logging and mining. The park extends from the shorelines of the fjordlike Slocan Lake at 1,750 feet to high alpine meadows and rugged spires reaching elevations of more than 9,300 feet. Many of the trails in the park are still primitive; some are accessible across Slocan Lake via canoe or boat. Water taxis operate out of New Denver.

Looking east from Jumbo Pass, Purcell Mountains (Hike 99)

Grizzly bears, black bears, moose, and a few mountain goats still roam within the borders of these two parks, although the most commonly seen critters are hoary marmots, pikas, and Columbian ground squirrels. High-elevation travelers might luck into some unfearing white-tailed ptarmigan, which turn completely white in winter. Grizzlies frequent the lush growth in low-elevation avalanche paths during spring. By late summer and fall, berry crops lure them to the high country. Kokanee Park rangers have closed some trails during the late season to avoid encounters between bears and hikers. The trail to Joker Lakes, featured in the first version of this book, has been abandoned altogether because of the potential for grizzly conflicts.

HIKES 98–100 Purcell Mountains/
St. Mary's Alpine Provincial Park

The spectacular but lightly explored crest of the Purcell Mountains divides the Kootenay Region of southeast British Columbia. The Purcells of the East Kootenay region, running north and south of Invermere, are relatively ignored, as visitors tend to follow the call of the paralleling Rocky Mountains and internationally recognized parks such as Banff and Jasper. The West Kootenay region, which includes the Selkirk Mountains and the west half of the Purcells stretching north and south from Nelson, is the focus of several hikes in this book. Hikers could concentrate many seasons of exploration here. Trails are few and far between. Routefinding and resource-fulness are often required.

The Earl Grey Pass Traverse is in the Purcell Wilderness Conservancy, an area protected in 1974 and enlarged in 1995 to 499,210 acres of glaciated peaks and prime grizzly bear habitat. The sanctuary is not enough to protect vast portions of the Purcells from high-elevation logging and a proposed mega-ski resort that are knocking at the wilderness boundaries. With few exceptions, however, the wild is still in place within the wilderness. In 25 miles from the east trailhead to Earl Grey Pass, only about eight decent campsites can be found among the ancient trees and devil's club in the steep-sided valley. None is suited to more than three tents. "We're not going out of our way to encourage use in the Purcell Wilderness Park," said Peter Mackie, British Columbia Parks manager in Nelson. "The trail maintenance isn't up to the standard you'll find in Kokanee Glacier or other parks. We use very few signs because it's more of a wilderness preserve."

St. Mary's Alpine Provincial Park is even wilder. The 22,650-acre preserve nestled against the southern boundary of the Purcell Wilderness Conservancy, became a Class A provincial park in 1973. It's managed as a true wilderness, with virtually no trail work inside its boundaries. Some of the area is reminiscent of Washington's Alpine Lakes Wilderness before anyone with boots set foot in it, especially at the end of September and early October when the alpine larch are blazing with yellow needles. The big difference between St. Mary's and the Alpine Lakes, however, is the absence of quotas or lottery drawings for access to this little-used area. Terrain does the crowd control.

Think of this area as a hand with fingers that are rocky ridges pointing toward the west. The west side of the park is a jumble of talus, where much of the off-ridge hiking is done on granite boulders rather than on dirt. Stands of trees, mostly alpine larch, sprout from the rocks. The east side of the park is lush and dense. Elevations range from 4,500 feet up to 9,500 feet at the summits of Mount St. Mary and Nowitka Mountain. Any of the sketchy trails that lead to the wilderness tend to fade to nothing. Hikers are on their own here.

A NOTE ABOUT SAFETY

Safety is an important concern in all outdoor activities. No guidebook can alert you to every hazard or anticipate the limitations of every reader. Therefore, the descriptions of roads, trails, routes, and natural features in this book are not representations that a particular place or excursion will be safe for your party. When you follow any of the routes described in this book, you assume responsibility for your own safety. Under normal conditions, such excursions require the usual attention to traffic, road and trail conditions, weather, terrain, the capabilities of your party, and other factors. Because many of the lands in this book are subject to development and/or change of ownership, conditions may have changed since this book was written that make your use of some of these routes unwise. Always check for current conditions, obey posted private property signs, and avoid confrontations with property owners or managers. Keeping informed on current conditions and exercising common sense are the keys to a safe, enjoyable outing.

—*The Mountaineers Books*

COLUMBIA RIVER BASIN

1 JUNIPER DUNES LOOP

Location: Columbia River
Status: Juniper Dunes Wilderness
Distance: 4.2 miles round trip
Hiking time: 3 hours
Difficulty: Easy
Season: Year-round
Maps: USGS Rye Grass Coulee, Levy SW, Levy SE, and Levy NE
Information: U.S. Bureau of Land Management,
     Spokane District

This wilderness is not likely to be a destination for masses of nature lovers. It has no towering peaks, trout-stuffed streams, or gin-clear lakes. Rather it is a small, parched nugget of unheralded nature naked to the dry winds that have shaped its character.

The Juniper Dunes Wilderness includes six groves of the largest concentration of western juniper trees in the state. But this is desert country. No fires are allowed and no drinking water is available. Perhaps most people would prefer to see it as a day hike, especially in early morning and late evening when wildlife is active. But by hauling in water for a small, clean camp, you can comfortably enjoy the peacefulness of this 7,140-acre sanctuary after the engine noise has left the edge of the wilderness, where off-road vehicles are allowed. All visits, however, are contingent on access restrictions that have a history of changing, depending on the experiences landowners have been having with visitors. Spring is the best season to visit this desert area, but it's vital that hikers check with the U.S. Bureau of

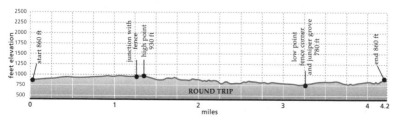

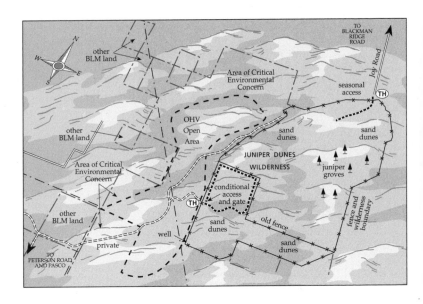

Land Management (BLM) office in Spokane to check the access status, and whether overnight parking is allowed.

From the first U.S. Highway 395 interchange coming into Pasco, Washington, from the north, take the Highway 395 exit toward Walla Walla. Drive 2 miles and turn left onto the Pasco-Kahlotus Highway. Drive 5.8 miles to a crop-spraying facility and airstrip and turn left on an unsigned gravel road listed on maps as Peterson Road. (If the paved road begins to make a sweeping right turn, you've gone about 200 feet past the turnoff.) Drive 4.1 miles on Peterson Road and turn right on a dirt road. Go about 100 feet to a parking area hidden in the sage. Do not proceed farther, if landowners are willing, unless equipped with an off-road vehicle or four-wheel drive; it is easy to get stuck in loose sand, especially when it is dry. From the parking area, follow the road past the big dunes used by off-road vehicle enthusiasts and bear right on the first prominent spur road. It's 3.5 miles from the parking area to the wilderness boundary. Vehicles may or may not be allowed as far as the boundary.

The dunes desert is ripe for wandering, with no designated trails. But the area is somewhat featureless to the untrained eye, and you could become disoriented. For a good introduction, hike along the road that crosses the wilderness boundary. Walk about 1.5 miles to an old fence line. Turn north and walk along the old fence line for 1 mile toward juniper groves. From there, you can retrace your steps with no danger of getting lost. Or continue, following the old fence as it heads west to the newer fence on the wilderness boundary. Follow this fence south to complete the loop back to the trailhead.

To reach the most scenic portions of the area, hike cross-country about 3 miles northeast toward the densest concentration of junipers and the fringe of the large 130-foot dunes that bank up against the northern boundaries of the wilderness. The scenery can change from year to year in this environment. Fires are not uncommon. A major one swept through the area in 1996.

Options: Wilderness access also is allowed from the north, driving south from Blackman Ridge Road on Joy Road (formerly known as Rybzinski Road), which ends just before the boundary. This access is on private land and cars cannot be left overnight. Seasonal closures are likely. Wise hikers check with the BLM before coming, and stop at the farmhouse near the end of the road to ask permission to park a vehicle for the day.

Juniper Dunes Wilderness

2 | STEAMBOAT ROCK LOOP

Location: Grand Coulee
Status: Steamboat Rock State Park
Distance: 4 miles round trip
Hiking time: 3–4 hours
Difficulty: Moderate
Season: March through November
Maps: USGS Barker Canyon, Electric City, Steamboat Rock
SE, Steamboat Rock SW
Information: Steamboat Rock State Park

Steamboat Rock is a spectacular basalt butte jutting up 800 feet from Banks Lake in central Washington. Generations before the Columbia River Irrigation Project pumped water from behind Grand Coulee Dam and created Banks Lake, Steamboat Rock was used as a landmark by Indians. Ditto for early settlers and modern pilots. Hikers can explore nearly 640 acres on top of the butte, from which they can contrast close views of the desert with the glaciated spectacle of the North Cascades in the distance. This hike can be made virtually year-round, although early morning is best in summer to avoid the heat. April and May are the best months to explore

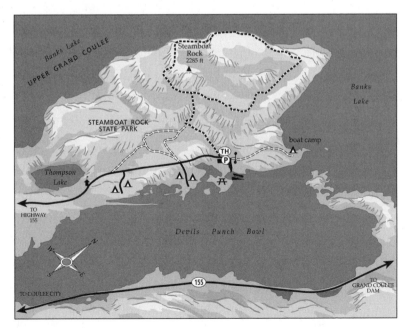

Hikers on Steamboat Rock above Banks Lake

this Columbia Basin scabrock country. Comfortable temperatures plus nesting waterfowl and eagles and a remarkable variety of wildflowers, from bitterroots to blooming cactus, provide pleasures hikers won't find in alpine country.

A band of mule deer resides on Steamboat. So do rattlesnakes.

From Coulee City, Washington, drive north on State Highway 155 about 16 miles to Steamboat Rock State Park, which is just south of Electric City and 10 miles south of Grand Coulee Dam. The park includes two popular campgrounds and a day-use parking area just north of the second campground.

The trail to the top of Steamboat Rock begins across the road from the boat launch parking area. The route leads up toward the east rim, gaining most of the elevation in the first steep pitch. Listen for the cascading call of the canyon wren. The trail is much gentler as it leads through a drainage from the east rim toward the west rim. Then it heads north up a short pitch to the top of the butte. Hikers can walk a clockwise loop around the perimeter of the relatively flat top of Steamboat Rock and return to the trailhead.

Drinking water and toilets are available at the campground and day-use

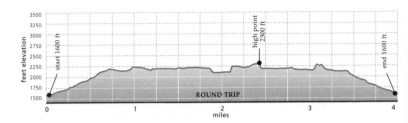

areas. Banks Lake is open year-round for fishing. It is particularly well known for its largemouth and smallmouth bass and walleyes, along with perch, whitefish, trout, crappie, and kokanee. Water sports such as wakeboarding are also popular.

Options: Interesting places to visit in the area include the Dry Falls interpretive center and several hiking routes out of Sun Lakes State Park just south of Coulee City on State Highway 17. The exhibits at Dry Falls tell the story of the Ice Age floods and geological phenomena that created the fascinating landscapes in this region. The center also houses an exhibit explaining the Blue Lake Rhino Cast discovered above Blue Lake.

•Lake Lenore caves are situated about 10 miles south of Dry Falls. A short hike from the parking area, well marked on Highway 17, leads to shelters used by prehistoric humans.

3 | NORTHRUP CANYON

Location: Grand Coulee
Status: Steamboat Rock State Park
Distance: 7 miles round trip
Hiking time: 3–4 hours
Difficulty: Moderate
Season: March through November
Maps: USGS Steamboat Rock SE, Electric City
Information: Steamboat Rock State Park

This little niche of Steamboat Rock State Park is largely overlooked by the fishing and boating crowds at the main campground and recreation area on Banks Lake. But nature has flourished here for years. This day-hiking jewel is a key bald eagle wintering area and a sanctuary for everything from deer and more than 65 bird species to bats, amphibians, and rattlesnakes. Northrup Creek is the only year-round stream flowing into Banks Lake, a reservoir created in the 1950s by the Columbia Basin Irrigation Project. But even this stream can disappear in drought years. Northrup Lake at the end of the trail is occasionally stocked with rainbow trout.

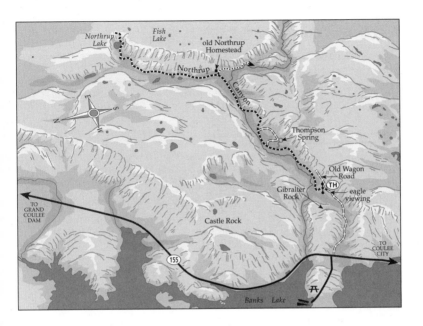

Take State Highway 155 north from Coulee City, Washington, or south from Grand Coulee. Along Banks Lake near milepost 19, turn east on a gravel road. Drive uphill past a gravel pit about 0.5 mile to the trailhead.

Before setting foot on the featured trail, note the 80-yard-long path heading north from the parking lot to a viewing area that's a winter hot spot for watching bald eagles. One of the canyon's two communal roosting areas is in the big Douglas firs and snags along the bluffs south of the trailhead. During winter, around 100 eagles can swoop into the canyon daily from 2 P.M. to 5 P.M. State biologists say this is the single most important winter roosting habitat in north-central Washington and likely attracts eagles from Banks Lake, Lake Roosevelt, and the Columbia River downstream. By May, however, hikers are likely to see more rattlesnakes than eagles.

The Northrup Canyon Trail starts out as an old road (notice piles of cans dumped by crews that built Grand Coulee Dam in the 1930s) heading up the creek. Pass under basalt cliffs that attract soaring hawks. At 2 miles, the route comes to a seasonal park residence and a decaying century-old cabin. At the park residence, bear left past the left side of the old chicken house and head up a single-track trail that becomes rocky with a few steep pitches. The trail leads up and down through open timber and out-croppings to Northrup Lake.

The canyon was homesteaded in 1874 by John Northrup, who planted the area's first orchard. By the turn of the century it had become popular for hikers, horse riders, and picnickers from Almira and Hartline. The area is lush with sage, a surprising variety of trees, and shrubs that form a green

Northrup Canyon, Steamboat Rock State Park

oasis in spring and display brilliant colors in fall. Washington assumed the land as an addition to Steamboat Rock State Park in 1976. Rules at the 3,522-acre park prohibit camping or campfires outside designated campgrounds. Pets must be kept on leash.

Options: Continue past Northrup Lake and up a scree slope for down-canyon views from a sage plateau.

•From the trailhead parking area, bear right on the Old Wagon Road Trail that was hacked out of steep canyon walls in the 1880s for stage and freight wagons running between Almira and Bridgeport. The road, which is rough with scree, leads up about 1.5 miles to canyon viewpoints before fading into cow trails leading to private land. The wagon road is closed from November 15 to March 15 to prevent disturbance to the eagles.

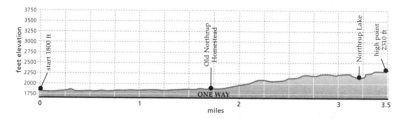

4 | ODESSA–PACIFIC LAKE

Location: Crab Creek
Status: Unprotected
Distance: 13–14 miles one way
Hiking time: 6 hours
Difficulty: Moderate
Season: March through November
Maps: USGS Pacific Lake, Sullivan, Irby, Odessa
Information: U.S. Bureau of Land Management,
    Spokane District

Farmers in this region of sagebrush and wheat fields still wonder what in blazes brings hikers to Odessa, Washington. And hikers who come in the heat of August will wonder why, too. In March, April, or May, however, the attraction is more obvious, as the desert blooms in this 12,000-acre stretch of rangeland secured by the U.S. Bureau of Land Management in the 1990s. Walk through sweet-smelling sagebrush, past secluded ponds, and in and out of shallow coulees lined by basalt columns. The area is part of the channeled scablands carved by Ice Age floods.

Most hikers will want to tackle this trail one way, starting from Odessa and hiking north to where a shuttle vehicle has been left at the Lakeview Ranch parking area near Pacific Lake. Be aware that hunters could be working this area from mid-October through early January.

To reach the south trailhead in Odessa, turn north off State Highway 28 onto Birch Street and cross the railroad tracks. Just past the Odessa Grange

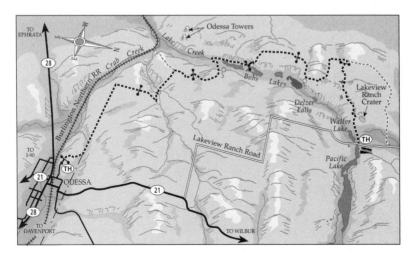

Supply, turn left on Alice Avenue. Follow the gravel road up a rock bluff to the trailhead near the city water treatment facility.

To reach the north trailhead at Pacific Lake, drive north from Odessa on State Highway 21 toward Wilbur. Go 2.8 miles and turn left (west) on Lakeview Ranch Road. Drive 5.1 miles on the gravel road to Lakeview Ranch. A caretaker's house is to the east of the road next to Pacific Lake, which is stocked with rainbow trout in non-drought years. The parking area is on the left next to shop buildings.

Consider this a desert hike, and a chance to get on the trail long before snow melts from the mountains. But even in spring, start trips as early as possible in the day to beat the potential heat and have the best chance of seeing active wildlife, such as mule deer, coyotes, marmots, hawks, songbirds, and waterfowl.

Bring plenty of water (although water could possibly be filtered from a stock-trough spring). Three liters wouldn't be too much. Wear brim hats, sunglasses, and sunscreen. Light, long-sleeve shirts as well as light pants tucked into socks will protect skin from sun and ticks, both of which are factors to be considered as seriously as the chance of rattlesnake encounters. By June, cheatgrass becomes another factor for people who don't like the feeling of a zillion needles sticking into their socks.

That said, the sage-country wildflowers that start to display in March and peak in late April through much of May are wonderful to behold after a long winter. Balsamroots and wyethia, cutleaf daisies, lupine, rock gardens full of bitterroots, nine-leaved desert parsley, larkspur, and yarrow are scattered among rabbitbrush, sage, bunchgrass, and plumes of canary reedgrass.

From the Odessa Trailhead, the route starts as a marked single track through the sage and basalt scablands, where male valley quail might be heard calling "chi-CAH-go." Go 0.5-mile and turn left (west) on the powerline road. This 2-mile stretch goes through the first of several rocky gardens of bitterroots that bloom in May. At a fence, head uphill and northward on a double track. Go through a gate; enjoy the westward view of the Lake Creek drainage and its confluence with Crab Creek. Steep banks above Lake Creek represent classic denning sites for coyotes and badgers.

At 5.2 miles, look across the Lake Creek drainage at basalt buttes called Odessa Towers, then plunge down a single track through crumbling basalt columns, past a spring and stock tanks (possible campsite) to Bobs Lakes.

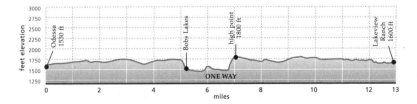

Male quail on scabrock along Odessa–Pacific Lake Trail

By summer, these can look more like "Bobs Salt Flats." Even in spring, hikers can often cross the fractured dry mud at this end of the lake. In wet periods, go a little farther to cross a bridge at the south end of the lake. Once on the other side, at 6.5 miles, watch for poison ivy as the trail leads north on the west side of the lakes. The route climbs, contours, and climbs again to the canyon rim and connects with a dirt road open to motor vehicles. The road bends and heads straight north on a somewhat boring stretch for 1 mile. In years of plentiful water, you can hike to the canyon rim in this stretch during spring and see water flowing over Delzer Falls, which is on private land. Most often, however, the falls are dry. The road-route bends east and down through white lupine (blooms in May) to the edge of Waukesha Spring, which is on private land.

At 10.6 miles, look for a road junction heading right (east). This non-motorized alternate route is the most scenic way to end the trip to Lakeview Ranch. But stretches of trail can be under water in the coulees, forcing rugged off-trail travel and minor routefinding challenges down to the double track in the valley floor that leads back to the ranch headquarters. If you are not up to that challenge, stay on the main route open to vehicles, which eventually curves eastward to Lakeview Road. Then turn south 0.5 mile to the trailhead. When viewpoints are encountered, scan for the several "craters" in the area that were caused during volcanic activity in which basalt flows cooled and collapsed.

Options: Hike from Lakeview Ranch cross-country along the rocky ledges on the south shore of Pacific Lake.

5 | OLD STAGE ROAD–MIDNIGHT RIDGE LOOP

Location: Kettle River Range
Status: Semi-primitive
Distance: 10 miles round trip
Hiking time: 6 hours or overnight
Difficulty: Moderate
Season: Mid-June through October
Maps: USGS Cooke Mountain, Copper Butte
Information: Colville National Forest, Republic District

The national recreation trail that rolls 30 miles along the crest of the Kettle River Mountains north from Highway 20 at Sherman Pass can be accessed from 17 trailheads (see Hike 6). This loop, however, is among the most diverse, enjoyable, and historical ways to visit the Kettle Crest. The route links two good trails from a single trailhead, making a trek to the crest an adventure in itself with no car shuttle required.

In 1892, the Washington State Legislature built a trail for wagons from Marblemount to Marcus. This first state highway attempted to connect commerce west of the Cascades with the expanding frontier of the Upper Columbia River. The demand for the road became more urgent in 1896 with the need to supply the mining boomtowns of the Republic gold fields. But this torturous route over the mountains proved to be impassable by freight wagon. It was abandoned in 1898, when an easier route was opened over Sherman Pass. From the west, Old Stage Road Trail 1 connects at the Kettle

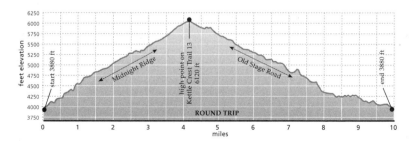

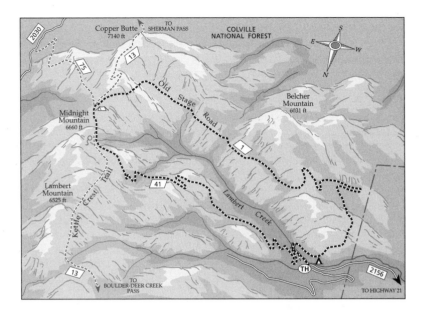

Crest with Trail 75, which goes down to the East Fork Mick Creek Road on the east side of the range. This 7-mile stretch is the only remnant of the road grade from the original state highway.

From the junction with State Highway 20 just east of Republic, Washington, drive north on State Highway 21 about 9 miles and turn right at milepost 171.7 onto County Road 546 (Lambert Creek). Eventually this becomes Forest Road 2156 as you drive a little more than 7 miles east to the trailhead and campground. (The road passes a pleasant car-camping spot at 6.6 miles.) This area generally is cathedral quiet, unless you happen to hit the same weekend as a scheduled group equestrian ride.

From the parking area at elev. 3,880 feet, don't go up the old trail through the elaborate Old Stage Road gate. Instead, cross the road and ford the north fork of Lambert Creek. Hike 0.3 mile along the south fork to a trail junction just before crossing a bridge. Bear left onto Midnight Ridge Trail 41, which leads 4 miles up to Kettle Crest Trail 13 at elev. 6,120 feet. The trail winds through alternating stands of dog-hair lodgepole pine swept by wildfire in the 1990s and through several marvelously adapted stands of old-growth pines, firs, and hemlocks. The armor of bark on these old giants enabled them to weather decades of forest fires and they continue to shade luxurious parks of grass, lupine, and other wildflowers. Eventually, the trail pushes up to aspen groves, hillsides of sagebrush, and stands of fireweed that will continue to bloom brilliantly until the burned forest areas mature. Yet the trail is so lightly used, it's best to hike this loop clockwise because the junction with Kettle Crest Trail 13 is faint and can be hard to find coming from the other direction.

Need water? Turn left on the Kettle Crest Trail and walk 0.3 mile to a tapped spring, reliable except possibly in late summer. Remember, even spring water should be purified. There's a tiny tent site just beyond the spring, but avoid the gully that floods in a thunderstorm. To continue the loop, hike south on the Kettle Crest Trail to a campsite in the saddle between Midnight Mountain and Copper Butte and the junction with the Old Stage Road. Trail 75 is the portion of the former wagon road that drops down the east side of the crest, but this loop trip follows Trail 1, which is the road to the west. The route angles down hillsides, where forest fires have left a more thorough impression while leaving better views of Midnight Ridge and the Kettle River Valley. The road completes the trip's traverse of the Lambert Creek drainage headwaters and drops down to the trailhead in 5.5 miles. Small tent sites can be found on this stretch in the three spots where the trail crosses the south fork of Lambert Creek. Limited cattle grazing is allowed here, helping keep the vegetation in check.

Options: From the saddle campsite, hike the Kettle Crest Trail north or south. Heading south gives quick access to good views from 7,140-foot Copper Butte.

Lupine blooming in the grassy parklands of Midnight Ridge

6 COLUMBIA MOUNTAIN LOOP (KETTLE CREST NORTH)

Location: Kettle River Range
Status: Semi-primitive
Distance: 8 miles round trip
Hiking time: 4 hours
Difficulty: Moderate
Season: Mid-June through October
Map: USGS Sherman Peak
Information: Colville National Forest, Republic District

The loop trip around Columbia Mountain could be considered a delicious meal in itself, or a juicy appetizer for future expeditions on the 30-mile north segment of the Kettle Crest National Recreation Trail, one of the premier backpacking routes in the Colville National Forest. (Also see Hike 7.) The trailhead, with easy access from State Highway 20, launches hikers toward the tops of rolling mountains and the flowered meadows of the Colville's largest roadless area. The abandoned cabin on Columbia Mountain is the oldest fire lookout still existing in this region, although its days are numbered.

The trailhead, which includes a picnic area and pit toilets, is on the north side of State Highway 20 at Sherman Pass 17 miles east of Republic, Washington, and 28 miles west of Kettle Falls, Washington. Sherman Overlook Campground is just east of the pass.

Walk north on Kettle Crest Trail 13 starting at elev. 5,575 feet. The route gains nearly 500 feet in the first 1.2 miles. Then it contours past a spur trail to a stock watering trough. At 2 miles, it's joined by Columbia Mountain Loop Trail 24 at elev. 6,120 feet. (From this point and back, the loop connection around the mountain is a relatively gentle 3.1 miles. Taking the spur to the summit adds 1 mile round trip.)

Turn right (east), go past a spring, and hike 0.5 mile on the spur across the west face of the mountain before coming to the junction with the loop. Hikers can follow their instincts in either direction, and the beautifully constructed trail will lead back to this point after contouring around the mountain with only a few brief episodes of elevation gain and loss.

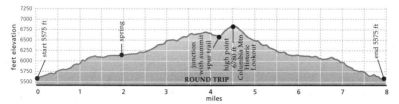

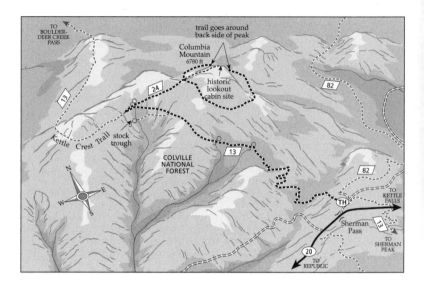

The high point of the trip, in more ways than one, is taking off from the northwest side of the mountain and hiking up the spur trail 0.5 mile to the broad 6,780-foot summit dappled with wildflowers in July. The deteriorating log cabin, a unique construction for forest fire lookouts, was built between 1914 and 1916. A dry campsite is along the trail just before reaching the summit. Consider timing the hike to descend in the glorious light just before sunset. Looking south, the silvery snags left from the 1988 White Mountain fire along Sherman Peak sometimes turn orange at sunset as though they are briefly ablaze again.

Options: Kettle Crest Trail 13 continues north 28 miles from Columbia Mountain to the paved road at Boulder-Deer Creek Pass east of Curlew, Washington. Hike the entire route in three to five days or bag segments separately using the numerous feeder trails that lead to the crest from east and west sides (see Hike 5). The Kettle Crest North has its ups and downs, with a cumulative elevation gain of 5,400 feet and 6,200 feet of loss. Water is sparingly available along this trail from springs, some of which are developed with stock troughs.

At about 4 miles from Sherman Pass, a PVC pipe provides spring water before the saddle at Jungle Hill. The first good campsite is at about 7 miles, about halfway between Jungle Hill and Wapaloosie Mountain. The site is an old outfitter's camp, nestled in a grove of trees about 100 yards past a spring. The trail climbs to the top of 7,140-foot Copper Butte, for a superb view from the tallest mountain in the area. There's a spring just off the east side of the trail about 1.2 miles north of Copper Butte and just south of 6,660-foot Midnight Mountain, where there's a campsite. Another spring is 0.3 mile past the junction with Midnight Ridge Trail 41.

Wapaloosie Mountain on the Kettle Crest north of Columbia Mountain

From the intersection of Trail 13 and Trail 30, it is 9-plus miles to the Boulder–Deer Creek Pass. The stretch has no good camping areas and few water sources. In a pinch, water is available from a stock trough along Trail 32 heading down to Forest Road 2160 northwest of Profanity Peak.

Additional topo maps needed for this stretch of the Kettle Crest include Copper Butte, Edds Mountain, and Mount Leona.

7 SHERMAN PEAK LOOP (KETTLE CREST SOUTH)

Location: Kettle River Range
Status: Semi-primitive
Distance: 5.3 miles round trip
Hiking time: 4 hours or overnight
Difficulty: Moderate
Season: Mid-June through October
Map: USGS Sherman Peak
Information: Colville National Forest, Three Rivers District, Kettle Falls Office

This southern section of the 43-mile Kettle Crest National Recreation Trail (also see Hike 6) heads south from Sherman Pass on State Highway 20 and goes 13 miles through the snags left from a 1988 forest fire, terminating just

Old Columbia Mountain Lookout, with Sherman Peak and Kettle Crest in the distance

past White Mountain, a Native American spiritual site. The trail is complemented with a segment featured here that forms the delightful 5.3-mile loop trip around Sherman Peak. Wildlife is abundant, including deer, coyotes, grouse, black bears, and songbirds, with signs of the elusive lynx. Listen for the shrill whistle of the varied thrush in the timber and the squeaks of pikas in the talus slopes. The Washington Department of Fish and Wildlife manages this region as a trophy mule deer area, which means it has a high ratio of mature bucks with antlers four-points or better on each side. Funds from sales of this guidebook helped volunteers build an overnight shelter south of Sherman Peak near Snow Peak in 1996.

The easiest access to the Sherman Peak Loop and Kettle Crest South is off State Highway 20 at Sherman Pass, which is 17 miles east of Republic, Washington, and 28 miles west of Kettle Falls, Washington. Sherman Overlook Campground is just east of the pass. (See "Options" for another access.)

From the Sherman Pass Trailhead at elev. 5,575 feet, the trail heads down

to the east and crosses Highway 20 southward to start zigzagging up Sherman Peak. At 0.7 mile, just before a bridge over a creek crossing, Trail 13 is intersected by Sherman Loop Trail 72. Continue straight and hike the loop clockwise. The northeast side of Sherman Peak is still lush and well timbered. But as the trail bends around the south side, more blackened, silvery snags dominate the landscape. In 1988, lightning on White Mountain started a fire that burned 20,126 acres. Summer flower displays of beargrass, lupine, Indian paintbrush, and fireweed have been phenomenal in subsequent years and should continue until the overstory develops again.

On the south side of Sherman Peak at 2.7 miles, Trail 13 junctions with Trail 72 again. To continue the loop, bear right onto Trail 72 and start heading north. Enjoy small patches of timber that escaped the flames. Cross a small creek on the north side of Sherman Peak, go through a bouldered slope, and join Trail 13 again. Turn left for the return to the trailhead at Sherman Pass.

Options: To get a different and more open perspective of the Sherman Loop, start on the west side of Snow Peak. From the junction of Highways 20 and 21 just east of Republic, go east on Highway 20 for 4.5 miles and turn south on Hall Creek Road (milepost 309.6). Drive 3.2 miles and turn left onto Forest Road 100. Drive 4.3 miles to the trailhead. The trail starts at elev. 5,800 feet and climbs 500 feet in 2.7 miles through the 1988 burn (little shade) to Kettle Crest Trail 13. Turn north 1.1 miles to connect into the Sherman Loop described above.

•Turn south 0.5 mile on Kettle Crest Trail 13 to a spring and the Snow Peak Cabin, which is available for rent through the Republic Ranger District.

•From either trailhead, you can hike the 13-mile south segment of the

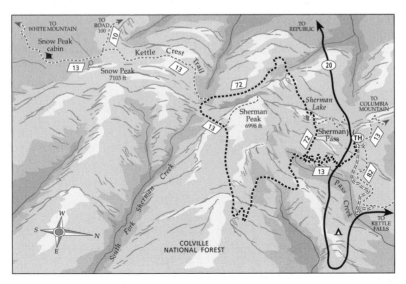

Kettle Crest Trail. Camping spots are available along the way, but dependable water sources are scarce south of Snow Peak Cabin. Check the ranger district for trail conditions through the burn, which is prone to deadfalls. Get a particularly pleasing vista from the southern ridge of White Mountain, site of a demolished lookout. Long before the Forest Service arrived, young Native Americans of what now are the Colville Confederated Tribes made a pilgrimage to the top of White Mountain as a rite of adulthood. Here they built rock cairns to commemorate the visions of their ceremonial retreat. Today, you can still see some of the cairns from the summit (a few, however, were stacked by bored Forest Service lookouts) and the area is still occasionally used by tribal members. Please respect the area and leave the cairns intact. The south trailhead is just south of White Mountain on Forest Road 250.

8 | HOODOO CANYON

Location: Kettle River Range
Status: Unprotected
Distance: 5 miles round trip
Hiking time: 3–5 hours or overnight
Difficulty: Moderately difficult
Season: May through October
Map: USGS Jackknife
Information: Colville National Forest, Three Rivers District,
Kettle Falls Office

This is a short day hike or overnighter through a lightly used and surprisingly lush area of the Colville National Forest. Hoodoo Canyon, which is near a popular developed campground, holds a cold, clear lake and a small world of wonders that seem to have been tucked away for hikers to explore.

From Kettle Falls, Washington, drive west on State Highway 20 across the Columbia River and turn right onto U.S. Highway 395 toward Canada. Drive north about 6 miles and turn west onto Forest Road 460 (Deadman Creek). Go about 6 miles and turn left onto Road 9565. Drive another 3 miles to the trailhead and parking area on the south side of the road.

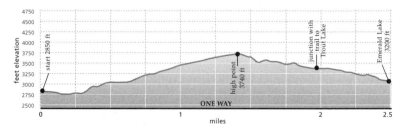

Hoodoo Canyon, with Emerald Lake in the distance

From the parking area, the trail begins at the edge of the timber. Don't be lured astray by game trails. Hoodoo Canyon Trail 17 descends quickly to a wide footbridge over Deadman Creek. The route is well maintained as it climbs through a stand of timber with abundant wildflowers. After about 2 miles, the trail breaks out of the timber with a view of Lily Lake, 500 feet below. Hoodoo Canyon is narrow with numerous rock outcroppings. The trail skirts the edge of the canyon, then descends at a trail junction,

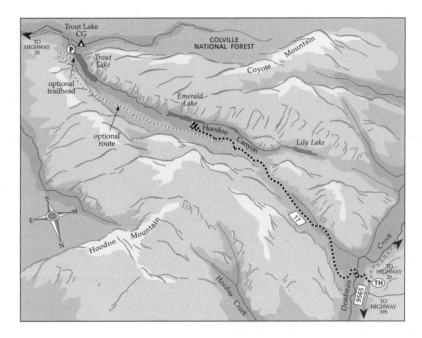

switchbacking the last 0.2 mile to Emerald Lake at 3,200 feet. Although the lake is a clear and cold 10–15 feet deep in early spring, it can dwindle to a small pond by late summer. Campsites are available only when water levels are down.

Options: An easier trail, well-constructed but less scenic, leads from the Emerald Lake area 2.5 miles to Trout Lake Campground.

9 | ABERCROMBIE MOUNTAIN

Location: Pend Oreille River
Status: Unprotected
Distance: 6.5 miles round trip
Hiking time: 4 hours
Difficulty: Moderately difficult
Season: Late June through early October
Map: USGS Abercrombie Mountain
Information: Colville National Forest, Three Rivers District, Colville Office

Abercrombie Mountain and its neighbors, Sherlock Peak and Hooknose Mountain, are the three prominent high points between the Columbia River on the west and the Pend Oreille River on the east. Hikers who reach their summits (also see Hike 10) enjoy panoramic views of these two major river valleys plus the Salmo-Priest Wilderness, Canadian peaks, and on a clear day, the North Cascades. Conservationists have proposed this area be designated wilderness.

From U.S. Highway 395 in Colville, Washington, drive east on Third Avenue toward Ione and State Highway 20. Near the edge of town, turn left (north) at the airport onto Aladdin Road and go about 2 miles to a Y, staying to the right toward Northport. Go nearly 24 miles (route becomes Northport Road 9435) to another Y, staying to the right toward Deep Lake on Road 9445. (This area also is accessible via forest roads over Smackout Pass from Ione, Washington.) Continue 7.3 miles, passing Deep Lake, and turn right (east) at Leadpoint onto Silver Creek Road 4720. Drive 0.5 mile and bear left at a Y, continuing on County Road 4720 about 1 mile, and cross a cattle guard onto national forest land. Drive 0.4 mile and turn left onto Road 7078. (Continuing straight onto Road 070 leads 1.3 miles to a camping area at Silver Creek Trailhead.) Drive 4.5 miles on Road 7078, turning right onto Road 300, a less-developed route that may be muddy in spots, and drive 3.3 miles up to the trailhead at the end of the road, where there's a small spot for camping.

Trail 117 begins as an old logging road at elev. 4,090 feet and gains 3,220 feet to the Abercrombie summit. Water is available in the first third of the route, but none is available higher on the mountain. At 1.4 miles, Trail 119

Descending Abercrombie Mountain

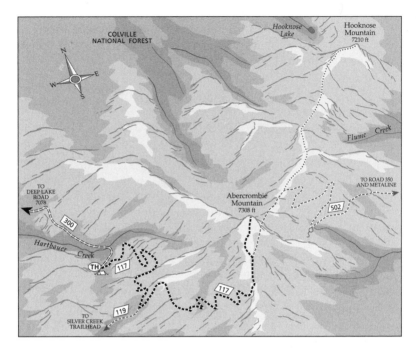

merges from the right. Head left (east), where a sign says it is 1.8 miles to Abercrombie. (Turning right would lead 6 miles down to Silver Creek Trailhead.) The trail is mostly gradual with switchbacks through the dry, open country of an old burn. At the ridge top, look for a large rock cairn, the first of several that mark the rest of the way along a faint trail north to the summit. The last 0.5 mile is fairly steep, but not overly difficult. A USGS survey marker has been installed at the 7,308-foot summit near the burned remains of a lookout tower.

Options: From the trail junction south of the summit, scramblers can extend the hike north, starting on Trail 502, then going off-trail along the ridgeline a little more than a mile to Hooknose Mountain, elev. 7,210 feet. The north face of Hooknose is sheer and impressive.

•Hikers willing to hike a trailless ridge could extend this into an 18-mile backpacking trip during early summer when lingering snow provides a water source for camping on the divide. Start from the spacious camping area and trailhead on the South Fork of Silver Creek at the end of Road 070, shown on Colville National Forest maps. From here, go up the switchbacking South Fork of Silver Creek Trail 123, crossing several creeks on the way to the ridge top at Gunsight Pass. Then bushwhack northerly along the ridge to Abercrombie Mountain Trail 117 and return on Trail 119 to the Silver Creek Trailhead. No defined trail has been built on the 3.4 miles of ridgeline, but the rugged terrain is open most of the way.

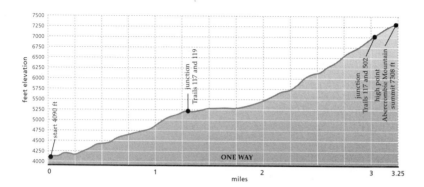

• Abercrombie also is accessible on the east side by following Forest Road 350, which takes off from the Boundary Dam Road northwest of Metaline Falls. The slow, rough road goes 7.5 miles to the trailhead for Flume Creek Trail 502, which heads 4 miles to the summit.

10 | SHERLOCK PEAK

Location: Pend Oreille River
Status: Unprotected
Distance: 7 miles round trip
Hiking time: 3–4 hours
Difficulty: Moderate
Season: Late June through early October
Map: USGS Deep Lake
Information: Colville National Forest, Three Rivers District, Colville Office

This is a switchbacking hike that breaks into open slopes to a scenic viewpoint on top of Sherlock Peak overlooking both the Columbia and Pend Oreille River drainages.

From U.S. Highway 395 in Colville, Washington, drive east on Third Avenue toward Ione and State Highway 20. Near the edge of town, turn left (north) at the airport onto Aladdin Road and go about 2 miles to a Y, staying to the right toward Northport. Go nearly 24 miles (route becomes Northport Road 9435) to another Y, staying to the right toward Deep Lake on Road 9445. (This area also is accessible via forest roads over Smackout Pass from Ione, Washington.) Continue 7.3 miles, passing Deep Lake, and turn right (east) at Leadpoint onto Silver Creek Road 4720. Drive 0.5 mile and bear left at a Y, continuing on County Road 4720 about 1 mile, and cross a cattle guard onto national forest land. Drive 0.4 mile and bear right

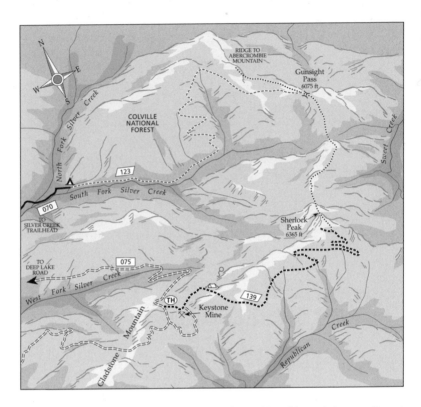

onto Forest Road 070. Drive about 0.5 mile to a Y and bear right onto Forest Road 075 (Windy Ridge). Drive nearly 5 miles to the trailhead.

Starting at elev. 4,500 feet, hike up an old road for 1.7 miles before joining the well-graded single-track trail that switchbacks to the ridge just below the 6,365-foot summit of Sherlock Peak. Camping is possible along the first section of trail and even near the summit, although spring water might have to be hauled some distance. From the top, enjoy views of the Columbia River Valley, the Salmo-Priest Wilderness, many peaks in Canada, and on a clear day, the North Cascades.

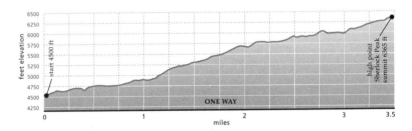

On the ridge south of Sherlock Peak

Options: Using a topo map, plot a cross-country hike through beargrass and sparsely timbered saddles 4 miles north to Abercrombie Mountain (see Hike 9). Or drop off the ridge at Gunsight Pass and follow the easy grade of Trail 123, which goes 7 miles down to Silver Creek Trailhead, where a shuttle car could be waiting.

11 HALL MOUNTAIN

Location: Sullivan Lake
Status: Unprotected
Distance: 5 miles round trip
Hiking time: 3 hours
Difficulty: Easy
Season: July through October
Maps: USGS Metaline Falls, Pass Creek
Information: Colville National Forest, Sullivan Lake District

Hall Mountain looms unobtrusively over the clear waters of Sullivan Lake. Gain most of the elevation for this hike in a vehicle, and contour across a mountain that's home for a band of bighorn sheep, plus deer, elk, and the occasional cougars and bears that prowl around to feast on them.

From Metaline Falls, Washington, continue north on State Highway 31 as it climbs 2 miles to the signed junction to Sullivan Lake. Turn right and follow this paved county road 4 miles to Sullivan Lake Campground area. Continue past the campground area on Forest Road 22 for 3 miles and turn

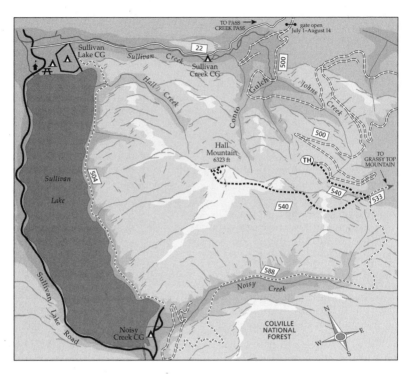

right on Johns Creek Road 500. Drive 7.5 rugged miles to the trailhead at the end of the road. Check with the ranger district for seasonal closures of this road, which typically is open to motorized vehicles from July 1 to August 14.

About 0.6 mile up the trail, there are two closely spaced junctions. Trail 533 is a pleasant ridge route east to Grassy Top Mountain (see Hike 12). Trail 588 is a steep trail plunging down to Noisy Creek Campground, and the best access to Hall Mountain if the Johns Creek Road is closed starting in mid-August. To reach Hall Mountain, head west on Trail 540. With most of the elevation gained on the access road, Trail 540 gains only 800 feet in the 2.5 miles to the summit. The trail is rocky in places but easy to follow. No water is available. Carry binoculars and hike early in the morning or late in the afternoon for the best opportunities to spot bighorn sheep.

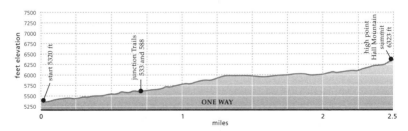

Bighorn sheep on Hall Mountain

Options: Make shuttle arrangements and hike steeply down off the west side of Hall Mountain on Trail 588 to Noisy Creek Campground at the south end of Sullivan Lake. Also, an excellent trail runs the 4-mile length of the lake's west shoreline from Noisy Creek to East Sullivan Lake Campground at the north end of the lake.

12 | GRASSY TOP MOUNTAIN

Location: Sullivan Lake
Status: Unprotected
Distance: 7.5 miles round trip
Hiking time: 4–5 hours or overnight
Difficulty: Moderate
Season: Late June through mid-October
Map: USGS Pass Creek
Information: Colville National Forest, Sullivan Lake District

This is an excellent ridge-running day hike for views of the Idaho Selkirks, the Priest Lake area, and portions of the Salmo-Priest Wilderness.

On Grassy Top Mountain

From Metaline Falls, Washington, drive north on State Highway 31, about 2 miles past the Pend Oreille River Bridge and turn right toward Sullivan Lake on County Road 9345. Drive southeast 4 miles to Sullivan Lake Ranger Station and campground. Turn left (east) on Forest Road 22 along Sullivan Creek for 5 miles to the junction with Road 2220. Turn right (south), continuing on Road 22 across Sullivan Creek and climbing for 7 miles almost to Pass Creek Pass, where the trailhead is situated at elev. 5,380 feet. Parking is limited to only a few vehicles along the road, (Note: Nearby to the north is a trailhead for Trail 512. See Hike 14.) Pass Creek Pass is also accessible from the Priest Lake, Idaho, area north of Nordman on Road 302.

Grassy Top National Recreation Trail 503 descends sharply to cross the

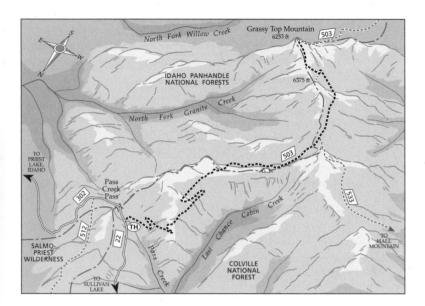

head of Pass Creek before climbing a well-kept path through heavy timber and below a towering granite ledge. One mile later the trail levels off through a thinning forest and acres of beargrass. Watch for an opening to the east of the trail: a good lunch spot and a possible campsite overlooking the North Fork of Granite Creek. Priest Lake and the Selkirk Crest can be seen in the distance. The trail continues gently on, wandering in and out of the timber along a ridge before connecting at 2.7 miles with Trail 533, which heads west to Hall Mountain. About 3 miles from the trailhead there's a choice of either following the trail the last 0.5 mile to Grassy Top, elev. 6,253 feet, or climbing a steep, unmarked trail up an open slope to a grand viewpoint at 6,375 feet.

Options: Groups with two vehicles can start this trip as described above and make a great ridge-hugging 8-plus-mile hike. Start on Trail 503 as described above. After 2.7 miles, turn right (west) and hike Trail 533 about 5.1 miles before turning right on Trail 540 to a shuttle vehicle at the Hall Mountain Trailhead (see Hike 11).

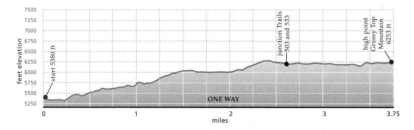

13 | CROWELL RIDGE

Location: Sullivan Lake
Status: Salmo-Priest Wilderness
Distance: 16 miles round trip
Hiking time: 2 days
Difficulty: Moderately difficult
Season: July through mid-October
Map: USGS Gypsy Peak
Information: Colville National Forest, Sullivan Lake District

This is a scenic, mostly treeless ridge hike in the Salmo-Priest Wilderness that involves about a mile of off-trail navigation through slopes of beargrass and talus to reach Gypsy Peak and Watch Lake. A shorter route to Gypsy Peak begins at Bear Pasture, but it is no match in scenery for the Crowell Ridge hike described here. Roads could be the limiting factor for some hikers. The road to Bear Pasture is closed to motorized vehicles from August 15 to November 20 each year and impassable to most passenger cars even when the gate is open. The road to the Sullivan Mountain Trailhead is very poor with water bars that could bump the bottoms of cars with low clearance.

From Metaline Falls, Washington, drive north on State Highway 31 about 2 miles past the Pend Oreille River Bridge and turn right toward

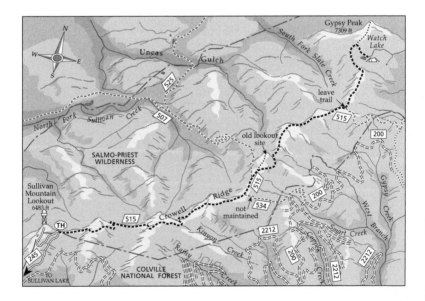

Watch Lake and Gypsy Peak, Salmo-Priest Wilderness

Sullivan Lake. Just before the Sullivan Lake District administration buildings, turn north at a sign for Sullivan Creek Highline and Crowell Ridge.
Follow Forest Road 2212 about 3 miles and turn left on Road 245 toward
Sullivan Mountain Lookout. Drive this rough road to the trailhead, which
leaves the north side of the road on a switchback just below the lookout.

Crowell Ridge Trail 515 starts at elev. 6,260 feet and weaves through
open timber before breaking out of the trees for most of its distance.
Roughly 5 miles from the trailhead, the trail heads decidedly downhill to
the northeast toward Bear Meadow. Using a topo map, leave the trail before it descends and follow the ridge north toward Watch Lake. Contour to
the east of the first knob after leaving the trail, then contour to the west
side of the ridge for about 1 mile over the talus until you come to the bowl
above Watch Lake. Descend to the saddle south of Gypsy Peak and then
down to the lake. The most impressive view of Gypsy, the highest point in
Eastern Washington at elev. 7,309 feet, is from the north, where its sheer
face looms over tiny Gypsy Lakes.

Carry plenty of water; no reliable source is available until the end of the
hike at Watch Lake. In dry years, even the lake can disappear by late summer. The camping areas are limited and fragile, definitely not suitable for
groups of more than six. The area around the lake can be boggy in July or
after heavy rains.

This is a popular elk, bear, and mule deer hunting area in the fall. Also
keep an eye out for bighorn sheep that frequent Crowell Ridge during
spring and summer.

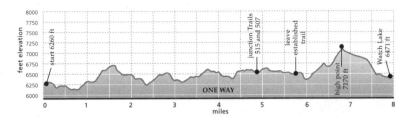

Options: The August 15 to November 20 closure of Forest Road 200, which provides access to the north end of Crowell Ridge Trail 515, provides a 10-mile loop hike opportunity. Follow Roads 22 and 2220 up Sullivan Creek, then turn left onto Road 2212 and park at the junction with gated Road 200. Hike up Road 200 about 2 miles, watching for neglected Trail 534 heading uphill just beyond Smart Creek. If this trail isn't apparent, consider bushwhacking up the steep slope to link with Crowell Ridge Trail 515. Then hike northeast, over Crowell Peak and drop down to the end of Road 200, which offers a pleasant return walk to the vehicles.

14 | SHEDROOF DIVIDE

Location: Salmo River
Status: Salmo-Priest Wilderness
Distance: 19 miles one way
Hiking time: 2 days minimum
Difficulty: Moderately difficult
Season: July through mid-October
Maps: USGS Salmo Mountain, Helmer Mountain
Information: Colville National Forest, Sullivan Lake District

Follow the backbone of the Salmo-Priest Wilderness on this up-and-down ridge hike along the Shedroof Divide bordering the west side of the Upper Priest River drainage. The trail skirts around or over five peaks and through open meadows with many pleasant views, although clearcuts have crept right up to the wilderness boundary in places. Water is scarce, particularly from late July through September. The hike is particularly enjoyable with a car shuttled to each trailhead and hiked from north to south. Several feeder trails from the west and east offer bailout points for shorter trips or longer loops.

To reach the north trailhead (also see Hike 15), drive east on Forest Road 22 from Sullivan Lake about 6 miles to the junction with Pass Creek Pass Road. Bear left toward Salmo Mountain on Road 2220 and go 14 miles (passing Gypsy Meadows and Road 270 to Salmo Mountain Lookout) to Salmo Pass Trailhead.

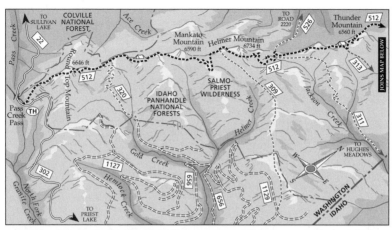

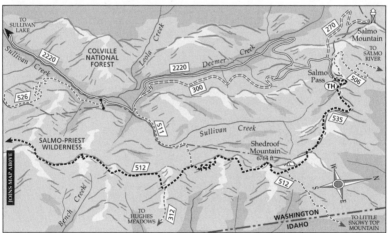

To reach the south trailhead (near the trailhead for Hike 12), drive east from Sullivan Lake on Road 22 about 6 miles. Turn right to continue on Road 22 toward Pass Creek Pass. The trailhead is a short way over the pass on the east side. Pass Creek Pass is also accessible from the Priest Lake, Idaho, area north of Nordman via Road 302.

From Salmo Pass, Trail 535 starts on a closed road for 1 mile before working south into the wilderness and up a ridge toward the high point of the trip at 6,590 feet along Shedroof Mountain. This is the first of five notable but not particularly uncomfortable climbs that lead around mountains named Thunder, Helmer, Mankato, and Round Top. Three campsites can be found along the Shedroof Divide. The first is about 3 miles from Salmo Pass Trailhead near the junction with Shedroof Divide Trail 512. A trickle of water can be found about 0.1 mile northeast on Trail 512. Continue the

Shedroof Divide, Salmo–Priest Wilderness

trip by heading south on Trail 512. A campsite near a weak spring can be found roughly halfway through the trip just south of Thunder Mountain near the junction with Trail 313. (This is 8.3 miles north of Pass Creek Pass Trailhead, and the most scenic stretch with peaks in every direction. Look for a scramble route up Thunder Mountain. Crowell Ridge and Gypsy Peak are to the west. The Selkirk Crest is to the east.) Another campsite with seasonal water is south of Mankato Mountain about 4 miles north of the Pass Creek Pass. The Shedroof Divide has no dependable water sources, although early season hikers should find sources near the campsites listed above as well as off Trail 512 near the junctions with Thunder Creek Trail 526 and Trail 311.

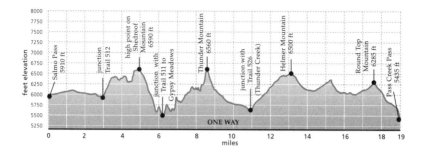

Options: Start the trip on Road 2220 at Gypsy Meadows and make a 14-mile loop with about 3,600 feet of elevation gain and loss using Trails 511, 512, and 526.

• A rugged 21-mile loop with 3,700 feet of elevation gain starts east of the divide up from Priest Lake at Hughes Meadows. If trails have been maintained (check with Priest Lake Ranger Station), hike Jackson Creek Trail 311 up 7.5 miles to a campsite on the Shedroof Divide. Walk north on Trail 512 for 6 miles to Trail 312. (A dry campsite is another 0.2 mile north on Trail 512.) Complete the loop by hiking Hughes Creek Trail 312 down 7.5 miles.

15 | SALMO-PRIEST LOOP

Location: Salmo River
Status: Salmo-Priest Wilderness
Distance: 19 miles round trip
Hiking time: 2 days minimum
Difficulty: Moderately difficult
Season: July through mid-October
Maps: USGS Salmo Mountain, Continental Mountain
Information: Colville National Forest, Sullivan Lake District

This loop exposes the Salmo-Priest for what it is: a lush nugget of wilderness that narrowly escaped development encroaching from every direction. The trail plunges down to the Salmo River and leads back up to airy peaks and ridges on the Washington-Idaho border. This is some of the wildest country left in Eastern Washington, among the state's last sanctuaries for grizzly bears, mountain caribou, wolves, and lynx.

From Metaline Falls, Washington, drive north on State Highway 31 about 2 miles past the Pend Oreille River Bridge and turn right toward Sullivan Lake. From Sullivan Lake, drive east on Forest Road 22 about 6 miles to the junction with Pass Creek Pass Road. Continue left on Road

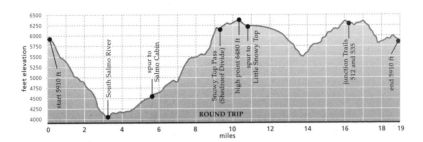

2220 toward Salmo Mountain. Drive 14 miles (passing Gypsy Meadows and the junction of Road 270) to the spacious Salmo Pass Trailhead. Parking and toilets are available. (This area is also accessible from Priest Lake via Pass Creek Pass.) The 1-mile stretch of road that once led to another trailhead has been closed with a gate and has become part of this hike.

The route begins on Trail 506 at 5,910 feet and immediately plunges downhill 3 miles on the most popular trail segment in the wilderness to the South Salmo River at 4,150 feet. It's an enjoyable walk, since the trail switchbacks downhill pleasantly through old-growth cedars and hemlocks, moss-carpeted logs, and lacey ferns. However, this north-facing slope can still be burdened with snow well into July. Good camping areas can be found on both sides of the river, which holds small cutthroat trout. (Some people overnight here and return the same way the next day.)

To continue the loop, cross the river and bear right at the junction with the unmaintained trail that heads left toward the Canada border. From the junction it's 2.3 miles to remains of the Salmo Cabin, which is an easy 0.2-mile walk down and to the right from the main trail. The cabin is situated by

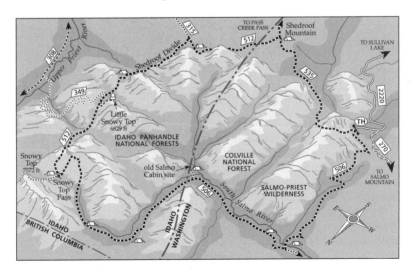

Looking south along Shedroof Divide from Snowy Top Mountain, Salmo–Priest Wilderness

a stream and a campsite. The cabin was built in the 1930s and used as a backcountry station until 1951. Hikers planning to do the loop in two days should push on at least another 3.5 miles to a decent campsite just below Snowy Top Pass. Water is abundant to this point. From here it's another 0.8 mile uphill to a better but dry campsite right at the pass on the shoulder of 7,572-foot Snowy Top Mountain. (Summit baggers should allow 2 hours from the pass to scramble to the top and back.) Water is not available at the pass and is scarce on Shedroof Divide, especially in August and September.

From the pass, continue south on the Shedroof Divide Trail 512 to the junction with the Little Snowy Top Trail, which leads 1 mile to the lookout above. The lookout, refurbished partly with funding from the original edition of this book, is open for public use. This is an excellent side trip, although plenty of good views of the upper Priest Lake area and Idaho Selkirks to the east and Crowell Ridge and Gypsy Peak to the west are yet to come on the main Shedroof Divide Trail. A few hundred yards past the Little Snowy Top junction is the junction to Priest River Trail 349, which switchbacks steeply 4.5 miles east to the river bottom. This is not recommended for people who value their knees. Continue hiking 6 miles, passing infrequent water sources to Shedroof Mountain. Leave the Shedroof Divide (there's seasonal water and a campsite near the junction) and head northwest on Trail 535 about 3 miles to the parking area.

16 SPOKANE RIVER LOOP

Location: Spokane River
Status: Riverside State Park
Distance: 5 or 6 miles round trip
Hiking time: 2–3 hours
Difficulty: Easy or moderate
Season: March through November
Maps: USGS Spokane NW, Airway Heights
Information: Riverside State Park

People of all ages, sometimes even during winter, come to enjoy this hike along the shores of the Spokane River beginning near the unique basalt formations known as the Bowl and Pitcher just northwest of Spokane. The trail leads away from the noise of the campground and picnic area, over a bridge above the rushing white water, to quiet retreats in Riverside State Park, which was established in 1933. Buttercups, grass widows, and balsamroot are among the many plants hikers enjoy during spring. Be extremely careful around the Bowl and Pitcher and Devils Toenail Rapids, where the water is particularly swift and dangerous.

From northwest Spokane, drive west on Francis Avenue to Assembly

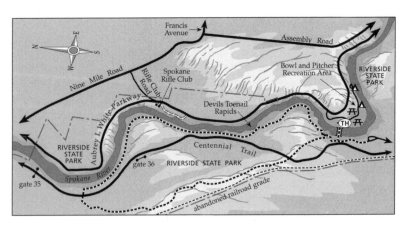

Footbridge and Spokane River rapids at the Bowl and Pitcher

Street, where Francis becomes Nine Mile Road. Continue northwest on Nine Mile Road 0.8 mile and turn left on Rifle Club Road toward Riverside State Park. Drive 0.5 mile and turn left on Aubrey White Parkway. Go another 1.3 miles to the Bowl and Pitcher Recreation Area and drive downhill toward the group campground. Hikers park in the day-use lot. Although this is a river trail, it can be hot and dry. No drinking water is available beyond the Bowl and Pitcher picnic area.

Walk the short way to the Spokane River and cross the suspension bridge over the frothing rapids to the trailhead. (Consider going left sometime to explore the pleasant mile of trail that heads upstream before connecting into a network of trails used by a horse-riding concession.) To hike the downstream section of this trail after crossing the bridge, bear right past the picnic shelter and continue up behind the rocks that form the huge Bowl and Pitcher basalt formations along the river. The trail becomes wide like a road; but after 0.3 mile it bends back toward the river, where you can hear the roar of Devils Toenail Rapid. Bear right, off the roadlike trail and onto a good footpath that leads to an overlook of the rapids. From here the trail continues downstream along the river, sometimes paralleling the paved Spokane River Centennial Trail.

Past the Spokane Rifle Club (across the river), the trail becomes wide like a road. At a Y, where the road goes left, bear right on the trail. The river bends to the north and the trail comes so low to the river that it can be

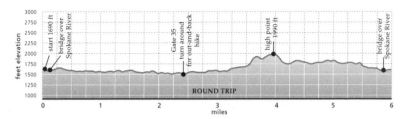

inundated for short periods during spring runoff. This area of the river, known locally as Little Vietnam, is lush and junglelike. Look for a spur heading steeply up to the left just before the trail comes to a buried pipeline that crosses the river. Hikers wanting the easiest walk can continue along the river for another few hundred yards to Gate 35 and turn around for a 5-mile round trip. (Note: The area west of the Centennial Trail at Gate 35 is a military reservation with trails that often can be explored. But the area occasionally is closed when training sessions are under way.) Hikers looking for the high road back can make a 6-mile loop as described below.

Much of these and a growing crop of other routes in Riverside State Park are shared with mountain bikers and horse riders. Park hours are 6:30 A.M. to dusk. Pets must be on leash.

Options: Take the spur trail as described above, cross the Centennial Trail, and head southwest across a flat. Cross a roadlike trail and make a sharp climb up to a bluff that offers a return route on a bench above the river. Turn left (south) on the bluff route and turn right at the next junction to continue heading southeast (upstream). At the next junction, a trail goes right up to a railroad grade that cuts through the bluff above. It's a good walk in itself. But to return to the Bowl and Pitcher Trailhead, go somewhat straight at this junction onto a footpath that winds its way down toward the suspension bridge and campground.

17 | DEEP CREEK CANYON LOOP

Location: Spokane River
Status: Riverside State Park
Distance: 4.6 miles round trip
Hiking time: 2–4 hours
Difficulty: Moderate
Season: March through November
Map: USGS Nine Mile Falls
Information: Riverside State Park

A dramatic range of scenery can be explored in this short hike up a side canyon from the Spokane River in Riverside State Park. Enjoy wildflowers

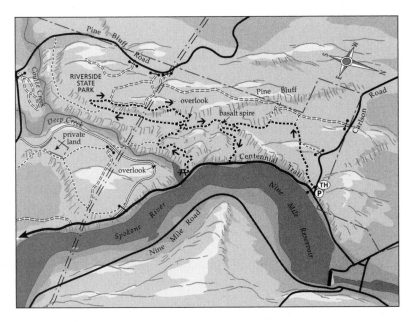

in the various habitats, ranging from the rubble of crumbling basalt near the mouth of Deep Creek to dark mossy forest to open ponderosa pine forest to cliff-edge overlooks of Nine Mile Reservoir on Pine Bluff.

From the corner of Assembly Street and Francis Avenue in northwest Spokane, Washington, head west on Francis Avenue, which eventually becomes Nine Mile Road (also State Highway 291). Go 6 miles and turn left (west) onto Charles Road. Cross the Spokane River at Nine Mile Dam and bear left onto Carlson Road. Drive nearly 0.5 mile to the Centennial Trail parking area.

All the paths in this area are worth exploring, although some simply run out a short way to another road. Detailed directions are given here to keep first-time visitors on a great introductory loop of the area.

From the parking area, cross Carlson Road to the trailhead and follow a dirt path that heads into the woods above the paved Centennial Trail (a wheelchair-accessible alternative and a pleasant walk in itself). The dirt trail soon heads uphill. At nearly 0.5 mile, turn left at a trail junction and begin contouring east on a sweet section of trail. At 0.8 mile, bear left at another junction, and head downhill. Note the tall, toothlike basalt spire on the way down to the junction with the Centennial Trail at 1.2 miles.

Turn right on the Centennial Trail (a former paved road at this point). In May, the area can be yellow with arrowleaf balsamroot and arnica. By mid-June, sticky geraniums plus wild rose, thimbleberry, and other shrubs are blooming. Ospreys are commonly seen along the river. Hike

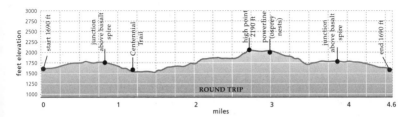

east to the picnic area at the mouth of Deep Creek at nearly 1.5 miles.

From the first bench at the west edge of Deep Creek picnic area, the trail heads up into a wasteland of basalt spires and scree that looks like the aftermath of bombing missions. The route switchbacks up a rough, rocky trail to a rim for a look down on Deep Creek. The trail twists below a tall basalt sentinel, then down to a trail junction at 1.8 miles. (The left trail heads down to a ford of Deep Creek.) To continue the route, bear right and head uphill a short way to another junction. Turn left, head steeply uphill 50 yards and bear left at yet another junction at 2 miles into the hike.

The trail eventually flattens and contours beautifully along a bench. Shortly after beginning an uphill grade toward Pine Bluff, note the junction for Trail 25 at nearly 2.5 miles. (This is a highly recommended side trip, heading left and down on Trail 25, which soon contours south along a bench to Pine Bluff Road.)

To continue the featured route, keep climbing up the grade, then switchback up to a grand overlook of the Spokane River Valley atop Pine Bluff at 2.6 miles. Hike north along the bluff (with the river valley on your right) past the first bench, then past a second bench. Pick up a double-track trail and continue north near the bluff. After passing under powerlines (look for osprey nests on the poles below), the trail heads downhill, becoming a glorious single track again.

At 3.2 miles, head left at a junction and walk 30 yards to a good overlook of Nine Mile Reservoir. Then go back and continue down the main trail to a familiar trail junction. Turn left, heading down a short steep stretch to another familiar junction at 3.3 miles. Turn left again, plunging downhill on a switchbacking trail into a ravine. The trail abruptly heads back uphill into a pleasant trail segment that winds through basalt rock formations and below mossy cliffs. Bear left at another familiar trail junction at 3.8 miles. Retrace the earlier walk, turning right at the next trail junction and walking downhill to the trailhead.

Much of this and other routes in Riverside State Park might be shared with mountain bikers and horse riders. Park hours are 6:30 A.M. to dusk. Pets must be on leash.

Opposite: *Along Deep Creek Canyon, Riverside State Park*

18 | LITTLE SPOKANE RIVER

Location: Spokane River
Status: Riverside State Park
Distance: 4 or 5 miles round trip
Hiking time: 3–4 hours
Difficulty: Moderate
Season: Late March through November
Map: USGS Dartford
Information: Riverside State Park

The Little Spokane River Valley is one of the most scenic and wildlife-rich areas in the Spokane area. During summer, few places in the United States have such a diversity of bird species. The spring-fed river is ripe with waterfowl and beavers and some fish, and the cover along the shores is thick enough to hold white-tailed deer and moose. Developers continue to circle the area like vultures, and some homebuilders out of touch with this ecosystem have shamelessly made no attempt to blend into the environment with their intrusive mansions on the upper slopes. But generations will always be thankful to former Spokane County Parks Director Sam Angove, along with river residents Morey and Margaret Haggin and others, who ended 15 years of buying, swapping, and negotiating to secure in 1985 a 1,500-acre preserve along the river that otherwise would have been privately developed and closed to the public. The Little Spokane River Natural Area, which has been expanded since then, is now managed by Riverside State Park.

Hikers should be gentle with this blessing. The Indian Painted Rocks near one trailhead hold delicate petroglyphs; waterfowl nest along the river in spring. Rules for this natural area are more restrictive than rules for the rest of Riverside State Park. Dogs, bikes, alcohol, fireworks, firearms, and camping are prohibited here. Also, no wading is allowed in the river's sandy bottom. Park hours are 8 A.M. to dusk.

The river trail is in two segments. The Indian Painted Rocks Trailhead is the midpoint, servicing both stretches. From Francis Avenue in northwest

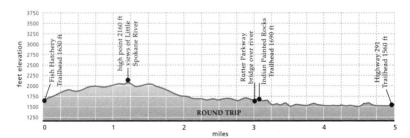

Spokane, turn north on Indian Trail Road and proceed 5 miles to Rutter Parkway. Stay to the right at a fork in the road and soon begin to head down toward the Little Spokane River. Drive past one trailhead, cross the bridge, and park in the Painted Rocks area. (If this parking lot is full, continue on Rutter Parkway to the trailhead that's a few miles upstream and 200 yards up the road that turns off to St. George's School.)

Upstream trail: To hike the upstream section of trail from Indian Painted Rocks, walk about 250 yards on the pavement back to the south side of the river and turn left (east) to the trailhead at a fence gate. The hike begins in a meadow and heads upstream along the Little Spokane River. The path soon enters woods from which the river can be seen intermittently. The variety in terrain makes this a pleasant hike from grassy meadows to coniferous woods to higher, drier, sunnier slopes. Watch for poison ivy near

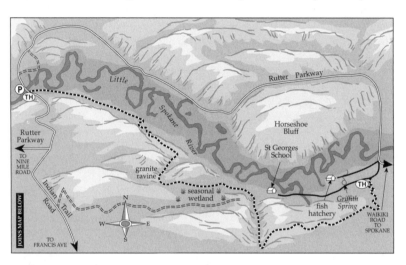

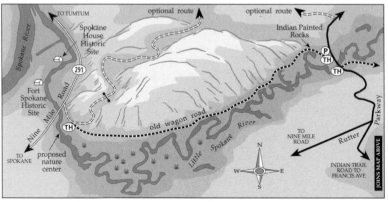

Paddlers seen from the Little Spokane River Trail

a small seasonal wetland about 0.8 mile into the hike after walking up a
ravine under cliffs of granite. Near a ridge overlooking St. George's School,
the main trail heads down for more than a dozen switchbacks. You could
continue from here to a parking area between the school and the state fish
hatchery (worth a visit), but most hikers return from here for a round trip
of 5 miles.

Downstream trail: Another easy hike, 4 miles round trip, can be made
along the trail heading west from the Painted Rocks, downstream along
the Little Spokane River toward its confluence with the Spokane River. The

hike is gentle, bordered by the river to the south and granite cliffs to the north, where rattlesnakes occasionally are found. The trail bends away from the river as a buffer to the once-active heron rookery in the cottonwoods about a mile downstream from Painted Rocks. Remnant nests might still be there, but the herons have moved their rookery upstream. Biologists would like to keep the trail away from the river in this area to give the herons an option to reestablish the rookery.

The route is colored with lupine, shooting stars, mountain bluebells, and other decorative wildflowers. Occasional side trails lead toward the river, where there is a splendid display of blooming yellow iris in June. The iris is not native. It was introduced by a river resident years ago and has spread up and downstream. Also in the area is camas, the roots of which were once gathered as a staple by Indian tribes. About 0.5 mile from the end of the trail at State Highway 291, the footpath widens into an old wagon road.

The Little Spokane flows into the Spokane River a short way from here. Nearby is the historic Spokane House, where international companies based their Inland Northwest fur-trading operations. Steelhead and huge Chinook salmon spawned in the Spokane and Little Spokane Rivers until Little Falls Dam blocked their passage in 1911.

Options: After hiking the downstream trail segment, you can return on a loop—7 miles total—via road paths in a section of land purchased through the Spokane County Conservation Futures program in 2000. Just before reaching State Highway 291, walk uphill on a paved road that leads northward to a subdivision. Go through the park gate and follow the dirt road closed to motor vehicles, heading north. A ridge walk offers good views of the Spokane River Valley before the road drops into a drainage and doubles back southeast to Rutter Parkway. Turn right and walk back on the pavement the short way to the Painted Rocks Trailhead.

19 | DISHMAN HILLS LOOP

Location: Spokane River
Status: Spokane County Parks
Distance: 2.5 miles round trip
Hiking time: 2 hours
Difficulty: Moderate
Season: March through November
Map: USGS Spokane NE
Information: Spokane County Parks Department

This route for explorers of all ages isn't meant to be just a hike. It's the beginning for years of enjoyment and exploration in Spokane's backyard. The Dishman Hills Natural Resources Conservation Area, 530 acres and

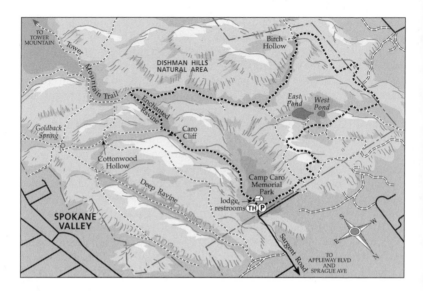

expanding, is a convenient reminder about the value of grassroots conservation involvement, which has secured this condo-proof preserve that's
nearly surrounded by development. It's crisscrossed with trails for easy
access to native flora and fauna and views of the Spokane Valley.

The area is particularly inviting in spring or fall, when wildflowers or
changing leaves splash the pine-studded hills with color. Wildflowers such
as grass widows and arrowleaf balsamroot bloom in April. Serviceberry
blossoms open in May followed by wild rose, ocean spray, and a who's-
who of the native plants that once flourished throughout the region.

The hills have four trailheads accessible by public land, including the
Edgecliff Park area on the west side of the hills at the end of 8th Avenue. On
the east side of the natural area, enter from Siesta Drive at 12th Avenue. The
most popular trailhead is on the north side of the hills at Camp Caro, which
has a large grassy area with playground equipment and restrooms. From
downtown Spokane eastbound on Interstate 90, take Sprague Exit 285 and
continue straight east on Appleway Boulevard 1.6 miles. Turn right (south)
on Sargent Road to Camp Caro parking. From I-90 coming from east or
west, take Argonne Exit 287. Go south on Argonne 1 mile and turn right
(west) on Sprague Avenue. Drive 0.3 mile and turn left (south) on Sargent
Road, across Appleway Boulevard and up to Camp Caro.

No camping or biking is allowed in Dishman Hills. Pets must be leashed.

The hike described here explores the north end of the hills. From the
passageway between Camp Caro's restrooms and meeting facility head
south away from the parking lot and angle left across the grass onto an
old road that continues to the old Boy Scout campsite. Hike up the steps
and follow the trail toward Goldback Spring. Spur trails have sprouted,

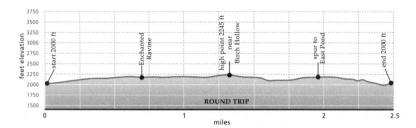

but stay on the main route. Pass a bench and note Caro Cliff. Take the first main trail heading right. This Pond Loop Trail heads into Enchanted Ravine, where moss-covered rock walls close in under Douglas firs. At the next junction with a main trail, bear right again, gradually gaining elevation. Just as the trail bends due north into open terrain and just *before* it heads down toward East Pond, turn left on a slightly less-used trail toward Birch Hollow. Continue gaining ground for views, including Beacon Hill to the north.

At the next main trail junction, consider exploring left to the aptly named Birch Hollow area, a haven for thimbleberries, ferns, and other plants, including poison ivy. To continue this route from the junction, go right, dropping onto an abandoned road.

Pass the junction with the trail to Edgecliff Trailhead, continuing straight and eventually bending right (east). A well-used spur trail heads right to East Pond, where birch and aspen can be brilliant with color in fall. (All ponds in the hills are bound to go dry during summer.) Here, too, it's common to see poison ivy, which wears attractive ranges of yellow, orange, and red colors in fall. Be sure to remind kids: "Leaves of three, leave it be!"

Most trails heading from East Pond eventually lead back to Camp Caro. This route continues east to a junction where it heads left and downhill on the so-called Short Trail to a fork. Go left. Then turn right on the next good trail to the park play area.

Dishman Hills Natural Resources Conservation Area is managed cooperatively by the Spokane County Parks and Recreation Department, Washington Department of Natural Resources, and the association, which hopes to beat developers and secure even more land that could make way for wildlife corridors and trails all the way south to Tower Mountain. (See Appendix C for contact.)

Options: Double the pleasure and the mileage by adding a second loop to this trip. From Enchanted Ravine, continue southward on the Tower Mountain Trail. (This will take some careful attention to the map while negotiating the numerous trail junctions. Maps available from Spokane County Parks Department are listed in Appendix C.) Bend west on the Eagle Peak Loop and enjoy the 360-degree view from Eagle Peak, elev. 2,425 feet. Go north on Ridge Top Trail, making a visit to Lost Pond, and go back to Enchanted Ravine, to reconnect with the loop described above.

Arrowleaf balsamroot in Dishman Hills Natural Area

Deep Ravine: The less formal trails heading north from Goldback Springs lead into Deep Ravine, the haunt of rock climbers. Come with plenty of water and wander. Although trails branch in many directions through the area, it's difficult to get lost for long in the hills, since numerous viewpoints allow hikers to orient to landmarks in the Spokane Valley.

Iller Creek: With an eye to the future, here's a hike at the south end of The Hills up Iller Creek toward Tower Mountain, which could someday be connected to the Dishman Hills if land purchases and easements can be arranged to make existing routes public. To reach the trailhead for the Iller Creek Conservation Area from where Argonne Road joins Sprague Avenue and Appleway, head south on Dishman-Mica Road. Turn right at the traffic light onto Schafer Road. Turn right on 44th and left on Woodruff Road. Then turn right on Holman Road and drive to the trailhead at the end of the public roadway. The trail goes uphill 2.5 miles to a pleasant ridge walk. Just south of the ridge are the lovely Rocks of Sharon, which conservationists have been trying to secure from private landowners.

20 | LIBERTY LAKE LOOP

Location: Spokane River
Status: Spokane County Parks
Distance: 7.5 miles round trip
Hiking time: 4 hours
Difficulty: Easy to moderately difficult
Season: Late May through October
Maps: USGS Mica Peak, Liberty Lake
Information: Spokane County Parks Department

Liberty Lake County Park is a popular picnicking area, with a swimming beach, cooking shelters, playground, campsites, and volleyball nets. But many people don't realize the park extends far beyond the facilities through a timbered mountain preserve. This hike meanders up Liberty Creek and along a hillside through the park before gaining nearly 1,200 feet in elevation. It's a mostly cool, quiet retreat, first through cottonwoods and ponderosa pines, then through Douglas firs and cedars.

Drive east from Spokane on Interstate 90. Take the Liberty Lake exit. Go straight (east) on Appleway Avenue 0.8 mile and turn right (south) on Molter. Go 1 mile and turn left on Valleyway. It is 2.3 miles from here to the entrance of Liberty Lake County Park. (Note that Valleyway becomes Lakeside Road when it bends to the right around the east end of Liberty Lake Golf Course.) Turn right off Lakeside Road at the park sign.

When the park is open, June through September, drive past the fee-collection booth straight to the day-use parking area and walk to the trail-head, which is at the southeast end of the camping area near RV campsite 21. During the months the park is closed, as in late May when spring wildflowers are blooming at lower elevations, leave vehicles on the hill above the park entrance by the water tower; hike down the road to the park entrance and through to the campground and trailhead.

The first portion of the trail offers easy hiking on an old road, crossing Liberty Creek on footbridges and passing several picnic sites. It's 2 miles to a large walk-in picnic area in a grove of old cedars. (Turn back here for an

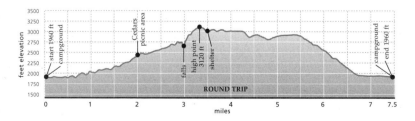

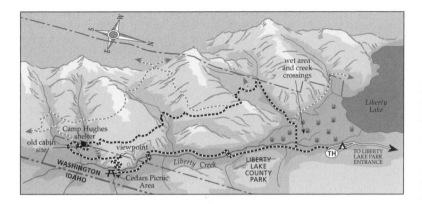

easy 4-mile round trip.) Cross the creek on the footbridge to the right and start switchbacking up the hillside. The trail narrows. On the last switchback, you will get a glimpse of Liberty Lake.

The trail leads out onto the side of a ridge with open views into Idaho and eventually into the woods again. The path soon works its way up to a log bridge (3 miles from the trailhead), complete with welcome handrails, that crosses high above a cool, cascading waterfall. During spring runoff, the waterfall pounds down with considerable volume. After crossing the bridge, the preferred trail contours around the ridge to the left and heads uphill. (An old switchbacking trail goes directly up the ridge.) The two

Liberty Creek Falls, Liberty Lake County Park

routes meet at a junction at an old cabin site and lead to an old road near the high point of elev. 3,120 feet. Turn right on this road, past the shabby Camp Hughes shelter, for a downhill return toward the campground. Once down to the meadow area, there are two more stream crossings, then a boggy or grassy stretch, depending on the season, before the trail returns to the trailhead.

Restroom facilities and drinking water are available only in the park campground area. While this area has these developed facilities, the trail leads into wild areas where bears and cougars have occasionally been seen.

21 MOUNT SPOKANE– THREE PEAKS LOOP

Location: Mount Spokane
Status: Mount Spokane State Park
Distance: Up to 14 miles round trip
Hiking time: 5–8 hours
Difficulty: Easy to difficult
Season: Mid-June through mid-October
Maps: USGS Mount Spokane, Mount Kit Carson
Information: Mount Spokane State Park

The featured route is a dandy that links three scenic peak vistas in the heart of 13,821-acre Mount Spokane State Park. The length of the full trip might be a little more than some hikers want to tackle, but don't overlook the easier options to this network of trails on the south slopes of Mount Spokane. Drive to trailheads higher on the mountain to eliminate elevation gain. Read on, there's something here for everyone.

From U.S. Highway 2 north of Spokane, turn east on Mount Spokane Park Drive (State Highway 206) to Mount Spokane State Park. From the Spokane Valley and Interstate 90, go north on Argonne Road, continuing north

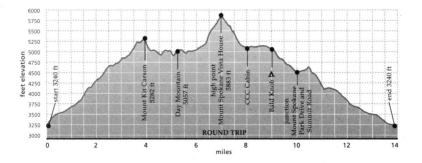

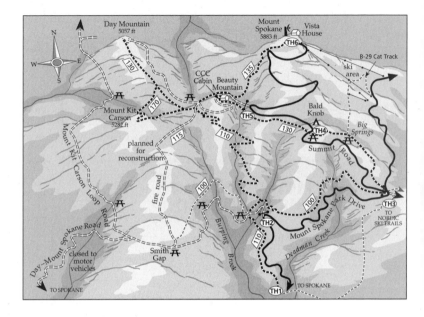

as Argonne becomes Bruce Road. Turn right at the junction with Mount Spokane Park Drive (Highway 206). The first and lowest trailhead for this hike is 0.2 mile past the park entrance and headquarters. (Summer hours: 6:30 A.M. to dusk.) For shorter and easier hike options, note five other trailheads:

Lower Mount Kit Carson Loop Road: Continue up Mount Spokane Park Drive nearly 2 miles from the park entrance to the hairpin turn parking area.

Sno-Park: Continue up the road 3 miles from the park entrance to the huge Sno-Park area. (Cross-country ski and mountain bike trails are to the right at the upper lot.)

Bald Knob: Turn left across from the Sno-Park lot and continue up the paved Mount Spokane Summit Road 1.2 miles to the Bald Knob Campground.

Upper Mount Kit Carson Loop Road: Continue on the Summit Road less than a mile from Bald Knob to the hairpin turn and the small parking spot at the gated dirt road. (Don't block the road.)

Summit: Drive to the end of the road at the summit area near the stone Vista House.

The full three-peaks hike starting on Trail 110 near the park entrance is a leg-testing endurance workout for climbers, backpackers, or other athletes, gaining and losing more than 3,100 feet elevation while hiking from open meadows to dark, old-growth timber. Wildflowers in dozens of varieties flourish during summer as well as huckleberries in some areas starting in late July. Beargrass is abundant and especially lovely in late June and early July. Trail signage at Mount Spokane is improving with a boost from funds generated by this book.

Sunset on Mount Kit Carson, Mount Spokane State Park

Bring plenty of water. The only potable source in the area is at the Civilian Conservation Corps cabin. And be prepared for mountain weather that can change quickly.

From the start of Trail 110, head uphill 1.8 miles on trail and old fire road (watch for trillium near wet areas) to a picnic spot by Burping Brook. Trail 110 crosses Mount Kit Carson Loop Road (closed to motor vehicles) and heads uphill 0.2 mile. Turn left on Trail 100/110. Go 0.2 mile and bear right on Trail 110. This is pleasant uphill walking for 1.6 miles, crossing Burping Brook, but the good trail could encourage high-speed downhill mountain biking. Beware.

At the trail junction, turn left and head uphill on Trail 115 (fire road), then turn right onto Trail 130. To bag Mount Kit Carson, go 0.3 mile on Trail 130, then turn left on Trail 170 for a 0.5-mile hike to the summit outcropping. Check out the view of the Spokane River Valley and perhaps the conical Steptoe Butte to the south. Had enough? Retrace the route back to the trailhead for a round trip of 9 miles.

Continue from the summit of Mount Kit Carsonon Trail 170 to Trail 130 junction and head left (northwest). The trail leads through timber before working up pleasantly through lush grass and lupine to rock outcroppings at the summit of Day Mountain. Lunch maybe?

Two peaks down, one big one to go. Backtrack, staying on Trail 130 to Trail 115 (fire road). Turn left and head down a short way to the junction with the Mount Kit Carson Loop Road, which is labeled as Trail 130. Cross the road onto Trail 135, which leads 1.5 miles to the Vista House and high point of the trip on top of Mount Spokane, elev. 5,883 feet. Lunch again? From here, the hike is mostly downhill.

Backtrack from the Vista House on Trail 135. Where the trail comes next to the Mount Kit Carson Loop Road, cut left (there may or may not be a path to the road) across the road and follow the dirt approach into the CCC cabin and picnic site. Water should be available. Just below the cabin, turn left (east) on Trail 130, a single track that parallels below the paved Summit Road and heads 1 mile to Bald Knob Campground.

Cross the Summit Road and look for Trail 130 north of the Bald Knob picnic shelter. Hike 1 mile down—starting on a road, joining the B-29 cat track, then bearing down to the right on a single track and eventually passing an equipment shed—to the junction with the Summit Road across from the Sno-Park lot. Turn right, crossing the Summit Road to a road gate and the start of Trail 100. This route leads 1.5 miles back to the junction with Trail 110. Déjà vu. You're back on familiar terrain. Turn downhill (south) on 110 and go 2 miles to the trailhead.

Until updates are available, USGS maps show trails that are no longer maintained and omit newer trails described in this hike.

Options: Parts of this hike can be picked up from any of the trailheads. Drive higher up the mountain to reduce the mileage and elevation gain/loss or shuttle vehicles to different trailheads. Check at park headquarters for map brochures.

The gentlest of the options would be heading west on Trail 130 from Bald Knob (trailhead 4). There's virtually no elevation gain in the 2-mile round trip to the CCC cabin. Or continue, using a short section of the Mount Kit Carson Loop Road to the vault toilet and trail junctions, to make a 5-mile round trip to Day Mountain.

22 | MINERAL RIDGE LOOP

Location: Lake Coeur d'Alene
Status: Unprotected
Distance: 3.3 miles round trip
Hiking time: 2–4 hours
Difficulty: Easy
Season: April through mid-November
Map: USGS Mt. Coeur d'Alene
Information: U.S. Bureau of Land Management,
    Coeur d'Alene Office

From humble beginnings at a picnic area on Lake Coeur d'Alene's Beauty Bay, a gentle ribbon of trail snakes its way up an arm of the mountain known as Mineral Ridge. This 3.3-mile trail, managed by the U.S. Bureau of Land Management, is one of the prettiest easy hikes in the Inland Northwest, suitable for a wide spectrum of hiking abilities. Hikers who are purely after exercise could put the trail away in less than 2 hours.

To reach the trailhead, drive 15 minutes east from Coeur d'Alene, Idaho, on Interstate 90 and turn off at Wolf Lodge Exit 22. At the stop sign, turn right toward Harrison. Drive 2.2 miles around the Wolf Lodge arm of Lake Coeur

Lake Coeur d'Alene's Wolf Lodge Bay from Mineral Ridge

d'Alene and look for the Mineral Ridge parking and picnic area on the left across from Beauty Bay. Water and restrooms are open here during summer.

Guide pamphlets often are available at the trailhead. They are keyed to each of the 22 trailside stations and explain basic principles of tree and plant identification, forest management, geology, and mining practices.

The trail gently switchbacks 1.5 miles to the top of the ridge, where there's a simple shelter called Caribou Cabin and an open area with a view of Wolf Lodge Bay, perfect for a snack or picnic. The ridge is honeycombed with old, shallow mining tunnels as well as pit mines, mostly obliterated

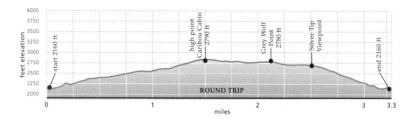

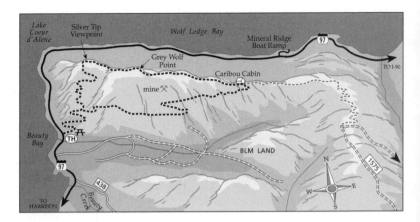

now. A side trail on the way to Caribou Cabin leads to the main entrance of a mine (now a favorite hideout for chipmunks).

From Caribou Cabin, the trail follows the ridge gently downhill past Grey Wolf Point to a splendid overlook of Beauty Bay at Silver Tip Viewpoint. (Hikers willing to stomp through snow in December often can use this vista to spot bald eagles, which visit Lake Coeur d'Alene each winter to feast on spawning kokanee salmon.) From this viewpoint, the trail switchbacks steeply down to the parking area.

23 | CUBE IRON MOUNTAIN LOOP

Location: Thompson River
Status: Proposed wilderness
Distance: 8.5 miles round trip
Hiking time: 6 hours or overnight
Difficulty: Moderate
Season: Late June through October
Maps: USGS Mount Headley, Priscilla Peak
Information: Lolo National Forest,
    Plains/Thompson Falls District

Quick access to mountain lakes makes this loop trip ideal for beginning back-packers or day hikers looking for routes with several length options. Camp at Cabin Lake and catch small cutthroat trout or scramble to Cube Iron Mountain, elevation 7,110 feet, for views into Idaho's Selkirk Mountains and Montana's Cabinets and Bitterroots. The name "cube iron" refers to the remnant cube-shaped pseudomorphs of pyrite crystals (fool's gold) found in rocks at some sites in the Cabinet Mountains. The pyrite here has been partially replaced by rusty red iron oxides, though you can sometimes find remnants of the original bright brassy pyrite in the cube cores. The cubes range in size. Choice ones are bigger than game dice.

From Thompson Falls, Montana, drive east on State Highway 200 and turn left (north) at milepost 56 onto a paved road along the west side of the Thompson River. Four miles from Highway 200, the pavement ends near a riverside campground. Pass another small campground at 5 miles. At 6.2 miles, bear left at a Y onto Road 603 (West Fork Thompson River). Drive another 7.5 miles to the Four Lakes Trailhead.

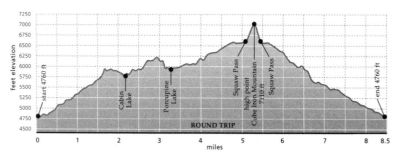

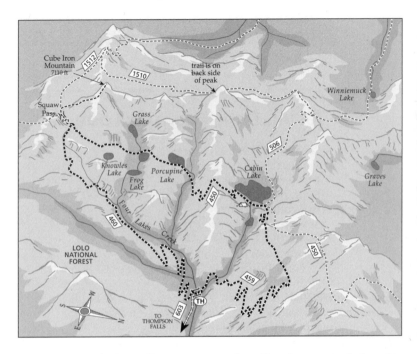

Start on Trail 459, walking past a small trailhead campsite before the route switchbacks in a reasonable grade up the side slope. At 2 miles, the grade levels. Go left at the junction with Trail 450. At 2.2 miles, come to a junction with Trail 506, which heads to Winniemuck Creek. (See "Options" below.) The 8.5-mile loop trip continues southerly a short way on Trail 450 to Cabin Lake.

To continue, stay to the left of the lake, hiking across the outlet to switchbacks leading over a saddle before dropping to Porcupine Lake. The terrain rolls from Porcupine past several other boggy lakes to the junction with Trail 460, which is about 3 miles from Cabin Lake. Day hikers and backpackers alike should hike up from the junction 0.2 mile to Squaw Pass. At the junction, go right onto Trail 1512 about 30 yards, where an unmaintained but well-defined trail heads steeply up a scramble route to a former fire lookout site on the summit of Cube Iron Mountain, elev. 7,110 feet.

Back at the junction with Trails 450 and 460, finish the last 3 downhill miles on 460 to the trailhead by hiking into a gully that shows obvious signs of spring avalanches. The trail heads into forest, where the last 2 miles of the route follow an old road that's been gated and designated for non-motorized use.

Options: Day hikers who want to do a longer 11-mile loop should head west on Trail 506 from the Cabin Lake area. Head south on Trail 1510 (the junction can be easy to miss) for great hiking on open sidehills and ridges.

Cube irons found by curious kids in the Cabinet Mountains
(Photo by Torsten Kjellstrand)

Turn east on Trail 1512 to Squaw Pass and then head out on Trail 460. Add 2.2 miles by going out Trails 450–459.

•From Squaw Pass, Trail 450 continues south along a ridge to Silcox Peak and Goat Lakes, another area worthy of exploration.

24 | REVETT LAKE

Location: Idaho-Montana Divide
Status: Unprotected
Distance: 4 miles round trip
Hiking time: 3 hours or overnight
Difficulty: Easy
Season: July through October
Maps: USGS Burke, Thompson Pass
Information: Idaho Panhandle National Forests,
  Coeur d'Alene River District, Wallace Office

This is a short, easy hike to a clear mountain lake above an area that was heavily mined beginning in 1882 when gold was discovered in Prichard Creek. The hike is especially popular with beginning backpackers and families. Small brook trout can be caught in the lake and huckleberries begin to ripen here in late July.

Outlet area of Revett Lake

From Interstate 90 just west of Kellogg, Idaho, take Kingston Exit 43 and head north on Forest Highway 9 (Coeur d'Alene River Road). Follow this paved road about 21 miles to a junction and bear left. Go 1.7 miles and turn right onto Highway 9, which climbs nearly 16 miles to Thompson Pass. (The road goes past Murray, the remains of a boomtown that once crammed thousands of people into the narrow valley. Consider visiting the historic Sprag Pole Bar/Museum.) Highway 9 winds along acres of dredged creek bed up to the Montana-Idaho border. At Thompson Pass, Revett Lake Road 266 branches off from the Blossom Lakes Trailhead parking area (see Hike 25) and heads southwest. Drive 1.2 miles to the end of the road where Revett Lake Trail 9 begins. No camping or water is available at the trailhead parking area.

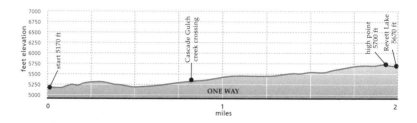

To reach the trailhead from Wallace, Idaho, head north on 6th Street past the historic railroad depot, under the I-90 bypass, across the Trail of the Coeur d'Alenes rail trail and onto Forest Road 456 toward Dobson Pass. This road is winding and steep, but paved. Drive over the pass and continue to the junction with Forest Highway 9 at the Coeur d'Alene River. Turn right onto Highway 9, bearing right at Prichard and heading up to Thompson Pass, which is 39 miles from Wallace. To reach the trailhead from Thompson Falls, Montana, use Forest Highway 7, clearly shown on Lolo National Forest maps.

Trail 9 to Revett Lake dives into the subalpine forest. The route curves around the ridge that divides Idaho from Montana, passing beneath steep, rugged talus slopes. In autumn, the slopes are ablaze with mountain ash and huckleberry, contrasting with the deep greens of hemlock, alpine fir, and spruce. The trail is well graded, wide, and easy to follow. It winds through stands of mature forest, crossing a lovely creek (Cascade Gulch) at about 0.8 mile on a split log bridge. A miniature waterfall can be seen here off to the left through the trees. The route then begins to climb gradually to the north, turning back to the south at its one and only switchback in a large talus slope. Passing in and out of trees and rocks, the trail finally gains the lip of the hanging valley where the lake lies in a bowl, nearly surrounded by steep slopes. The outlet stream is to the left of the main trail in a swampy meadow. Camps are strung out along the outlet side of the lake, the better ones in the trees above the lake. The shoreline is rocky, with thick brush and trees in most places. The trail ends near a small, swampy beach littered with driftwood.

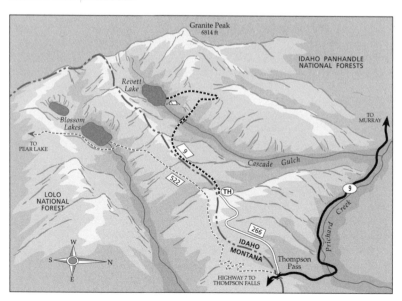

25 | BLOSSOM LAKES

Location: Idaho-Montana Divide
Status: Unprotected
Distance: 6 miles round trip
Hiking time: 3 hours or overnight
Difficulty: Easy
Season: July through October
Map: USGS Thompson Pass
Information: Lolo National Forest,
Plains/Thompson Falls District

The fairly easy 6-mile round trip to Lower Blossom Lake can be extended into a longer hike of a little more difficulty to Pear Lake or even to Glidden Ridge and beyond. These lakes are off the beaten track of hikers heading to more glamorous areas in the Idaho Selkirks to the north and the Cabinet Mountains to the east. But they have their own quiet charm.

From Interstate 90 just west of Kellogg, Idaho, take Kingston Exit 43 and head north on Forest Highway 9 (Coeur d'Alene River Road). Follow this paved road about 21 miles to a junction and bear left. Go 1.7 miles and turn right onto Highway 9, which climbs nearly 16 miles to Thompson Pass. (The road goes past Murray, the remains of a boomtown that once crammed thousands of people into the narrow valley. Consider visiting the

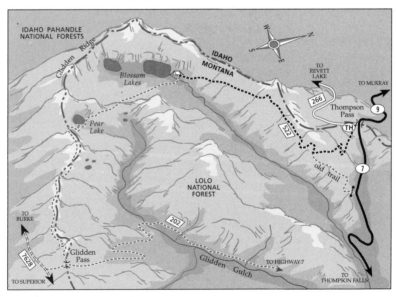

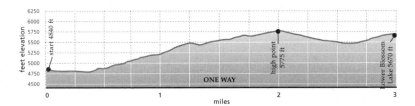

historic Sprag Pole Bar/Museum.) Highway 9 winds along acres of dredged creek bed up to the Montana-Idaho border. Pull into the paved parking area and trailhead at the pass on the south side of the highway. The old trailhead for Blossom Lakes, used mostly for stock, is 0.5 mile farther east on the highway. Thompson Pass and nearby Revett Lake Trailhead can also be reached from Wallace, Idaho and Thompson Falls, Montana (see Hike 24).

Trail 522 contours south for about 0.5 mile before making a camel-hump climb up the broad ridge and descending down toward the lake. The forest consists of small, subalpine timber, mainly hemlock with some white pine, whitebark pine, lodgepole pine, Sitka spruce, Douglas fir, western larch, and alpine fir. The trees are small and thick, so views are scarce. After climbing most of the trek's 950-foot gain in two gradual steps, this remarkably straight trail curves around to a view, about 0.2 mile short of the lake. Standing on glacier-carved bedrock, you can look out toward the northeast and the heavily forested ridges of Driveway Peak. The trail soon begins to contour above a creek set in a narrow, precipitous, rocky gorge, only a short way from Lower Blossom Lake.

The trail passes through campsites on the northeast side of the lake. Looking over to the western side of the lake, the ridge rises up to 6,629 feet, a wall of broken talus, cliff bands, scattered trees, and brush. The eastern and southern edges of the lake are heavily wooded. One lonely camp sits high on a rocky knoll above the western side of the outlet stream with a lovely view of the lake. There is no trail to Upper Blossom Lake, although you can bushwhack through heavy brush and rock outcroppings to reach it.

A dam was built at Lower Blossom Lake in 1883 to store water for placer mining operations at Murray. Near Lower Blossom Lake, the trail crosses an old diversion canal, which was dug by Chinese laborers. This canal, which was never used, can be traced all the way to Thompson Pass.

Options: To extend the hike (9 miles round trip), stay on the trail, which climbs steadily up the side of a hogback ridge, again through thick timber and past rock outcroppings for about 1 mile, topping out at about 6,240 feet. The trail then drops down to a narrow, rocky basin where tiny Pear Lake nestles under a sheer 500-foot cliff. Pear Lake offers virtually no place to camp. The lake basin, sitting as it does on a shadowy north slope, could hold snow for a long time in a cool year. The lake looks stagnant, although one small inlet creek gurgles down a talus slope at the southwest end of the lake.

Lower Blossom Lake (Photo by Liz Escher)

From here, the trail climbs steeply up to the ridge, topping out close to 6,600 feet. The trail follows the ridgeline, dropping slowly down, until it intersects with Trail 201 at Glidden Pass. Glidden Gulch Trail 201 goes to the right to a trailhead at Cooper Pass, or it goes down to the left, plunging along the creek to Highway 7. Hike or shuttle back up the highway to make a complete loop from the start of the Blossom Lakes hike.

26 | SIAMESE LAKES LOOP

Location: Idaho-Montana Divide
Status: Proposed wilderness
Distance: Up to 25 miles round trip
Hiking time: 2–4 days
Difficulty: Moderate to difficult
Season: Early July through September
Maps: USGS Bruin Hill, St. Patrick Peak, Schley Mt.
Information: Lolo National Forest, Ninemile District

Legendary forest fires of 1910 changed lives for a generation in the Inland Northwest. But the changes to the landscape will endure for centuries, as this hike so vividly displays. Walk up a drainage under thick cedars and hemlocks that were already old when they survived the "Great Blow-up." Climb to quaint little lakes nestled in the rock of the Bitterroot Divide. Consider options to bag a peak or cruise the scenic ridge on the Stateline National Recreation Trail along the Montana-Idaho border. Then take the moderate way out and backtrack to the trailhead, or complete the loop with a more difficult stream-crossing odyssey down a drainage that had been devoured by the holocaust. This final leg reveals how an uncommon diversity has risen from the ashes, and why this area deserves protection as the Great Burn Wilderness.

From Interstate 90 east of Superior, Montana, take Fish Creek Exit 66 and turn south on Fish Creek Road. Drive 0.9 mile and bear right at the Y onto North Fork Fish Creek Road. Go a short way and bear left along Fish Creek a total of 10 miles from I-90, following signs to Hole in the Wall Lodge. Turn right onto Forest Road 7750 toward West Fork Fish Creek and continue another 6.7 miles to Clearwater Crossing Campground and

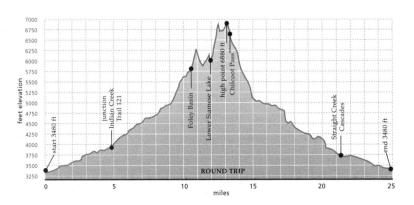

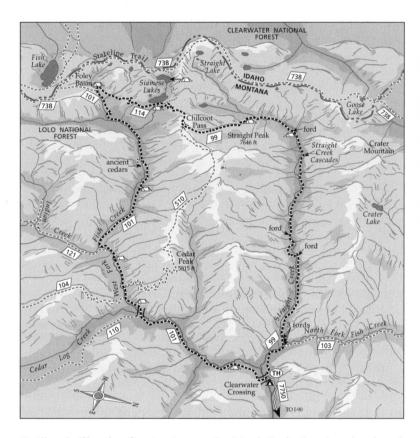

Trailhead. (Shortly after turning up the North Fork, there's a developed campground and a point of interest: the biggest recorded ponderosa pine in Montana.)

Begin the hike with a "drunken sailor walk" across the swinging walkway over West Fork Fish Creek. To get started on the right foot, tents or other wide objects carried outside of a backpack must be strapped onto the top half of the pack in order to clear the very narrow footbridge. Then switch on the cruise control for a lovely and gentle hike up well-maintained Trail 101 under cedars close to the creek. Pass a possible campsite at 0.8 mile. At about 3 miles, pass the junction with Cedar Log Lakes/Schley Peak Trail 110. Cross the bridge to the other side of the creek, passing a good campsite at a spiffy fishing-swimming hole, and then continue upstream. Pass the junction with Indian Ridge Trail 104. A few hundred yards farther, pass Trail 510 (see "Options" below). Then go past the junction with Indian Creek Trail 121 at about 5 miles. (This trail can be linked with Trail 110 to make a loop trip to Cedar Log Lakes area, but the long pull from the bottom appeals mostly to horse riders.) From here, Trail 101 up the West Fork becomes a little more volatile with more ups and downs. The lush growth of plants and wildflowers begins engulfing stretches of the trail as it passes through avalanche slopes. Cow parsnip and the occasional devil's club grow in a subalpine environment. Gape at a remarkable grove of ancient cedars. Camping is possible several times in the first 5 miles of this trail, but sites are harder to find thereafter.

At 11.5 miles, the trail forks. Trail 101 continues left 1.5 miles to Stateline National Recreation Trail 738 and a short drop over the divide to Fish Lake. Siamese Lakes Trail 114 angles to the right into a meadowy and sometimes buggy basin. One last campsite with water is at the dogleg in the trail at Foley Basin before the route heads up about 2 more miles to Lower Siamese Lake. This stretch of trail is deceptively up and down. The lake is in a rugged bowl with a waterfall cascading down from Upper Siamese Lake. Both lakes are stocked every seven years or so with cutthroat trout. Horse riders have had a particularly heavy impact on the large campsite at the lower lake outlet. A smaller site is a 50-yard bushwhack north from the outlet.

This area is worth a layover day (see "Options"). Some hikers may want to backtrack to the trailhead, but adventurers might prefer to continue the loop, even though it requires at least six stream fords, and maybe a couple more depending on the availability of natural fallen-log bridges.

Continue up from the lake, switchbacking steeply at first and then traversing for a total of 1.6 miles from the lower lake to Chilcoot Pass. Note the junction with Trail 510 to Cedar Peak (see "Options"). Look north to Crater Mountain, then drop steeply down the pass on Trail 99 into Straight Creek, which is a different world in many ways from the West Fork. Hiking the 9.5 miles from Chilcoot Pass down Straight Creek, which has easy water access but fewer camping opportunities, can be challenging early in the hiking season when flows are still high. None of the six major stream crossings has a bridge, although logs and rocks are usually exposed enough for easier crossing by August. Four of the fords are in the last few miles to the confluence with the North Fork of Fish Creek, which is just 1 mile from the trailhead. Depending on the relationship your feet have with your hiking shoes, consider cruising right through these last crossings. Higher upstream, it's probably wiser to ford in sandals or wading shoes.

About 4 miles down from Chilcoot Pass, the trail passes Straight Creek Cascades, a series of terraces that make an impressive lunch spot. Pause here to notice the enormous biodiversity. Recall that West Fork Fish Creek has old-growth cedar and hemlock reminiscent of Pacific Northwest forests. Straight Creek, however, was burned intensely during the 1910 fire. A century later, visitors can marvel at the impacts of fires that took out almost every standing piece of timber, especially on the Crater Mountain side. Only shrubs and grasses have reestablished. On westbound Interstate 90 just west of Lookout Pass, an historic site marker gives more information and cause to ponder the magnitude of the fire. (See "Great Burn" listings in the Index.)

Beargrass above Lower Siamese Lake, proposed Great Burn Wilderness

Hole in the Wall Lodge near the trailhead has modern cabins, a restaurant, and offers horse trail rides and pack trips. In the mid-1800s, outlaws used this area as their hideout for nearly 20 years. Two rock ledges that run down to the creek conjured up the image of "riding through a hole in the wall." Bootleggers also plied their trade here.

Options: Although not particularly pleasant, it's possible to make a shorter loop from Siamese Lake back to Clearwater Crossing Trailhead by taking Trail 510 from Chilcoot Pass. But hikers must endure 52 switchbacks on a monster downhill, losing 3,200 feet in a few miles to West Fork Fish Creek. Note that the trail passes on the south side of "Cedar Peak," which is a misnomer. It's actually a "point" that probably wouldn't have been named at all if it hadn't been for the fire lookout erected there after forest fires had eliminated the trees. Now it's reforested with 100-foot subalpine firs and hemlocks, and virtually no vistas. Meanwhile, there's a true peak that's unnamed east of 7,646-foot Straight Peak.

• Highly recommended is a trek to Upper Siamese Lake following the faint route that angles up the slope on the north end of the lower lake. Extend this hike into a full day trip or more by following a better trail from the upper lake to Stateline Trail 738. Go north on this ridge-running National Recreation Trail for spectacular views and access to other lakes.

• A longer loop taking advantage of the scenic stateline ridge can be made by continuing north from Upper Siamese Lake on Trail 738 about 7 miles to Goose Lake, and then hiking 12 miles back to Clearwater Crossing Trailhead on North Fork Fish Creek Trail 103. This trail is longer than Straight Creek Trail, but it has some redeeming values, such as fewer fords, an unofficial spur trail to the Trio Lakes near the state line (see Hike 65), and halfway down, a remnant of the historic Greenwood Cabins, built in the late 1800s. Up to 20 Chinese miners lived here in a futile search for gold. Bootleggers later used the place. Campsites are available.

• A different loop can be made by going south from Upper Siamese Lake on Stateline Trail 738 to Mud Lake area and then looping back on the Indian Creek or Indian Ridge Trails (Trails 121 and 104, respectively).

• Want the easiest alpine hike in the area? Drive back from Clearwater Crossing and navigate up South Fork Fish Creek Road 343 for the long climb to Schley Mountain Trailhead and take the easy, family-friendly hike into Kidd Lake. Extensions could go to Mud and Cedar Log Lakes.

27 | HEART LAKE

Location: Idaho-Montana Divide
Status: Proposed wilderness
Distance: 6 miles round trip
Hiking time: 3–4 hours or overnight
Difficulty: Moderate
Season: Mid-June through late October
Maps: USGS Straight Peak NW, Hoodoo Pass
Information: Lolo National Forest, Superior District

Some backpackers consider this a model mountain trek. Hike into an area proposed as part of the Great Burn Wilderness and camp at the largest alpine lake in this western Montana portion of the Bitterroot Mountains. Walk a reasonably easy 3 miles to a high lake, make camp, and behold the opportunities for scenic side trips to the lofty, rocky ridge above without the heavy pack. The trip can be extended to visit Pearl or Dalton Lakes or made into a loop.

From Interstate 90, take Exit 47 at Superior, Montana, and head east on Diamond Road (State Highway 257), which parallels the south side of I-90. The pavement eventually ends and becomes Forest Road 250 (Trout Creek). It's about 20 miles from Superior (passing Trout Creek Campground) up to the Heart Lake Trailhead and parking area on a switchback in the road.

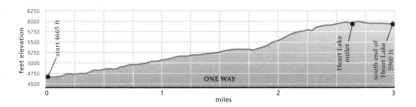

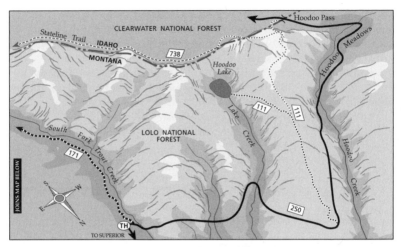

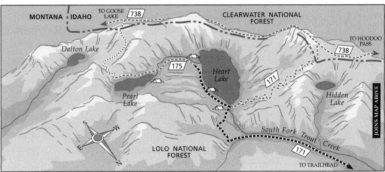

Well-used Trail 171 follows the South Fork of Trout Creek and crosses several small tributary streams and wet spots in the drainage. The hike is reasonably gentle, gaining about 1,130 feet in 3 miles through timber and grassy meadows. The undergrowth is thick, but the trail usually is well brushed. Just before reaching the lake, note a trail coming down from the right from the Stateline National Recreation Trail above (see "Options"). Hike halfway along Heart Lake to one campsite. There's another one at the far end of the lake. The lake holds cutthroats and brook trout.

Options: For a worthwhile day hike, follow the trail up the steep, rocky headwall west of the lake, switchbacking up 900 vertical feet to the ridge and Stateline Trail 738 (see Hike 65). At points the trail is faint and difficult to locate, but the ridge is distinctive, still mostly treeless from the Great Burn of 1910. Look for rock cairns marking the trail. From above at elevations ranging from 6,700 feet to nearly 7,000 feet, reap the reward of a fantastic view over Montana to the east and Idaho to the west. Although there is water all the way to Heart Lake, the ridge above the lake is dry.

Heart Lake with Pearl Lake in the distance, proposed Great Burn Wilderness

• Continue past Heart Lake through lush vegetation about 1 mile to Pearl Lake, which is perched on a mostly open bench with an outlet campsite. The trail skirts the length of the lake, and around the far end it climbs through wildflowers toward a saddle overlooking Dalton Lake. Return, or make a loop by scrambling up the faint unmaintained trail through the heather and the impacts of fire and avalanche to join the Stateline Trail on the ridge. Head west 1 mile toward Hoodoo Pass and the overlook of Hidden Lake, and drop down on the trail back to Heart Lake.

28 | HUB LAKE

Location: Idaho-Montana Divide
Status: Unprotected
Distance: 6 miles round trip
Hiking time: 5 hours or overnight
Difficulty: Moderate
Season: July through early October
Map: USGS DeBorgia South
Information: Lolo National Forest, Superior District

A quick weekend trip with easy access off Interstate 90, the 3-mile trail to Hub Lake begins as a pleasant stroll through a grove of ancient cedars.

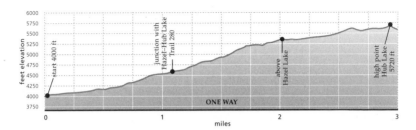

Then it does some serious climbing as it follows Ward Creek and crosses other small creeks to a couple of small campsites at the lake. Hikers have the options of following the trail farther, climbing to excellent viewpoints at Ward or Eagle Peaks.

On Interstate 90, drive east of DeBorgia, Montana, 7.5 miles and take Exit 26. (Unfortunately, drivers westbound out of St. Regis, Montana, will not find Exit 26. They must take Exit 25, then go back on the freeway eastbound 1 mile to Exit 26.) Once off the freeway, drive south on Ward Creek Road 889 nearly 6.5 miles. The trailhead is on the right side of the road just before it crosses Ward Creek.

Trail 262 follows Ward Creek about 1.2 miles up to the junction with Hazel-Hub Lake Trail 280. About 0.2 mile before the junction, however,

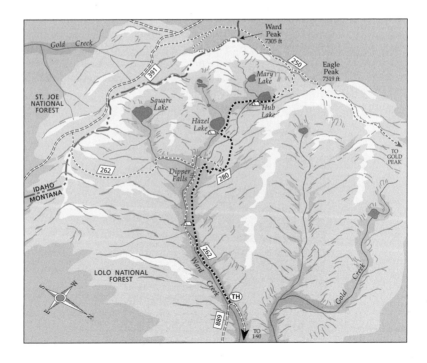

Hub Lake from trail to Up Up Ridge

listen for Ward Creek's 60-foot cascade down Dipper Falls. The trail is fairly gentle for the next mile to a 100-foot spur trail heading south to Hazel Lake. This lake holds fish, but it is brushy. Trail 280 climbs more steeply for the last mile up to Hub Lake. It passes through a flower-studded meadow flanked by Ward and Eagle Peaks. The trail traverses northeast through a draw for 0.8 mile to the lake's outlet.

Several places are suitable for camps, including the outlet area, where the remains of an old mining cabin can still be found nearby. Late in the season, the meadows at the upper end of the lake dry up enough for camping.

Options: Kill time by fishing for the lake's small cutthroat trout, or follow the faint trail up through wildflowers 930 feet to the junction with the lightly used Up Up Ridge Trail at elev. 6,650 feet in the saddle between Ward and Eagle Peaks. It's about 2 miles up from Hub Lake and south on the ridge and a scramble up the open south side to the top of Ward Peak, elev. 7,305 feet.

29 | ST. REGIS LAKES

Location: Idaho-Montana Divide
Status: Unprotected
Distance: 4–6 miles round trip
Hiking time: 2–4 hours or overnight
Difficulty: Moderate
Season: Late June through mid-October
Map: USGS Lookout Pass
Information: Lolo National Forest, Superior District or
   Idaho Panhandle National Forests, Coeur d'Alene River
   District, Wallace Office

High and easy access off Interstate 90 makes this a popular weekend trip to a scenic mountain lake area. The hike is easy, except for the fairly steep last 0.5 mile up to the main St. Regis Lake. The round-trip distance can be shortened to about 4 miles if you want to drive as far as possible. But many visitors prefer to walk the rough access road along the upper St. Regis River. This is Bitterroot Mountains huckleberry country; bring an extra "empty" water bottle in late July and August.

From I-90 on the summit of Lookout Pass (Montana-Idaho border), take Exit 0 and head south. Turn right at the stop sign and then turn left at the junction (away from the ski area). Head downhill just short of 1 mile and turn right on a gravel road. Drive 0.1 mile to the first trailhead. Continue past this trailhead 0.1 mile to another trailhead. People who don't have four-wheel-drive vehicles should use one of these two trailheads. If you must drive as far as possible, continue west from the first trailhead, passing brushed-over remains of mining dating back to 1910, and drive the rough road about 1.7 miles to the trailhead a short way down a spur road. This is where the footpath begins for St. Regis Trail 267. Round-trip distance from here is 4 miles.

Trails from the first two trailheads (one on each side of the creek) merge

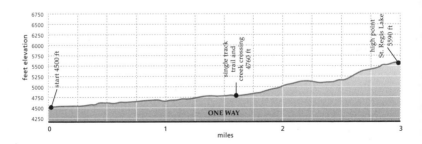

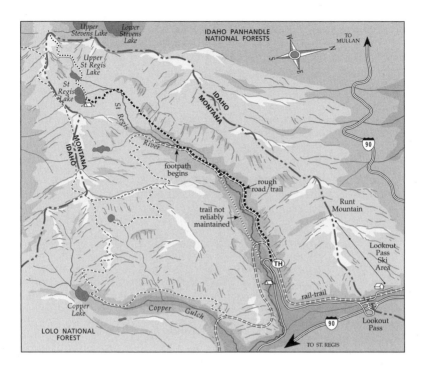

in less than 1 mile to follow the rough road described above about 0.5 mile to where the main footpath begins. The trail drops down, crosses the creek (no bridge), and continues west 0.8 mile to the base of a headwall. From here the trail climbs with a couple of switchbacks for 0.5 mile to the main lake. This lake is brushy, with only a couple of campsites on the north shore. The upper lake is small and boggy. The main lake holds hungry brook trout. The lakes and river were named by Father Peter DeSmet in 1842 for St. Regis de Borgia, another Jesuit Priest.

Options: Take the crude trail from the main lake to the upper lake, climb out of the brush zone and scramble steeply up southward to the ridge, where it becomes an easy walk toward Stevens Peak (great as a day hike), and a nifty view down on Upper Stevens Lake (see Hike 30).

Huckleberries, common in the Bitterroot Mountains

IDAHO PANHANDLE NATIONAL FORESTS

COEUR D'ALENE RIVER DISTRICT

30 | STEVENS LAKES

Location: Idaho-Montana Divide
Status: Unprotected
Distance: 5 miles round trip
Hiking time: 4 hours or overnight
Difficulty: Moderate
Season: Late June through mid-October
Map: USGS Mullan
Information: Idaho Panhandle National Forests,
Coeur d'Alene River District, Wallace Office

Popular among weekend campers, this hike quickly leads from Interstate 90 to an area of quiet alpine lakes in the western reaches of the Bitterroot Mountains. The lakes are situated at the brink of timberline below Stevens Peak and just a ridge west of St. Regis Lakes (see Hike 29). Stevens Peak was named in the 1800s by Captain John Mullan for Isaac Stevens, governor of Washington Territory and later a general in the Civil War. Stevens reportedly climbed the peak in 1853 to get a lay of the land. Good choice, since it's the highest peak in the area.

Heading east on Interstate 90 from Wallace, Idaho, take East Mullan Exit 69. Turn left at the stop sign and drive north over the freeway. At the next stop, turn right on State Highway 10 and go east about 1 mile, passing the Lucky Friday Mine, to Shoshone Park junction. Bear right (south) at the fork, crossing over I-90, and follow Willow Creek Road 1 mile to a parking

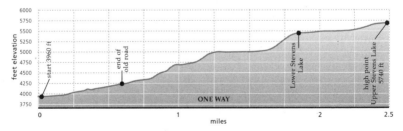

area at the abandoned railroad right-of-way that's now a rail-trail east to Lookout Pass. (Note the nearby trailhead for Trail 138 to Lone Lake, a nice day hike.) Begin the hike to Stevens Lakes by walking across the trackless railroad bed. Bear left onto a spur road. Continue up the road almost 1 mile until you pass the second switchback. Look for the trailhead on the right at the third switchback. Vandals rip off the trail signs as fast as the Forest Service can put them up, so keep a sharp eye out for a trail that might not be signed.

East Fork Willow Creek Trail 165 begins at about elev. 4,400 feet and heads up a steep slope, across a rockslide, and into the forest. Less than 1 mile later, it breaks out of the timber into a large basin surrounded by precipitous slopes and a stunning waterfall, which is powered by water from Stevens Lakes. The trail leads across East Fork Willow Creek and climbs steeply up the hillside, rising 350 feet in 0.2 mile to Lower Stevens Lake, where several campsites can be found. The trail continues along the west shore and climbs a small rise to Upper Stevens Lake and several more campsites. Small rainbow trout can be caught in both lakes and the alpine scenery is better than might be expected for so little effort. Expect to see pockets of snow in the shadows of treeless spires well into July.

Sunrise on upper Stevens Lake and Stevens Peak

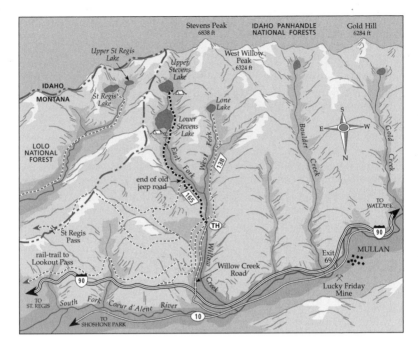

Options: Scramble up the ridge to the west of the lakes to 6,838-foot Stevens Peak for spectacular views of other lakes in the region.

31 | CHILCO MOUNTAINS

Location: Coeur d'Alene River Basin
Status: Unprotected
Distance: 9.6 miles round trip
Hiking time: 4–5 hours
Difficulty: Moderate
Season: Mid-May to early November
Maps: USGS Bayview, Spades Mt.
Information: Idaho Panhandle National Forests,
   Coeur d'Alene River District, Fernan Office

From the summit of Chilco Mountain, you can see Lake Pend Oreille and Lake Coeur d'Alene, mountain waters that are as beautiful as they are big. The hike is an alpine escape for people visiting one of the Idaho lakes. Although motorized use is increasing, few people hike this route to one of the most often seen but still largely unrecognized peaks in the area.

From Coeur d'Alene, head north on U.S. Highway 95 toward Sandpoint. Drive about 15 miles and turn right onto Bunco Road. (The intersection is at milepost 446 across from Silverwood.) Drive about 13.3 miles, staying on Bunco Road, which becomes Forest Road 332. Look for a trailhead sign on the right at the junction with Forest Road 385. Concrete posts mark the entrance to Trail 14.

The maintained trail climbs and switchbacks through timber for 1.8 miles until it reaches the ridge running north from Chilco Mountain, one of the highest peaks in the area at elev. 5,635 feet. Here the trail splits. Go left 0.2 mile to the summit of Chilco Mountain, site of a dismantled fire lookout. Enjoy, then backtrack and take the other trail fork and switchback down and across the west face of the mountain. The trail drops to Chilco Saddle, where off-road vehicles often approach the ridge, and then climbs to South Chilco Mountain, elev. 5,661 feet. (Mileage for this hike is based on returning from here, although you could continue south 1.6 miles to Forest Road 406 at the head of Chilco Creek. See "Options" below.)

A fire lookout was built on South Chilco in 1915 and abandoned in 1939. Chilco had a lookout and a cabin built in 1948 and dismantled in the late

Chilco Mountain, Lake Pend Oreille in background
(Photo by Sam Schlieder)

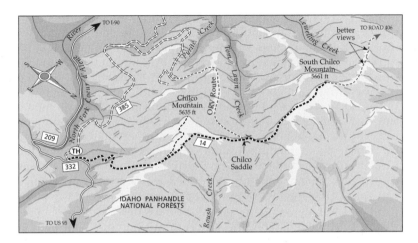

1950s. No water is available along the trail, although there are sites suitable for camping in the saddle between the two summits and on top of South Chilco.

Options: Hike this route in the opposite direction or make a 3.5-mile round trip to the top of South Chilco by approaching from the south trailhead. At Interstate 90 in Coeur d'Alene, head north toward Sandpoint on U.S. Highway 95. From the intersection with Appleway Avenue, drive north 10 miles on US 95 and turn right (east) on Ohio Match Road (milepost 441.1). Take mileage reading here and continue on Ohio Match Road, which becomes gravel. At 3 miles, bear left at junction with Tree Farm Lane, cross cattle guard, and continue on Forest Road 206. At 7 miles, turn left (north) at T (near gauging station) onto Forest Road 437 along East Fork of Hayden Creek. At 14 miles, go around sweeping left turn (past steel powerline tower), then make immediate left turn onto Road 406, which leads nearly 1 mile to the trailhead at elev. 4,320 feet. The trail goes steadily uphill with no water sources to the three summits of South Chilco. The highest summit is timbered. Get better views from other high points. Look south to Spades Peak fire lookout, southwest to Hayden Lake, west to Mount Spokane in Washington, and northeast toward the Cabinet Mountains in Montana.

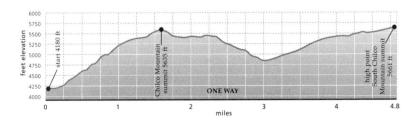

32 | INDEPENDENCE CREEK

Location: Coeur d'Alene River Basin
Status: Unprotected
Distance: 15 miles round trip
Hiking time: 8 hours or overnight
Difficulty: Moderate
Season: July through September
Maps: USGS Cathedral Peak, Faset Peak
Information: Idaho Panhandle National Forests,
    Coeur d'Alene River District, Fernan Office

Once runoff is over and the sun bears down in July and August, this is an appealing hike for visitors in Upper Coeur d'Alene River country. This National Recreation Trail, which once crossed Independence Creek 19 times, was pegged for reconstruction in 2003 to reduce the number of fords to four. But that's still enough to cool your heels. Sneakers are important footwear to wear or carry on this hike. Much of Trail 22 still follows the route of one of the first mining wagon roads in the area. The hillsides are

Independence Creek (Photo by Sam Schlieder)

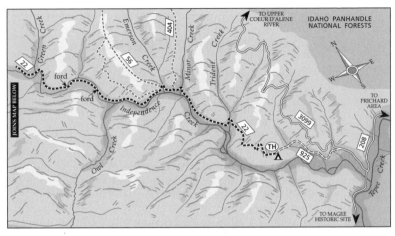

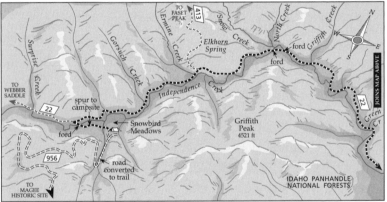

studded with decaying snags from the Great Burn fires of 1910. Watch for signs of black bears, deer, elk, coyotes, hawks, and owls.

The best access is from Interstate 90. Take Kingston Exit 43 just west of Kellogg, Idaho, and head north on Forest Highway 9 (Coeur d'Alene River Road). Drive about 21 miles, bear left at the junction and continue along the Coeur d'Alene River on Road 208. Go another 26 miles to where the road turns into gravel and becomes Road 6310. Continue for 3.3 miles and turn right on Road 3099 (just before crossing Independence Creek). Go 0.3 mile and turn left on Road 925 to the start of Trail 22, where there is a camping area and vault toilet.

From Independence Creek Campground (elev. 2,960 feet), Trail 22 leads away from the creek and makes its most strenuous gain in elevation. The first 0.5 mile is a 350-foot climb through a forest of lodgepole pine and Douglas fir before dropping back down to the creek. From this high point, and others along the way, you'll have a good view of the meandering creek

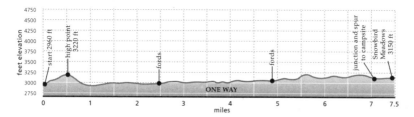

below. The trail follows the creek through forest and open meadows where picnicking and camping sites can be found.

Crossing small Trident Creek, the trail levels and stays closer to Independence Creek. At 1.2 miles, pass Minor Creek and the junction with Trail 404. In another 300 yards, the trail crosses Emerson Creek and a junction with Trail 56. Both trails are used primarily by hunters in fall. Continue up Independence Creek on Trail 22, crossing a meadow and making the first of four creek crossings not changed by the trail reconstruction. Pass the site of an old splash dam and soon you'll cross back to the north side of the creek. (Early spring crossings could be tricky with high, fast water. Later, the rocks can be slick. Bring a walking staff.) The trail enters a meadow and then traverses the base of the canyon ridge, crosses Green Creek and Griffith Creek, and returns to ford Independence Creek twice in quick succession.

At this point, reconstructed Trail 22 stays on the north side of the creek (avoiding the original route of 12 crossings in 2 miles). Pass the junction with Trail 413, which originates on Faset Peak. Cross Ermine and Gorsuch Creeks. Trail 22 soon drops down near the creek to a junction with a spur that doubles back on the old route across Independence Creek to a large meadow and camping area. Snowbird Meadows has gone through periods of desecration from off-road vehicles. But the area is healing now that access roads have been closed to motorized use. Trail 22 is fairly uneventful from here west to the Webber Saddle Trailhead. Most hikers prefer to picnic or camp at Snowbird Meadows and return.

33 | UPPER COEUR D'ALENE RIVER

Location: Coeur d'Alene River Basin
Status: Unprotected
Distance: Up to 14 miles one way
Hiking time: Up to 8 hours or overnight
Difficulty: Easy
Season: May through October
Maps: USGS Cathedral Peak, Jordan Creek
Information: Idaho Panhandle National Forests,
    Coeur d'Alene River District, Wallace Office

Coeur d'Alene River National Recreation Trail 20 appeals to day hikers, overnighters, and fly fishers alike. It parallels the Upper Coeur d'Alene River, sometimes running high above the stream, for about 14 miles. The trail most logically is broken into two sections: The south segment begins off paved Coeur d'Alene River Road 208 and heads 5.7 miles north to Jordan Camp. The north segment begins at Jordan Camp and goes more than 8 miles to Road 3099 near Marten Creek. Both hikes pass through Great Burn areas devastated by the 1910 fire.

(Be aware that locals call the Upper Coeur d'Alene River the "North Fork of the Coeur d'Alene River." Most Forest Service and USGS maps officially show the Coeur d'Alene River north of Interstate 90 as having three forks: the main stem, the North Fork, and the South Fork. People who live in this region, however, refer to the Coeur d'Alene River above the South Fork as the North Fork. What most maps list as the North Fork—the stream that meets the main channel about 5 miles north of Enaville—is known as the Little North Fork.)

South segment: The south portion of Coeur d'Alene River Trail 20 is 5.7 miles one way from the Coeur d'Alene River Road to Jordan Camp. The trail generally skirts high above the river, but you can slip and slide down several steep places to the cool water to fish or camp. The river is one of Idaho's top

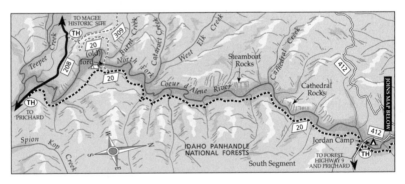

Overlooking south section of the Coeur d'Alene River Trail

catch-and-release fishing streams for west-slope cutthroat trout. Service-berries, huckleberries, and wildflowers are profuse in some areas.

From Interstate 90 just west of Kellogg, take Kingston Exit 43 and head north on paved Forest Highway 9 (Coeur d'Alene River Road). It's a total of 49 miles to the south trailhead, following the Coeur d'Alene River north about 21 miles and bearing left onto Road 208 continuing upriver for about 28 miles. (The road passes several national forest campgrounds on the way, including Kit Price, Devil's Elbow, and Big Hank.) Two trailheads have been available for the south segment: the newer trailhead just before a bridge across the Coeur d'Alene River and the older one a short way far-ther, just before the end of the pavement between mileposts 25 and 26. The old trail may be abandoned, even though it has offered a nifty family back-packing opportunity.

The newer trailhead leads immediately up and over some rock outcroppings and stays on the east side of the river, avoiding the need to ford. The second trailhead is the beginning of Trail 309 and the old source for Trail 20. Follow this route for a 0.25 mile and bear right at the trail junction

toward Trail 20. Depending on whether the Forest Service continues to clear Trail 20, the route leads over a hump and back down to the river. Several worn paths here lead to campsites, perfect for short family overnighters, on the west side of the river. However, to link up with Trail 20, the river must be forded. This is easy and pleasant after runoff, which sometimes isn't until late June or early July. It can be cold and foolish early in the season. Then you must scramble up to the newer version of Trail 20, which contours high above the river, coming back close to it only twice in the remaining 4.5 miles to Jordan Camp. Scenic attractions along the trail include Steamboat Rocks and Cathedral Rocks, which tower above the river. Water is frequently available along the trail. Incidentally, Spion Kop, the unusual name of a mountain east of the trail near Jordan Camp, was named after a famous battle in the Boer War. *Kop* is a South African term for mountain.

North segment: To hike the 8-mile north portion of the trail, exit I-90 as described above, drive about 21 miles and bear left on Road 208. Drive 6 miles, passing Avery Creek picnic area. Just before Shoshone Work Center, turn right onto Road 412. Drive 22.2 miles—past Berlin Flats Campground, over Jordan Saddle—to Jordan Camp Campground area. The trailhead is just east of the bridge. (Consider shuttling another vehicle to the end of the trail on Road 3099 near Marten Creek.)

Trail 20/52 heads northwest, climbing high at first, but generally staying much more intimate with the Upper Coeur d'Alene River than the south segment of Trail 20. From the trail junction just before the Alden Creek ford, Trail 20 drops left off the ridge and crosses a broad meadow. The trail here is somewhat faint and boggy in the spring. A good campsite is just past the meadow. The route follows a former jeep trail for a short way. It rounds a bend in the river and crosses a slope of talus near Deer Creek, where some impressive rock formations loom above the river. (Scramble up for a sentinel's vantage and a lunch spot complete with rock stools.) The trail climbs gently to a point several hundred feet above the river and levels. The slopes here are sparsely timbered allowing good views. Just before Sluice Creek, the trail passes several camping places on a flat bench near the river. More campsites can be found past Clark Creek on a forested bench across the river. (Beware: the smooth rock slab at the Clark Creek crossing is slick.) The trail roller-coasters to Wren Creek, where it levels out through the forest and finally ends at Road 3099 near the concrete foundations indicating the former location of Beaver Work Center.

PRIEST LAKE DISTRICT

34 | UPPER PRIEST RIVER

Location: Upper Priest River
Status: Proposed wilderness
Distance: 16 miles round trip
Hiking time: 2 days
Difficulty: Easy
Season: Mid-June through late October
Map: USGS Continental Mountain
Information: Idaho Panhandle National Forests,
    Priest Lake District

A dark, dank trail through a virgin red cedar forest awaits hikers out for a long walk accompanied by the musical rumble of the Upper Priest River. The river is part of the federal Wild and Scenic River System and reaches into an area proposed as an addition to the Salmo-Priest Wilderness.

From Priest River, Idaho, drive north on State Highway 57 about 37 miles to Nordman. Continue another 14 miles on Forest Road 302 (Granite Creek) to Stagger Inn Campground. Now drive 1.6 miles and take the middle fork at the road junction onto Road 1013. Drive nearly 12 miles and look for the trailhead sign and parking area on the left side of the road. (Drivers who start up a sharp switchback have gone about 0.5 mile too far.)

The trail is constantly ambushed by springs and streams, and often visited by deer and the occasional moose and grizzly bear. About 5.4 miles upstream, pass the junction with Trail 349, which goes up mercilessly to the Shedroof Divide. Campsites can be found at several spots, including

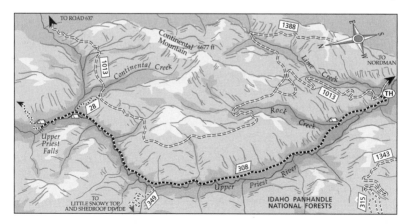

Upper Priest River (Photo by Chuck Kerkering)

Rock Creek and Malcom Creek. Camping also is available at Upper Priest Falls (also called American Falls), but these sites tend to be dirty and over-used generally by less than ethical visitors who occasionally come in on the short 2.3-mile route from farther up Road 1013. These hikers save time getting to Upper Priest Falls, but they miss one of the best lowland hiking trails in Idaho.

The last 0.8 mile of trail to the tumbling 40-foot falls is maintained to a lesser standard. Anglers should check Idaho Fish and Game Department fishing regulations for rules that protect endangered bull trout.

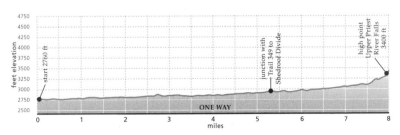

35 UPPER PRIEST LAKE– NAVIGATION TRAIL

Location: Upper Priest River
Status: Upper Priest River Scenic Area
Distance: 11 miles round trip
Hiking time: 6–7 hours or overnight
Difficulty: Easy
Season: Late May through October
Maps: USGS Priest Lake NE, Upper Priest Lake
Information: Idaho Panhandle National Forests,
    Priest Lake District

Easy road access to a gentle trail that gains very little elevation en route to developed campsites along a huge mountain lake combine to make this a dependable backpacking trip for a wide range of hikers. No roads access Upper Priest Lake, but canoes, kayaks, and power boats can get there via The Thorofare that links the upper lake with Priest Lake.

From Priest River, Idaho, drive north on State Highway 57 about 37 miles to Nordman. At the fork at Nordman, turn right toward Reeder Bay

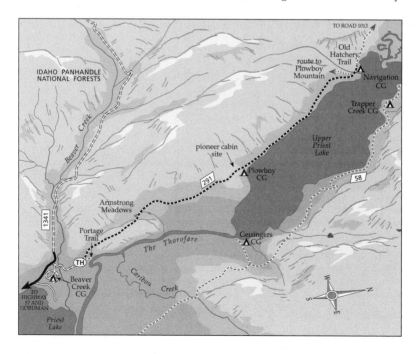

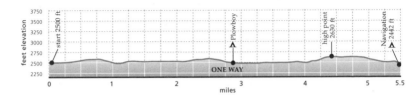

and continue north along the west shore of the lake to Beaver Creek Campground. Turn into the campground entrance and follow the signs to the trailhead parking area. Here there are vault toilets along with the start of a 0.2-mile canoe portage trail that heads down to The Thorofare between Priest and Upper Priest Lakes.

From the Beaver Creek Trailhead, Trail 291 heads into a cedar forest. After about 1 mile, it skirts Armstrong Meadows and a beaver pond. It then ducks back into the woods. Although it has a few uphills and downhills, the elevation gain in this portion of the hike is negligible.

About 0.2 mile before Plowboy Campground, pass what's left of a pioneer cabin from earlier days when settlers lived around the lake. Continue on to Plowboy, which is situated on the shore of Upper Priest Lake. The campground has several picnic tables, fire pits, and pit toilets, used by both hikers and boaters. Other scattered campsites can be found in the area.

It's a total of about 2.7 miles to Plowboy Campground, the halfway point to Navigation Campground, which is reached by continuing northwest on the trail along the undulating shore of Upper Priest. Navigation has vault toilets and numerous campsites. Picnic tables in this area were destroyed

Upper Priest Lake from Plowboy Campground (Photo by Sam Schlieder)

by unusually high winds in a 1976 summer thunderstorm that blew down hundreds of trees. The area was closed for several years before it could be cleared.

Anglers should check Idaho Fish and Game Department fishing regulations for special rules in this area designed to protect endangered bull trout.

Options: To explore the northerly extension of the trail to the Plowboy Trailhead (formerly called the Hatchery Trailhead), cross Deadman Creek and follow the trail on the north bank. (A shuttle vehicle could be left at the north trailhead by bearing left at Nordman onto Forest Road 302. Drive to the end of the pavement, continue past campsites at Stagger Inn and Granite Falls, and bear right on Road 1013. A mile past Hughes Meadows turnoff, go right to the trailhead for Plowboy Trail 295. From the trailhead, it's 4 miles to Navigation Campground, but the route is not as scenic as the walk in from the south trailhead.)

• A 2-mile trail leads from Navigation Campground to the top of Plowboy Mountain and the minimal remains of an old lookout. About 50 feet east of the lookout is an open area with an excellent view of the Selkirk Mountains. This Plowboy trail continues down the other side of the mountain with many switchbacks, coming out at the Plowboy Mountain Trail 295 Trailhead, located about 2.5 miles west of Beaver Creek Campground.

• From Beaver Creek Campground at Tule Bay, the Lakeshore Trail winds 7.5 miles south, hugging the shores of Priest Lake and offering access to several walk-in beach camping sites. The trail offers a good view of Chimney Rock across the lake on the Selkirk Crest (see Hike 51). Two other access points to the Lakeshore Trail are along the road between Beaver Creek and Nordman.

36   UPPER PRIEST LAKE– TRAPPER CREEK

Location: Upper Priest River
Status: Upper Priest River Scenic Area
Distance: 10 miles round trip
Hiking time: 6–7 hours or overnight
Difficulty: Easy
Season: Late May through October
Map: USGS Upper Priest Lake
Information: Idaho Department of Lands at
        Cavanaugh Bay and Idaho Panhandle National Forests,
        Priest Lake District

Priest Lake visitors can get away from the crowds at the main lake with this hike to a lightly used area at the north end of Upper Priest Lake. Vehicles

Trapper Creek Trail to Upper Priest Lake (Photo by Chuck Kerkering)

are not allowed in this area and no water skiing is allowed on Upper Priest, making it more the playground of hikers, anglers, and canoeists. It once was the playground of mountain caribou and grizzly bears, both of which are now endangered but still clinging to existence in this region.

From Priest River, Idaho, drive north on State Highway 57 about 37 miles to Nordman. At Nordman, bear left at the Y, staying on Highway 57, which becomes Forest Road 302. The pavement ends after nearly 4 miles. Continue on Road 302 past Stagger Inn Campground. (The Roosevelt grove of ancient cedars and Granite Falls are worth a stop.) Less than 2 miles past the campgrounds, the road forks three ways. Take the middle fork, staying on Road 1013 as it winds through the forest. Stay on the main road, passing the turnoffs to Hughes Meadows and several other spur roads for about 3 miles and turn right onto Forest Road 655. The trailhead for Trapper Creek Trail 302 is nearly 0.5 mile east on this road.

The trail leads gently through a cedar forest, breaks into some openings, and heads back into the woods. It's a peaceful hike with some ups, downs, and bridges over most stream crossings. The trail emerges at the northeast shore of Upper Priest Lake, 4 miles from the trailhead. A short distance before arriving at the lake, there is a dilapidated cabin, reminiscent of the early history of the area, which was busy with miners and trappers. From the lakeshore you can see Navigation Campground across the lake to the west and Plowboy Mountain, which dominates the west shore (see Hike 35). (Plowboy Campground is not visible from here.) The trail

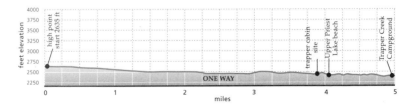

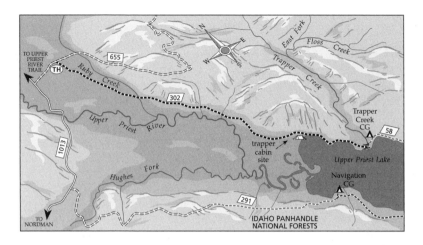

continues eastward, skirting the shore for 1 mile to Trapper Creek campsites.

Options: From Trapper Creek campsites, Trail 58 leads all the way to Lionhead Campground at the north end of Priest Lake, with a spur leading off to Geisingers campsite at the outlet of Upper Priest.

37 | LOOKOUT MOUNTAIN

Location: Upper Priest River
Status: Unprotected
Distance: 5 miles round trip
Hiking time: 3–4 hours or overnight
Difficulty: Moderately difficult
Season: Late June through mid-October
Map: USGS Caribou Creek
Information: Idaho Department of Lands, Cavanaugh Bay

The north face of Lookout Mountain is a nearly vertical 200-foot cliff forming a broad U shape often admired by hikers and canoeists looking up from Upper Priest Lake. The summit of Lookout Mountain provides a magnificent view of Priest Lake, Upper Priest Lake, and a long swath of the Selkirk Mountains crest. The Forest Service designated the peak a fire observation point in 1921 and erected the first lookout house on the summit in 1929. After the first lookout was unstaffed for 30 years, a new tower was built by the Idaho Department of Lands in 1977. In 1983, volunteers began restoring the original lookout. Age has been winning the battle. No stranger to fire, the lookout was a little too close for comfort to a blaze that lightning ignited on Lookout Mountain itself in 2001.

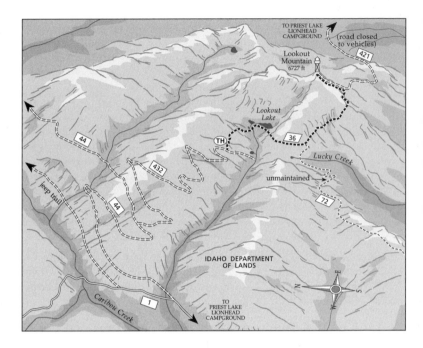

From Priest River, Idaho, drive north on State Highway 57 about 22 miles and turn right on Dickensheet Road toward Coolin. Drive 5.3 miles to Coolin and turn right on East Shore Road toward Cavanaugh Bay. Continue another 24.4 miles, passing Lionhead Campground, and turn right on Road 44. Head uphill 2.5 miles and continue right on Road 432 another 3.2 miles to the trailhead. The route begins at 5,200 feet and heads 0.7 mile uphill to Lookout Lake at 5,564 feet. The lake is the only year-round reliable source of water on the trail. Three small campsites are situated along the trail on the west side of the lake. The lakeshore itself is marshy, with a boulder field along the south end. Overnighters often camp here and day hike to the summit.

From the lake, follow the trail about 0.5 mile to a junction with an unmaintained trail. From here, go left and up about 1.2 miles to the summit of Lookout Mountain. The last 0.2 mile to the summit is on a steep jeep road.

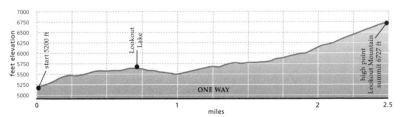

Above Priest Lake in the granite rubble of Lookout Mountain

At the top, you will find an outhouse in a clump of trees west of the lookout structures and a stunning but dangerous drop-off to the north.

Options: Make a loop of sorts by hiking down Road 421, closed to motor vehicles, to Lion Creek Road 42, where shuttle vehicles could be waiting at the gate.

38 | HUNT LAKE

Location: Selkirk Crest
Status: Unprotected
Distance: 2 miles round trip
Hiking time: 2–3 hours or overnight
Difficulty: Moderately difficult
Season: July through September
Map: USGS Mt. Roothaan
Information: Idaho Department of Lands, Cavanaugh Bay

Don't be misled by the short mileage on this hike. The effort involves more hopping than walking, since the route from the trailhead to the lake weaves up a talus slope, marked by painted arrows and cairns. Many hikers will love this hike, but not if they have weak ankles. Some might prefer to tent camp at the full-service campgrounds along the east shore of Priest Lake at Indian Creek or Lionhead State Park and make Hunt Lake a day trip without the weight of a pack.

There's an advantage to a trail through huge granite boulders. The Idaho Department of Lands is a timber agency, not a recreation agency. Thus, trails on state land between Priest Lake and the Selkirk Crest are rarely maintained. But while other state land trails are often covered with

Hunt Lake, Idaho Selkirk Mountains

brush and blowdowns (unless volunteers are active), this trail needs no maintenance.

From Priest River, Idaho, drive north on State Highway 57 about 22 miles and turn right on Dickensheet Road toward Coolin. Drive 5.3 miles to Coolin and turn right on East Shore Road toward Cavanaugh Bay. Continue 7.3 miles past Cavanaugh Bay and turn right onto Hunt Creek Road 24, which leads to the trailhead. Logging activity in this area creates spur roads and route changes, making detailed directions from here unreliable. (The best bet is to stop at the Idaho Department of Lands office next to the

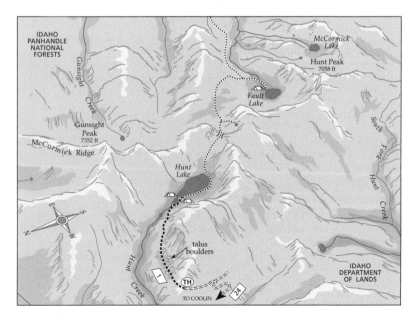

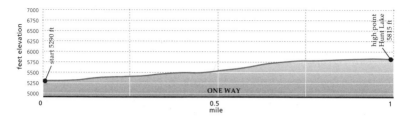

airstrip at Cavanaugh Bay for a look at the latest road map.) Head 4 miles up Road 24, bear right and continue on Road 24 for 1.2 miles (crossing Hunt Creek at 0.4 mile) to a junction. Bear left onto Road 24/241 for 3.5 miles to the trailhead.

A post marks the trailhead and the trail runs only a few yards before it hits the boulders. Cairns or arrows painted on the rocks mark the trail every 50 to 100 feet. Only a few short stretches get down to earth along the route.

No water is available until Hunt Lake, which offers fair fishing for small cutthroat trout. Two campsites are at the outlet end with room for a tent or two at the far end near the inlet. The rest of the lake is surrounded by brush and boulders.

Options: From Hunt Lake, scramblers with routefinding experience can climb over the rocks and through shoreline brush to Gunsight Peak, elev. 7,352 feet. Easier is the bushwhack along the west shore, across and up a talus slope at the southeast end of the lake and through the prominent pass to Fault Lake at the edge of the 1967 Sundance Burn (see Hike 52).

BONNERS FERRY DISTRICT

39 | IRON MOUNTAIN LOOP

Location: Kootenai River
Status: Unprotected
Distance: 10.5 miles round trip
Hiking time: 4–6 hours
Difficulty: Difficult
Season: Late June through October
Maps: USGS Clifty Mountain, Leona
Information: Idaho Panhandle National Forests,
   Bonners Ferry District

Steep trails that discourage riffraff lead to lofty views of the Kootenai River Valley from Iron Mountain. Once the elevation is gained, the open-ridge

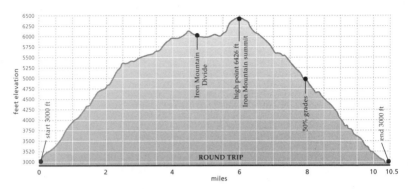

hiking is delightful in this lightly used niche of the Idaho Panhandle National Forests. Camping near a murky water source is an option at Divide Lake. But the trails leading in and out of this area, obviously designed for creatures with four legs, lend this route beautifully to leaving the freight behind, hiking with a light day pack, and then car-camping along roads below. Grizzly bears could be encountered in this region.

From the north side of Bonners Ferry, Idaho, just before crossing the railroad bridge, turn east on Ash Street. Drive 0.4 mile and bear left on Forest Road 24 (Cow Creek) toward Rocky Mountain Academy. Go 0.5 mile and bear left at the Y, continuing on Road 24. Go nearly 3 miles and turn left, continuing on Road 24. Go 3 miles and pull out on the curve with a great view of the Kootenai River Valley plus the Selkirk Mountains to the west. See how old bends in the river are now rich farmland? Now continue driving nearly 11 miles and turn right on Road 408. Go 3.2 miles and bear left down Road 628 (milepost 15.8) toward East Fork Boulder Creek. Drive 0.5 mile, passing the trailhead for Middle Fork Boulder Creek Trail 180, to a gate and the start of Trail 176.

Hiking the divide south of Iron Mountain

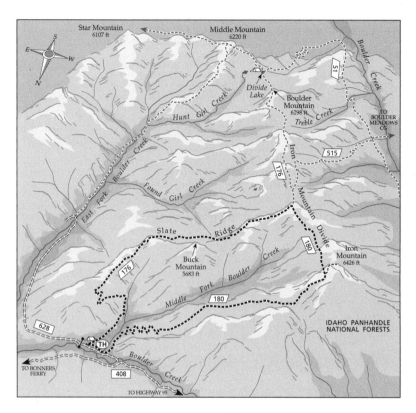

These trailheads and a trailhead mentioned in the "Options" below are also accessible from U.S. Highway 95 about 6.5 miles south of Bonners Ferry from Twentymile Road and Forest Road 408, but the route east of Boulder Creek can be rough.

Buck Mountain Trail 176 heads south from the road and climbs steadily, gaining 3,000 feet of elevation in 4.7 miles. Get in a rhythm. Relief will come. Above tree line, on the Iron Mountain Divide at the junction with Trail 180, turn south for an excellent optional side trip, 5 miles round trip, along the ridge to a shallow marshy pothole called Divide Lake. This is the only reliable source of water on the ridge in the late season. Bring a water purifier.

To continue to Iron Mountain, head north on Trail 180. Near a small, sparsely timbered saddle (with a dry campsite), look for a spur trail heading northwest up to the top of Iron Mountain, elev. 6,426 feet.

Back at the saddle, Trail 180 heads east about 3.5 miles downhill to Road 628. Hiking poles will be handy. The trail grade is fairly gentle at first, but the middle section is steep, with grades exceeding 50 percent, before tapering off again into switchbacks for the last stretch of downhill.

Hike the spur road a short way to Road 628. Turn right and walk 0.2 mile to the starting point.

Options: The loop could be done counterclockwise, depending on whether you wanted to negotiate the steeper trail (Trail 180) going up or down.

• The trip could be lengthened by hiking through the gate at the trailhead, following Road 628 for 3 miles, and then taking Trail 136 up the East Fork Boulder Creek 4.3 miles (seems farther) to Middle Mountain. The trail can be difficult but not impossible to follow to the divide and the junction with Trail 176.

• Make a west-side-based 12-mile loop to the south end of this divide by driving east from US 95 south of Bonners Ferry as described above. Go over Twentymile Pass south of Black Mountain and turn south on Road 427 to the campground at the end of the road in Boulder Meadows. Hike the trail up Boulder Creek and turn left (east) on Smythe Trail 515, climbing to Trail 176. Turn south on the divide for 2.5 miles and then drop westward off the ridge near Divide Lake on Timber Trail 51. Hike down to a junction and turn right (north) continuing on Trail 51, which becomes an old logging road down to Boulder Creek. Eventually, you will turn left back to the campground or go straight to another trailhead at a gate and parking area just north of the campground.

• Hikers coming from the Sandpoint, Idaho area might want to make variations of these hikes, accessing from Highway 200 east of Kootenai and heading north to connect with Forest Road 280 (Grouse Creek). Drive to the trailhead and hike Trail 488 toward Calder Mountain and then Divide Lake.

40 | WEST FORK LAKE

Location: Selkirk Crest
Status: Proposed wilderness
Distance: 12 miles round trip
Hiking time: 8 hours or overnight
Difficulty: Moderate
Season: Mid-June through September
Maps: USGS Smith Peak, Shorty Peak, Caribou Creek, Grass Mountain
Information: Idaho Panhandle National Forests, Bonners Ferry District

This trail leads past West Fork Cabin, which is open to public use with a woodstove and room for about six adults. The trail also visits West Fork Lake and Hidden Lake, the largest high-mountain lake in the Idaho Selkirks. West Fork Lake is situated in a remote area where hikers can climb to views of country in which grizzly bears and mountain caribou have

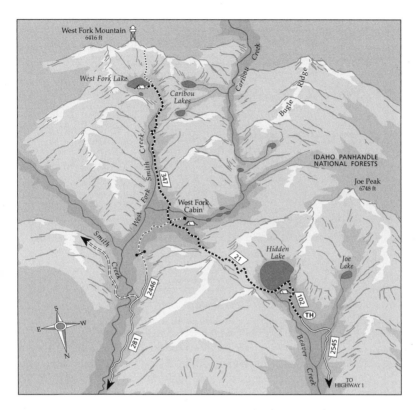

found their last remaining refuge in this region. The presence of these rare species (incidentally, mosquitoes are *not* rare here) has been triggering management options such as road closures. Check with the Bonners Ferry Ranger District for updates.

From the north side of Bonners Ferry, Idaho, head north on U.S. Highway 2/95. Drive 15 miles and bear left onto Highway 1. Drive 1 mile and turn left toward Copeland. Cross the Kootenai River and turn right (north) on West Side Road. After 9 miles, the paved road bends left and becomes Forest Road 281 (Smith Creek). At the end of the pavement is an overlook of Smith Falls Hydroelectric Plant. From here, drive 1.3 miles and bear right on Road 655 toward Hidden Lake. (Left fork leads to another trailhead and

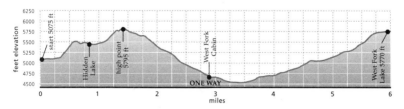

West Fork Lake, Idaho Selkirk Mountains (photo by Jerry Pavia)

a shorter but less scenic route to West Fork Lake.) Go 2.5 miles, passing the Shorty Peak turnoff, and bear left at a fork onto Road 2545. Drive nearly 3 miles and bear right, uphill, to the trailhead.

Begin on well-used Trail 102, which switchbacks steeply through an old burn. After 0.2 mile it begins to level off for the next 0.5 mile to Hidden Lake, which is stocked with rainbow trout. Plenty of campsites are available. Continue around the outlet side of the lake, then head steeply up the toughest section of the hike about 1 mile, overlooking the lake, to a trail junction. Bear south and tie into Trail 21. Hike down from the saddle about 2 miles through brushy areas (and an area of big cedars until Crown Pacific Timber Company whacked them in the 1990s) to West Fork Cabin, which is well used and open on a first-come, first-served basis. After the original cabin burned to the ground in 1998, the cabin was rebuilt by volunteers and many contributors, including the trail fund from sales of this guidebook. Continue south 0.3 mile and bear right at the junction onto Trail 347 toward West Fork Lake and mountain. Cross a branch of West Fork Smith Creek, heading down through ferns and old cedars that have been spared by the chain saws and up through some granite talus and boggy areas about 2.5 miles to a junction. The main trail heads left to campsites at the lake, which is stocked with cutthroats. The other fork of the trail leads up an unmaintained route to the old lookout site on West Fork Mountain for views of West Fork Lake, Smith Peak, and Lions Head. The West Fork Lookout was one of two on the Panhandle forests that was made by a windmill company and adapted for day use as a lookout. The other was on Saddle Mountain to the north.

Options: From the ridge above West Fork Lake, navigate the short way to Caribou Lakes, scooped out of granite benches.

41 | LONG CANYON LOOP

Location: Selkirk Crest
Status: Proposed wilderness
Distance: 35 miles round trip
Hiking time: 4–5 days
Difficulty: Moderately difficult
Season: July through September
Maps: USGS Smith Peak, Pyramid Peak, Shorty Peak, Smith Falls
Information: Idaho Panhandle National Forests, Bonners Ferry District

A classic Inland Northwest backpacking experience, this trip leads up beneath ancient cedars, hemlocks, and white pines through and above the very last major unlogged drainage of the Idaho Selkirks. Then it climbs up to a lake-studded ridge and plunges back to the Kootenai River Valley on the longest uninterrupted trail network in the region.

Long Canyon is flanked by two of the three highest mountains in northern Idaho, Smith Peak at 7,653 feet and Parker Peak at 7,670 feet. (The highest in the Idaho Selkirks is Fisher Ridge at 7,709 feet, not to be confused with lower Fisher Peak, 7,580 feet.) Within Long Canyon are four lakes, three of which are stocked with grayling or cutthroats, but they are reached only by difficult bushwhacking from the main trail through dungeons of

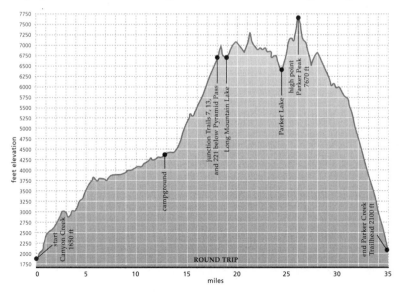

devil's club. Long Canyon Creek holds some small rainbow and brook trout. The main Long Canyon trail, called Canyon Creek Trail 16, has been rebuilt and maintained since the early 1980s by several Bonners Ferry–based volunteer groups, including hikers and horsepackers. Increased recreational use could force the Forest Service to impose restrictions to protect grizzlies. Check with the ranger district for updates.

From Bonners Ferry, drive north 15 miles on U.S. Highway 2/95 to the junction with State Highway 1. Bear left on Highway 1 and turn west at the Copeland turnoff. From here it's 10 miles—crossing the Kootenai River and heading north at the West Side Road junction—to Canyon Creek Trail 16. The hiking loop ends at the trailhead for Parker Creek Trail 221, which is on the paved West Side Road a little more than 3 miles southeast of the Trail 16 Trailhead. A shuttle car or bike can be left there.

From the parking area, walk up a short way on an old road that becomes Trail 16. Carry plenty of water, since it's about 4 dry miles from the trailhead before the route comes close to the creek. Listen for the sound of Smith Falls below. The first section of trail winds pleasantly through the timber before bending back south toward Long Canyon Creek and the steep slopes that helped preserve this grand drainage from logging. The trail then becomes a combination of ups and downs through ocean spray and ninebark on a dry hillside. At 2.4 miles, remains of an old cabin are above the trail; a pond is below. From the first campsite by the creek, head up again. Around mile 7, look for evidence of old marten trap sets on trees along the trail. Bridges span bogs of fern and devil's club a short way before the next campsite (3-plus miles up from the first creekside campsite) and the first crossing of Canyon Creek. This ford can be difficult (65 feet across) in high water during June, although log crossings might be available. (Water is abundant along the trail from this point on to Pyramid Pass.)

Past 9 miles, there's another crossing of Canyon Creek and another campsite. The quietness is rarely disturbed beyond here, except perhaps

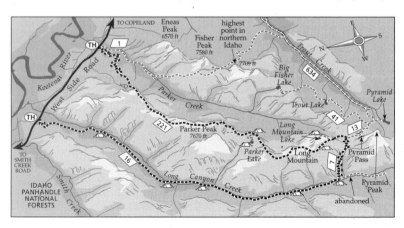

Tributary of Long Canyon Creek, Idaho Selkirks (photo by Jerry Pavia)

by the shrill whistles of the varied thrush. At mile 11, note the huge old cedars and white pines that were toppled to the ground by a microburst. At mile 12.8, there's a huge campsite before crossing the unnamed creek that flows out of Smith Lake.

At 13.5 miles, Trail 16 passes a little campsite and crosses Long Canyon Creek the third time 0.5 mile before coming to the junction with Trail 7 at elev. 4,520 feet. (Trail 16 is no longer maintained very far beyond this junction because of forest management decisions protecting grizzly habitat.) Head up Trail 7, switchbacking toward westward views of Smith Peak, then southward views of Pyramid Peak. From the junction with Trail 16, Trail 7 climbs 1,850 feet in 4 miles to a junction about 0.5 mile below Pyramid Pass. Turn left onto Trail 221, which heads north and steeply uphill to a saddle and a scenic alpine setting on Parker Ridge. This ridge above Long Canyon is graced with several easily accessed lakes, usually stocked with grayling or cutthroat trout. Allow time to scramble ridges through heather, beargrass, and huge white granite boulders for incredible views of the Selkirks and the entire Parker Creek drainage down to the Kootenai Valley. From here it's about 16 miles to the Parker Creek Trailhead, but 7 miles of it are scenic ridge-walking.

Down from the saddle, a side trail leads to campsites at Long Mountain Lake. Hike another 3 miles, enjoying views of peaks as far as the Cabinet Mountains in Montana and the Canadian Rockies, to a trail heading down 0.6 mile to Parker Lake. A smaller crowd of mosquitoes tends to share the campsite on the ridge. (It is important to stock up with water at the lakes for the rest of the trip. After passing Parker Lake (about 10 miles from the end of the trail), the only dependable water is at a spring at a switchback 5 miles from the Parker Creek Trailhead.) Continue on Trail 221 to the junction with a lightly used but excellent trail that leads 0.5 mile to Parker Peak. At 7,670 feet, it's the second highest point in northern Idaho and the former site of a fire lookout built in 1939. You've come too far not to make this side trip. From here, the trail begins a rugged 2-mile, switchbacking descent off Parker Peak. Once out of the boulder field below, the trail begins a steady descent to the Kootenai Valley through a parklike lodgepole forest. The last part of the route is a long series of switchbacks that help hikers avoid rock ledges.

42 | FISHER PEAK

Location: Selkirk Crest
Status: Proposed roadless
Distance: 11 miles round trip
Hiking time: 5–6 hours
Difficulty: Moderately difficult
Season: Mid-June through early October
Map: USGS Pyramid Peak
Information: Idaho Panhandle National Forests, Bonners
   Ferry District

Here's a hard and healthy day hike into one of the Selkirk Mountains' last truly wild and unroaded areas. This is officially recognized as habitat for grizzly bears and endangered mountain caribou. After gaining 3,170 feet in elevation to the summit, breathe a well-deserved sigh of relief and look into Parker Canyon, a wilderness candidate and one of the few significant unroaded drainages left in northern Idaho.

At Bonners Ferry, Idaho, take the City Center exit off U.S. Highway 2/95. Head west on Riverside Street along the Kootenai River, following signs to the Kootenai National Wildlife Refuge. At nearly 5 miles, bear right on West

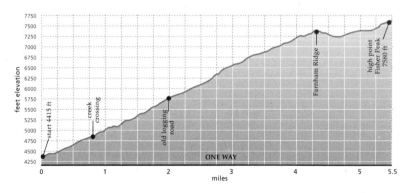

Looking over the Kootenai Valley and into Canada from Fisher Peak

Side Road and pass the refuge headquarters. About 15 miles from Bonners Ferry, turn left onto Forest Road 634 (Trout Creek). Follow the Trout Creek Road west for 5.3 miles up to the very limited parking along the road at the trailhead. This area is also accessible from north of Bonners Ferry through the Copeland junction.

Trail 27 to Fisher Peak begins at elev. 4,415 feet and heads steadily uphill. The grade is not unreasonably steep, but it is often relentless and becomes faint in some places. Cairns help define the trail in these sections. About 0.7 mile up, the trail crosses a stream that could be difficult to ford during runoff. This is the only reliable water source on the hike.

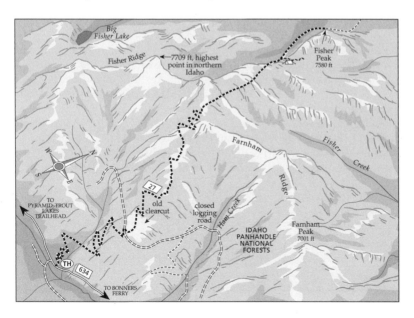

At about 2 miles, the trail crosses an old road and clearcut, and then gets better with each mile. It proceeds up to struggling white bark pines on Farnham Ridge, where the views are better and the trail becomes gentler until the last 0.2 mile past two false summits to the rewarding vista waiting atop Fisher Peak, elev. 7,580 feet. Remains of a lookout are scattered about. A few miles to the north, the Kootenai River flows into Canada. Looking south, notice unnamed "Fisher Ridge": at elev. 7,709 feet, it's the highest point in the Idaho Selkirks.

43 | TROUT–BIG FISHER LAKES

Location: Selkirk Crest
Status: Proposed roadless
Distance: 7 or 12 miles round trip
Hiking time: 4 or 8 hours or overnight
Difficulty: Moderate
Season: Early July through early October
Map: USGS Pyramid Peak
Information: Idaho Panhandle National Forests, Bonners
  Ferry District

Many hikers consider this one of the premier overnight trips in Idaho's Selkirk Mountains. The trails lead to open ridges with excellent views, and backpackers can set their sites for one or two nifty mountain lakes.

At Bonners Ferry, Idaho, take the City Center exit off U.S. Highway 2/95. Head west on Riverside Street along the Kootenai River, following signs to the Kootenai National Wildlife Refuge. At nearly 5 miles, bear right on West Side Road and pass the refuge headquarters. About 15 miles from Bonners Ferry, turn left onto Forest Road 634 (Trout Creek). Go 9 miles to the well-marked trailhead. Improvements to this road have greatly increased recreational use by hikers and horse riders. Parking is restricted to 10 slots at the trailhead, and the length of stay and group size are limited. No parking is allowed along the road. Check with the ranger district for updates.

Trail 13 heads uphill about 0.5 mile to a junction. (See Hike 44 regarding

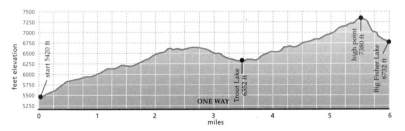

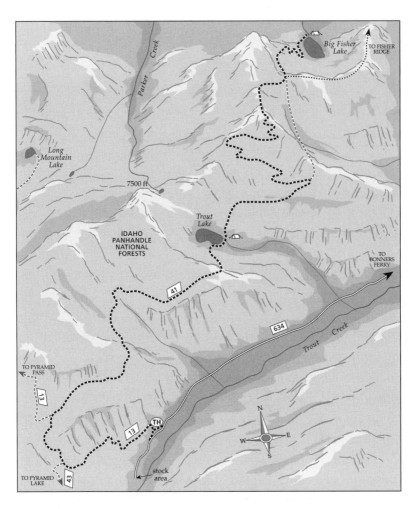

the trail to the left.) Bear right on Trail 13 following the signs toward Pyramid Pass. At the next intersection, bear right to Trout Lake. Most of the trail is wooded with occasional open sections as it skirts a ridge in the 3.5 total miles to Trout Lake. Virtually no water is available along the trail. The trail levels out and then drops 300 feet to the lake and several campsites. The lake is stocked with rainbow trout, sometimes cutthroats. The hike to Big Fisher Lake covers another 2.7 miles and takes about 2 hours. The trail has been rerouted up to the ridge and there are more switchbacks than are shown on old topo maps. There is no water along the trail. After climbing the ridge, a steep, rocky section of trail drops almost 700 feet into a granite cirque, where the lake is situated in the shadow of Fisher Ridge. Here there are plenty of campsites, also cutthroat trout.

The outlet at Trout Lake, Idaho Selkirk Mountains

Options: From Trout Lake, backtrack up the trail toward the trailhead until it levels and then make the easy scramble up to the 7,500-foot ridge above the lake for good views.

• From the trail just before it drops down into Big Fisher Lake, a much more difficult full-day scramble can be launched toward Fisher Peak along the rugged Fisher Ridge (see Hike 42).

44 | Pyramid–Ball Lakes

Location: Selkirk Crest
Status: Proposed wilderness
Distance: 4 miles round trip
Hiking time: 3–4 hours or overnight
Difficulty: Easy
Season: Early July through early October
Map: USGS Pyramid Peak
Information: Idaho Panhandle National Forests, Bonners
Ferry District

Backpackers and day hikers have not been able to keep the secret about this reasonably easy high-lakes route. The trail leads to lakes sunk into rocky cliffs near the crest of the Selkirk Mountains in settings you normally would have to hike much longer distances to enjoy in this region. It takes less than an hour to reach Pyramid Lake; it's less than an hour more up to tiny Ball Lakes.

At Bonners Ferry, Idaho, take the City Center exit off U.S. Highway 2/95. Head west on Riverside Street along the Kootenai River, following signs to the Kootenai National Wildlife Refuge. At nearly 5 miles, bear right on West Side Road and pass the refuge headquarters. About 15 miles from Bonners Ferry, turn left onto Forest Road 634 (Trout Creek). Follow Trout Creek

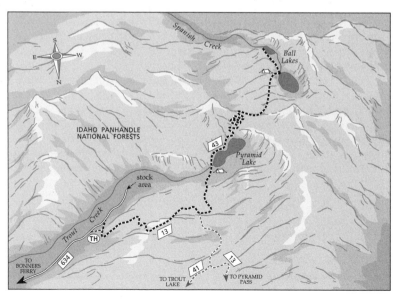

Ball Lake, Idaho Selkirk Mountains (photo by Jerry Pavia)

Road west for 9 miles to the well-marked trailhead. Improvements to this road have greatly increased recreational use by hikers and horse riders. Parking is restricted to 10 slots at the trailhead, and the length of stay and group size are limited. No parking is allowed along the road. Check with the ranger district for updates.

Trail 13 heads uphill about 0.5 mile to a junction. Turn left onto Trail 43 toward Pyramid Lake. (See Hike 43 for the trail heading to the right.) From here the trail winds gently uphill about 0.5 mile to Pyramid Lake. The shallow lake is in a cirque of rock cliffs and stocked with rainbow trout. Campsites are available for about six tents. The trail continues around the east shore of Pyramid Lake and up another mile, mostly switchbacks, to Ball Lake, stocked with cutthroats. Little Ball Lake might have grayling.

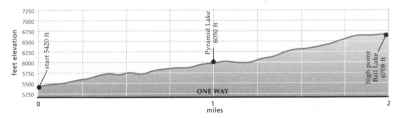

Options: The ridge above Ball Lakes is ripe for off-trail exploring.

●From the junction near the trailhead, follow Trail 13 north about 2.2 miles to Pyramid Pass, where additional hiking could be extended to Parker Ridge or Long Canyon (see Hike 41).

45 | MYRTLE LAKE

Location: Selkirk Crest
Status: Proposed wilderness
Distance: 9.6 miles round trip
Hiking time: 6 hours or overnight
Difficulty: Moderately difficult
Season: Early July through early October
Maps: USGS Roman Nose, The Wigwams, Smith Peak
Information: Idaho Panhandle National Forests, Bonners
Ferry District

This tiny off-the-beaten path lake is surrounded by timber. The route starts in private timber company land and it's not as scenic or popular as other Selkirk Mountains lakes that seem to hang from steep granite cliffs. But therein lies the attraction to many hikers. The lake is named for the periwinkle, also known as "myrtle," with its pinwheel petals and outlined star in the center of the bloom. The weird thing is that myrtle isn't native to the Selkirks.

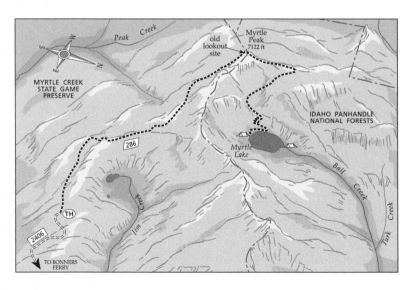

Myrtle Lake, Idaho Selkirk Mountains

At Bonners Ferry, Idaho, take the City Center exit off U.S. Highway 2/95. Head west on Riverside Street along the Kootenai River, following signs to the Kootenai National Wildlife Refuge. After nearly 5 miles, bear right and pass the refuge headquarters. Drive another 1.5 miles and turn left on Forest Road 633 (Myrtle Creek). Drive 10.8 miles and, shortly after crossing the bridge over Jim Creek, drive about 2.5 miles up Road 2406 to a parking area. The road can be brushy, depending on logging schedules. Pass several spur roads and switchback up to the end of the road to the trailhead.

The trail begins as an old skid road through the brush, but within a few hundred yards Trail 286 becomes a scenic footpath. It heads relentlessly uphill on a southeast exposure that can be hot on sunny summer days. After about 1 mile, the trail winds through slabs of rock. The tread is often difficult to find, but hikers have maintained a system of rock cairns. As it nears the top of the Selkirk Crest, the trail offers views of Kent and Harrison Lakes. The trail leads to a scenic grassy pass just under the old Myrtle Peak lookout platform. As late as mid-July, the trail from this point and down a ridge to a saddle above the west side of the lake can be covered with snow. Generally, there should be no problem glissading or kicking steps over this short stretch. Approaching the saddle, keep a sharp eye out for the trail,

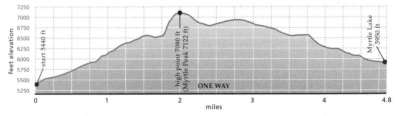

which plunges sharply over the steep ridge to the right toward the lake. Finally the trail winds through an open forest to the lake, which has a small campsite at the north end. The shoreline is brushy and boggy, but fishing can be good for small cutthroat trout.

46 TWO MOUTH LAKES

Location: Selkirk Crest
Status: Proposed wilderness
Distance: 9 miles round trip
Hiking time: 4 hours or overnight
Difficulty: Moderate
Season: Late June through early October
Map: USGS The Wigwams
Information: Idaho Panhandle National Forests, Bonners
　　　Ferry District

This area of the Selkirk Crest is wild and stunning. It has been officially classified as prime habitat for several endangered species, including the

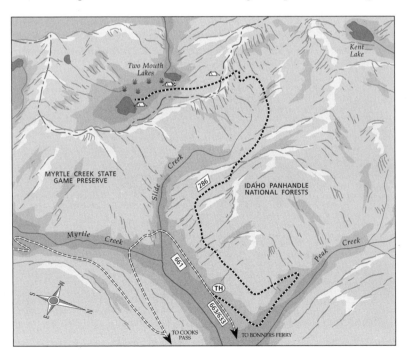

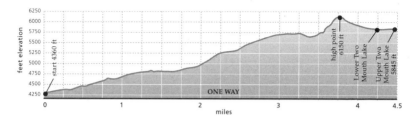

mountain caribou. Help keep it that way by camping on flat rock rather than on vegetation. While visiting this area in the 1980s, the author photographed several mountain caribou that had been ear-tagged after being relocated from British Columbia to jump-start Idaho's struggling recovery program. The sighting was reported to Idaho Fish and Game Department researchers, who went to the area three days later and found that one of the caribou had been killed and was being devoured by another endangered species—a grizzly.

At Bonners Ferry, Idaho, take the City Center exit off U.S. Highway 2/95. Head west on Riverside Street along the Kootenai River, following signs to the Kootenai National Wildlife Refuge. After nearly 5 miles, bear right and pass the refuge headquarters. Drive another 1.5 miles and turn left on Myrtle Creek Road 633. Drive about 10 miles up the main road.

Begin hiking on Road 658, which is barricaded at Road 633. Hike about 0.5 mile and look for a sign marking a skid road heading uphill to the left. Follow this skid road, which eventually becomes Trail 268 in the Slide Creek basin. (Slide Creek can gobble up about 100 feet of the trail early in

Main Two Mouth Lake, Idaho Selkirk Mountains (photo by Cris Currie)

the year, making it difficult to negotiate.) The trail winds around the basin and climbs a pass before dropping down to the lakes from the north. This trail is reasonably easy to follow if maintained to keep the alders cut back. Before dropping down to the lakes, consider hiking the open ridges for spectacular views. Lower Two Mouth Lake, stocked with cutthroat trout, is beautiful and interestingly shaped, sitting right on the Selkirk Crest. Campsites are limited since the surrounding area is marshy. One or two campsites are also available near the outlet of Upper Two Mouth Lake. The Forest Service asks hikers to minimize use of the marshy areas between the two lakes because of their fragile nature.

Increased recreational use in this area could force the Forest Service to impose restrictions to protect grizzlies. Check with the ranger district for updates.

47 | BOTTLENECK LAKE– SNOW LAKES

Location: Selkirk Crest
Status: Proposed roadless
Distance: 7 miles round trip
Hiking time: 4–7 hours or overnight
Difficulty: Moderately difficult
Season: July through early October
Map: USGS Roman Nose
Information: Idaho Panhandle National Forests,
Bonners Ferry District

This trip is especially appealing to hikers who like to scramble up and beyond trail's end for lofty views of the Selkirk Crest. Bottleneck Lake itself is a sight to behold, with limited camping nestled below granite cirques.

Drive north from Sandpoint, Idaho, on U.S. Highway 2/95 and turn west into Naples. Bear right on Deep Creek Road. Continue north 5.7 miles and turn left toward Snow Creek Road. Drive 2 miles to a Y and take the gravel road to the left. Drive 9.5 miles on Forest Road 402 (Snow Creek) to the trailhead just past Cooks Pass Road. Trail 185 officially begins here, heading up a primitive road that eventually splits into trails of variable

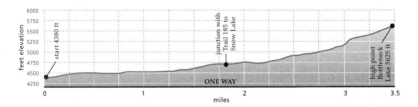

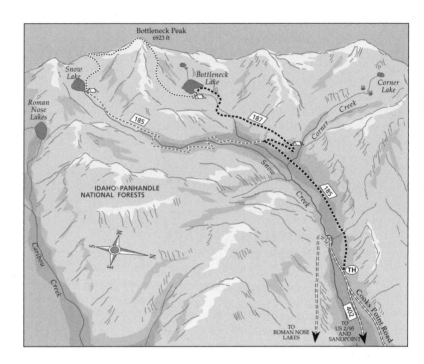

quality. (Snow Creek Road is also accessible from Bonners Ferry via West Side Road.)

From the trailhead, walk about 1.8 miles to a fork. Trail 185 branches left 2 miles by old road and 1 mile by trail to Snow Lake, which offers the easiest access to a scramble route to Bottleneck Peak, elev. 6,923 feet.

Trail 187 to Bottleneck Lake makes a sharp switchback to the right up the hill to a possible campsite where the road once ended. From here, it's about 1.5 miles to Bottleneck Lake. The footpath varies from great to wretched and will remain so until the Forest Service decides to change its course through a few wet areas. Two camping areas are available at the lake.

Bottleneck Peak begs to be climbed. Bushwhack around to the southeast corner of the lake to the bottom of the talus. Scramble up the talus to the cliff that rings the cirque and walk toward the base of the peak. Access to the ridge top is achieved via a narrow chute just before the peak, although it's not necessarily for rookies. The fastest way to the summit is to follow the northeast ridge, but this also involves a couple of moderately exposed maneuvers. A longer alternative is to go down the other side along the ridge, contouring below the east face, and climb the brushy slope to the south ridge. From the summit, the view of the east slope of the Selkirk Crest from Harrison Peak to Hunt Peak is impressive. Also be sure to walk south along the ridge top for a view of Snow Lake and Roman Nose.

Looking down on Bottleneck Lake from Bottleneck Peak

Options: Hike to Snow Lake, stocked with cutthroat trout, and devote a morning or afternoon to scrambling up the slope west of the lake, gaining nearly 900 feet in elevation, and making an excellent ridge walk north to Bottleneck Peak.

48 | Roman Nose Lakes

Location: Selkirk Crest
Status: Proposed roadless
Distance: 3–4 miles round trip
Hiking time: 2–3 hours
Difficulty: Easy
Season: Mid-June through early October
Map: USGS Roman Nose
Information: Idaho Panhandle National Forests,
    Bonners Ferry District

A compact, heavily used trail system in the shadow of 7,260-foot Roman Nose Peak gives hikers a quick-fix alpine adventure in a region lush with huckleberries in August and September. Drive directly to an alpine lake and campground, while trails lead to two more lakes. Because the distance is only 1 mile from the trailhead to the next lake, expect company not usually

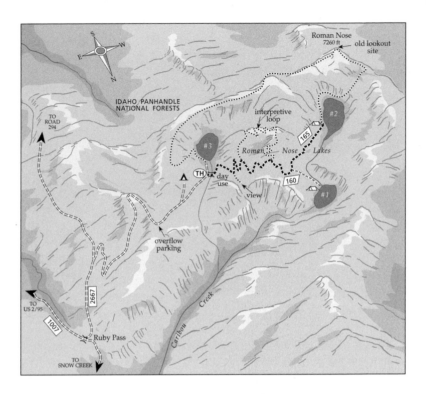

associated with backcountry travel. But the terrain is captivating, with plenty of opportunities for scrambling away from the beaten track.

Drive north from Sandpoint, Idaho, on U.S. Highway 2/95 and turn west into Naples. Bear right on Deep Creek Road. Continue north 5.7 miles and turn left toward Snow Creek Road. Drive 2 miles to a Y and take the gravel road to the left. Drive 9.5 miles on Forest Road 402 (Snow Creek), passing the turnoff to Cooks Pass Road, and bear left onto Road 1007. Drive 7.3 miles, over Caribou and Ruby Passes, and turn right toward Roman Nose Lakes on Road 2667. Go 0.5 mile and bear right at the Y. Drive another mile to the overflow parking area. Continue 0.5 mile, passing the campground turnoff, to the trailhead near Roman Nose Lake 3.

Camping at the main lake near the trailhead is allowed only at the

Roman Nose Peak after the lookout collapsed in 1999

designated camping area. The limited parking area at the main lake, stocked mostly with rainbow trout, can be full on summer weekends, forcing latecomers to park farther up the road in the overflow area. From the trailhead, at elev. 5,875 feet, cross a footbridge and head uphill. At the first junction, a spur trail leads right to a scenic overlook, where you can see water cascading from Roman Nose 1 (the lower lake). Bear left to another junction. Day hikers may prefer the newer scenic interpretive loop that contours to the left. The loop trail switchbacks numerous times, maintaining a gentle grade to the route's high point, elev. 6,410 feet, with views of the lower lake. From the first loop trail junction, backpackers may prefer to follow Trail 165 directly uphill for the shorter route to the backcountry lakes, which hold brook trout and the occasional stocked bull or rainbow trout. The trails lead through huckleberries, wild rhododendron, mountain ash, elderberry, subalpine fir, various wildflowers, and silvery snags, monuments of the great Sundance forest fire of 1967.

All the trails merge at two close junctions. Just below the junction of the scenic interpretive loop trail and Trail 160, you can either head south on Trail 165 to Roman Nose 2 (upper lake) under the precipitous face of Roman Nose Peak or north to the lower lake. Both have small campsites.

Options: The upper lake offers good side-trip possibilities, including a 1,000-foot scramble to Roman Nose Peak, which stands out on the Selkirk Crest from populated viewpoints farther south, including Lake Pend Oreille. Fire lookouts were fixtures on the peak starting in 1917. But the most recent lookout tower, built in 1955, toppled from weather and neglect in October 1999.

SANDPOINT DISTRICT

49 | HARRISON LAKE

Location: Selkirk Crest
Status: Proposed wilderness
Distance: 5–7 miles round trip
Hiking time: 4 hours or overnight
Difficulty: Moderate
Season: Late June through early October
Maps: USGS The Wigwams, Roman Nose
Information: Idaho Panhandle National Forests,
    Bonners Ferry and Sandpoint Districts

One of the most ruggedly beautiful alpine lakes in the Selkirk Mountains, Harrison Lake, at the headwaters of the Pack River, offers plenty of rewarding options for scrambling up granite talus to higher elevations for views into key habitat for endangered grizzly bears and mountain caribou. The lake, the second-largest high mountain lake in the Selkirks (Hidden is bigger), is accessible by two trails.

South route: This mostly easy round trip of 5 miles is shorter than the hike below, but gains more altitude, about 1,440 feet total. The same maps

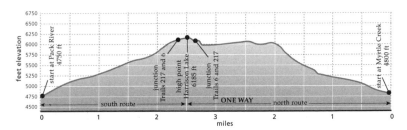

Harrison Lake basin from the flank of Harrison Peak, Seven Sisters Peaks in distance

are applicable to both hikes, but the north route is managed by the Bonners Ferry Ranger District.

From Sandpoint, Idaho, head north on U.S. Highway 2/95 toward Bonners Ferry. Drive 10.5 miles, cross the Pack River Bridge, and turn left onto Road 231 (Pack River). Drive about 20 miles (very rough in some places, four-wheel drive recommended)—past a great view of Chimney Rock and, a few miles later, a stunning Yosemite-like dome of granite—to the trailhead where the road dead-ends near one of the highest and most remote vault toilets on the Sandpoint Ranger District.

Trail 217 climbs steadily, following an old jeep road much of the way. It crosses at least two dependable streams for water. Large slabs of granite dominate the scenery until the lake, in its grand cirque, comes into view.

North route: At Bonners Ferry, Idaho, take the City Center exit off U.S. Highway 2/95. Head west on Riverside Street along the Kootenai River, following signs to the Kootenai National Wildlife Refuge. After nearly 5 miles, bear right and pass the refuge headquarters. Drive another 1.5 miles

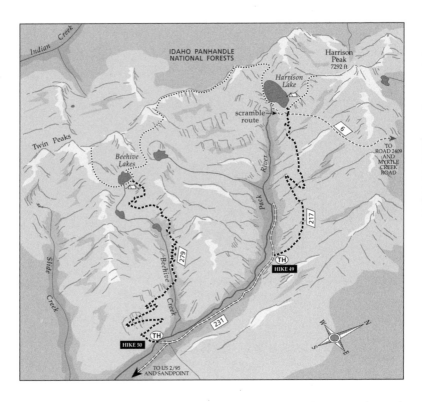

and turn left on Forest Road 633 (Myrtle Creek). Drive about 14 miles and turn right on rougher Road 2409 (Upper Myrtle Creek) and drive as much of the 1.5 miles to the trailhead as possible.

Trail 6 is an old skid road for about a mile. After the third creek crossing (negotiated by hopping rocks), the trail can be wet for a short stretch. Soon the trail leaves the roadbed, heading up the hill.

The first third of the trail can be brushy. It leads gently uphill with a few short, steep sections. At the top of the ridge, the trail narrows again and wanders along almost level. It crosses a few rock slabs where it is marked with cairns, and drops down into the Pack River drainage (great view here) to the junction with Trail 217 coming from the south. Pay attention here. Coming back, it is easy to miss this trail junction and head out Trail 217. (Just before the trail crosses the rock slabs is a good place to go cross-country to scramble up 7,292-foot Harrison Peak.)

From here it's 0.25 mile to the lake, although it's the steepest part of the hike. Several overused campsites and a pit toilet are situated near the lake, which is stocked with cutthroat trout. Early visitors are likely to find the campsites under snow in mid-June.

Options: See Hike 50.

50 | BEEHIVE LAKES

Location: Selkirk Crest
Status: Proposed wilderness
Distance: 9 miles round trip
Hiking time: 6–8 hours or overnight
Difficulty: Moderately difficult
Season: Late June through early October
Maps: USGS The Wigwams, Roman Nose
Information: Idaho Panhandle National Forests,
  Sandpoint District

A rough road takes hikers high up toward the Selkirk Crest for reasonably easy access to these high mountain lakes. The waters are cut into the granite shoulder of the crest and can be surrounded by snow in late June. The lakes in this area are stocked with cutthroat trout, which seem to cope with the area's healthy mosquito crop better than those hikers who do not come equipped with repellents and long-sleeved shirts and pants.

From Sandpoint, Idaho, head north on U.S. Highway 2/95 toward Bonners Ferry. Drive 10.5 miles, cross the Pack River Bridge, and turn left onto Road 231 (Pack River). Drive about 19 miles, staying on Road 231. (Four-wheel-drive recommended.) Look for the sign for Beehive Lakes Trail 279 and bear left down the road to the trailhead. (Nearly 15 miles up the

Upper Beehive Lake, Idaho Selkirk Mountains

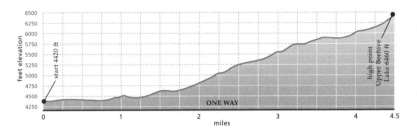

Pack River Road there's a good view of Chimney Rock on the Selkirk Crest to the west. See Hike 51.)

Hike across the Pack River on a footbridge and head up Trail 279. The route begins as an old road that dwindles to a trail. Continue up, through a high meadow and into a timbered area, where the trail switchbacks up a steeper slope. Cairns and arrows help you navigate through rock slabs and eventually to the rocks surrounding the lake. The area is worth exploring, not only to see all three lakes but also to scramble to the Selkirk Crest for a view. Bushwhacking is required to visit another one of the Beehive Lakes, locally known as Little Harrison Lake.

Options: A rugged but rewarding 10-mile loop can be made by hiking to Harrison Lake on Trail 217, scrambling to the Selkirk Crest, and hiking the trailless granite rubble south to Beehive Lake. (The treeless peaks in this area of the Selkirk Crest are called the Seven Sisters.) Hike Trail 279 back to Pack River Road for the mile-long walk up the road to the Harrison Lake Trailhead.

51 | CHIMNEY ROCK

Location: Selkirk Crest
Status: Unprotected
Distance: 4 or 11 miles round trip
Hiking time: 3 or 6 hours or overnight
Difficulty: Moderately difficult
Season: July through early October
Map: USGS Mt. Roothaan
Information: Idaho Panhandle National Forests, Priest Lake
and Sandpoint Districts and Idaho Department of Lands

Chimney Rock is the most distinctive formation on the Selkirk Crest. Visible from Priest Lake and portions of U.S. Highway 2/95 north of Sandpoint, it's one of the few mountain features just about every hiker in the region can identify. Bagging it has been a rite of passage for rock climbers since 1934, when a group of Seattle climbers led by Byron Ward made the first recorded ascent of the 360-foot rock column to the 7,124-foot summit.

Two distinct routes lead to Chimney Rock, a relatively easy one from the Priest Lake side (west) and a longer route in from the Pack River side (east), which is favored by visitors coming from the Sandpoint, Idaho area.

West route: From Priest River, Idaho, drive north on State Highway 57 about 22 miles and turn right on Dickensheet Road toward Coolin. Drive 5.3 miles to Coolin and turn right on East Shore Road toward Cavanaugh Bay. Continue 7.3 miles, cross the Hunt Creek Bridge and bear right onto Road 24 (Hunt Creek). Drive about 4.5 miles on the main road and bear left onto Road 2. Follow this main road up 1.5 miles and bear right onto Road 25. Drive about 3.4 miles to the junction of Roads 2/254 and turn

East side of Chimney Rock, Idaho Selkirk Mountains

right. (The road deteriorates here for the last mile, possibly requiring high-clearance vehicles.) The last 0.5 mile of rugged road crosses a south-facing slope to the informal trailhead.

The trail is easy to follow from the end of the road, even though it is not shown on recent USGS or Forest Service maps. The first 1.5 miles are gentle, but the route becomes steep as it heads up the west ridge of Mount Roothaan. (The mountain was named by Jesuit missionaries after a Dutchman who was once Father General of the Jesuits.) Once on top of the ridge, Chimney Rock will be in sight. Some people turn around here. Others scramble the ridge up to Roothaan's 7,326-foot summit, or—if they have hauled water—there are a couple of small campsites. To continue the

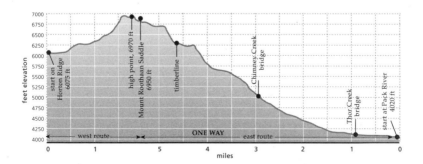

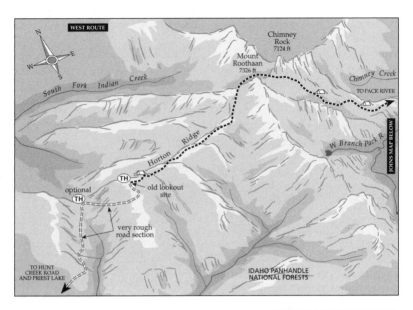

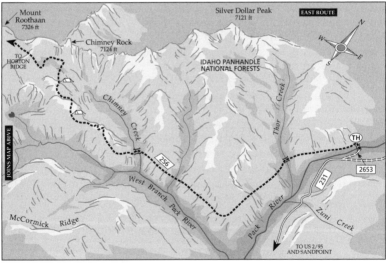

remaining 0.7 mile to Chimney Rock and cross to the east side, the most direct route hugs the rocks to the right and sidehills across talus directly to the saddle north of Roothaan. This is a north-facing slope, however, that can hold snow and make travel dangerous without an ice ax well into July. Another more difficult route bears left and drops faintly through 20 feet of rocks before becoming obvious again. The trail plunges to the bottom of a

cirque with several small, fragile campsites and water seeps. From here you must scramble through the talus to the base of Chimney Rock.

East route: Round-trip hiking distance is 11 moderately difficult miles, gaining 2,250 feet to the end of the "trail" and the beginning of scrambling options over granite boulders. Obtain information from the Forest Service Sandpoint Ranger District.

From Sandpoint, follow U.S. Highway 2/95 north for 10.5 miles and turn west onto Road 231 (Pack River). Follow Pack River Road 17 miles (very rough near the end) and turn left (west) onto Forest Road 2653. Drop downhill to the trailhead and primitive campsite at the West Fork.

Hike across the dilapidated bridge and go left on an old logging road, contouring the slope 2 miles before bearing up to the right on another old road. The trail, which can be overgrown, eventually bears left, crosses a bridge, and heads up the hillside on a route marked by flags and rock cairns. This is a climbers' route, maintained by users through huckleberry bushes, small beargrass meadows, and across huge granite slabs where you must keep a sharp eye out for the next cairn.

The route crosses a large bench and a smaller one, the only two decent camping areas. At the head of the canyon, the trees fade away and Chimney Rock is in clear view. Make your own route up and to the left (walk on the granite boulders and slabs and spare the fragile wildflowers) toward the saddle between the Chimney Rock ridge and Mount Roothaan. The scenery is stunning in every direction. Be sure to take drinking water along. Little potable water is available, especially in late summer.

52 | FAULT LAKE

Location: Selkirk Crest
Status: Unprotected
Distance: 12 miles round trip
Hiking time: 6 hours or overnight
Difficulty: Moderate
Season: Late June through early October
Maps: USGS Mt. Roothaan, Dodge Peak
Information: Idaho Panhandle National Forests,
   Sandpoint District

This unconventional hiking route leads toward two lightly visited alpine lakes on the Selkirk Crest in an area ripe for bagging Hunt Peak and other off-trail exploration. The trail is uniquely suited for day-trippers who want to combine hiking and mountain biking.

From Sandpoint, Idaho, head north on U.S. Highway 2/95 for 10.5 miles and turn left (west) on Road 231 (Pack River). Drive 12 miles and turn left

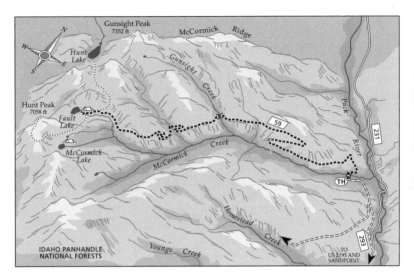

onto Road 293. Drive 1.2 miles, continuing straight past the next Road 293 junction, to the trailhead at the bridge over McCormick Creek.

The 6-mile route into Fault Lake includes 4.4 miles of former logging road that's gradually evolving into a single-track trail. The grade is moderate, making it perfect for backpackers who want a long, gentle approach to the Selkirk Crest. However, the grade is also ideal for mountain biking, putting the crest and several peaks within easy reach of day-trippers. Mountain bikers with intermediate skills might have to walk short sections of the route going up. But on a bike, the 4.4-mile return takes only about a half-hour at safe speeds.

From the trailhead, cross the bridge over McCormick Creek and follow the old road as it eventually bends left and up the McCormick drainage with views ahead of Hunt and Gunsight Peaks. At 4.4 miles, the old road gives way to a trail that climbs out of the thinning timber to a plateau where the forest still hasn't recovered from the Sundance forest fire that roared through the area in 1967. The final 1.5 miles to Fault Lake are steeper and

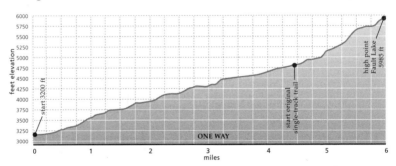

From Hunt Peak, looking at Fault Lake, Selkirk Crest, and Sundance Burn

more rugged. Camping is very limited here, but a steel food cache is provided to protect food from bears. Lakes in this area are stocked with cutthroat trout.

Options: Scramblers can hop granite boulders (there's no trail) southward to the moonscape around McCormick Lake and even climb to the summit of Hunt Peak for views of Priest Lake to the west and Chimney Rock to the north. Camping is possible at McCormick, but the treeless terrain near the crest leaves camps vulnerable to wind.

• Off-trail hikers can find their way northwest from Fault Lake through a pass south of Gunsight Peak to Hunt Lake (see Hike 38).

53 | LAKE DARLING– MOUNT PEND OREILLE LOOP

Location: Lake Pend Oreille
Status: Unprotected
Distance: 8 miles round trip
Hiking time: 5–6 hours or overnight
Difficulty: Moderate
Season: Mid-June through early October
Map: USGS Mt. Pend Oreille
Information: Idaho Panhandle National Forests,
    Sandpoint District

Hikers out for this 8-mile loop trip can enjoy a spectrum of attractions usually found only on multi-day backpacks, including a good chance to see moose. The route ranges from timbered trails to a shallow mountain lake and up to the high open views from Mount Pend Oreille.

From Sandpoint, Idaho, drive east toward Clark Fork on State Highway 200 about 12 miles. Just east of milepost 42, turn left (north) on Road 275 (Trestle Creek). Drive about 16 miles (passing a small campground at 4.4 miles and the turn to Lunch Peak Road 1091 at about 12 miles) and turn left onto Road 419 (Lightning Creek). Go for another mile to a parking area just below the trailhead for Trails 52 and 161. Park here or bear left and head up the Gordon Creek side road another 50 yards to the trailhead.

Trail 52 to Lake Darling has a good tread and rises gently to gain 680 feet of elevation in 2 miles. Allow about 1.5 to 2 hours to hike to the lake, especially early in the hiking season when the last 0.5 mile of trail from the intersection of the South Callahan Creek Trail 54 may be wet with snowmelt. Several campsites are available along the east shore of the lake. The shoreline can be boggy and buggy, which is enough to make the unprepared boogie.

Some hikers might choose to retrace their steps back to the trailhead for a round trip of 4 miles. But to complete the 8-mile loop, continue around the north side of the lake and head west on Trail 52 to the intersection with Trail 67. For a recommended side trip to the top of Mount Pend Oreille, turn right, make the switchback, and cross along the west side of the mountain

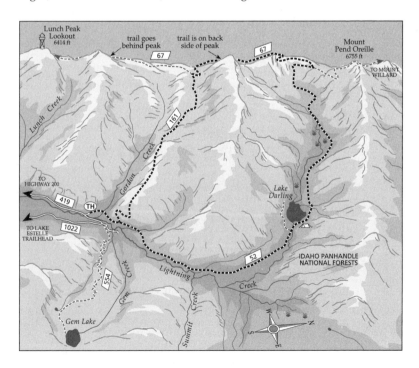

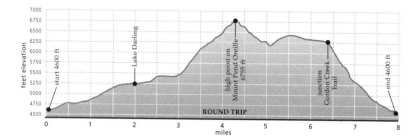

until the trail comes to the northwest ridge. Just before the trail starts heading downhill, make a sharp right turn and look for the faint route heading up the ridge to a pile of talus. From this summit at 6,755 feet, the north end of Lake Pend Oreille and Sandpoint are visible to the south, the Selkirk Crest to the west, Mount Willard to the north, and the snowcapped peaks of the Cabinet Range are to the east. Signs of an abandoned lookout tower can still be found on the summit. Much easier to find are the flowering beargrass, lupine, and arnica in July and the huckleberries in August.

To continue the loop, drop off the mountain and head south on Trail 67 toward Lunch Peak about 1 mile to a trail junction. From here, it's a nice 2-mile ridge hike continuing on Trail 67 to Lunch Peak, which is accessible by road and has a one-story lookout that's available for rent through the Sandpoint Ranger District. This makes a great end (or beginning) to the trip for a group with two vehicles. Otherwise, turn east and hike down Gordon Creek Trail 161 about 2 more miles, losing nearly 1,700 feet in elevation to

Mount Pend Oreille summit with Mount Willard in distance

the trailhead. This last 2-mile section of trail is not maintained to the same standard as Trail 52 and can be brushy at the end of the three-year maintenance interval.

Options: Gain most of the elevation in a vehicle and start hiking from Lunch Peak, elev. 6,400 feet, for a spiffy ridgeline walk, 4 miles round trip, to Mount Pend Oreille.

• Hikers who aren't in a big hurry can make an interesting side trip to beautiful Char Falls on the way home. From the junction of Trestle Creek and Lightning Creek Roads, continue south on Lightning Creek Road about 0.5 mile to a large turnout on the east side of the road. (This trail is not marked; if you come to Quartz Creek, you've gone 0.5 mile too far.) The falls can be heard from the turnout in the road. Walk downhill about 0.5 mile to the east on an old logging road until Lightning Creek can be seen. Some rigs have found ways to drive here and camp. A trail leads a short way down to the falls. Be careful; the slopes are very steep and Lightning Creek has a lightning-fast current in this area.

54 | LAKE ESTELLE–FOUR LAKES

Location: Lake Pend Oreille
Status: Unprotected
Distance: 5.4 miles round trip
Hiking time: 3–4 hours or overnight
Difficulty: Easy
Season: Mid-June through mid-October
Maps: USGS Mt. Pend Oreille, Smith Mt., Benning Mt.,
    Trestle Peak
Information: Idaho Panhandle National Forests,
    Sandpoint District

An easy, well-maintained 2.7-mile hike into Lake Estelle gives hikers an opportunity to get into high country without much sweat or difficulty. Estelle is the queen of four lakes in this area. Side trails to Blacktail and Moose Lakes offer the added opportunity of sampling other small brook-trout waters. Moose Lake, which is marshy and not high on the list of

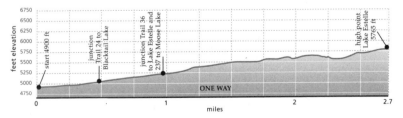

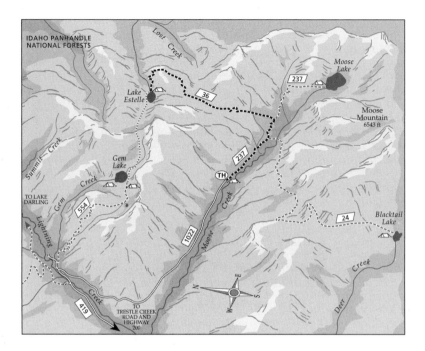

choice camping areas, is as easy to reach as Lake Estelle by trail but almost 400 feet lower in elevation. Yes, moose often are found throughout this area. Nearby Gem Lake provides another good excursion, either from a separate trailhead or via an optional scramble route from Estelle. The trails are heavily used, so be prepared for company on foot and on horseback, and perhaps occasional illegal access by motorcyclists.

From Sandpoint, Idaho, drive east toward Clark Fork on State Highway 200 about 12 miles. Just east of milepost 42, turn left (north) on Road 275 (Trestle Creek). Drive about 16 miles (passing a small campground at 4.4 miles and the turn to Lunch Peak Road 1091 at about 12 miles) and turn left onto Road 419 (Lightning Creek). Continue left a little more than 1 mile northeast (across a bridge over Lightning Creek) and follow Road 1022 (Moose Creek) southeast for 2 miles to the trailhead and a campsite with a vault toilet at the end of the road.

Trail 237 begins in uninspired fashion in a section of forest ringed by nearby clearcuts. However, the scenery quickly improves. From the trailhead it is about 3 miles to Lake Estelle, 2.5 miles to Moose Lake or 3.2 miles to Blacktail Lake. About 0.5 mile up the trail, keep an eye out for Trail 24, a well-graded route heading right (south) to small, shallow Blacktail Lake, elev. 5,542 feet. A little less than 1 mile from the trailhead, Trail 237 continues to Moose Lake, elev. 5,437 feet, while Trail 36 bears north toward Lake Estelle, elev. 5,765 feet. The right fork to Moose Lake is the easiest of the two, with a

Lake Estelle and the pass to Gem Lake

trail about as smooth and usually as obstacle-free as a bowling lane. Moose Lake, although marshy, is worth seeing for its setting, being nestled into a large open meadow about 1 mile from Moose Mountain.

The main route heading north climbs gradually for 2 miles through timber and rock outcroppings (worth a scramble) to Lake Estelle, a sequestered alpine lake sheltered on three sides by slopes of brush, carved rock, and scree. The scenic high point is nearly 1 mile past the Moose Lake junction, where the crisp and rugged ridge of hills that make up the Cabinet Mountains can be seen to the east. There's plenty of freedom to explore nearby terrain. From the campsites on the east shore of the lake, look across the water to a steep talus slope. It takes about 30 minutes to follow the angler trail around the north side of the lake and scramble up this slope 900 feet in elevation where you can follow a westward course (without a marked trail) about 0.8 mile down through old timber and wildflowers to Gem Lake. (See "Options" for a way to Gem Lake by trail.)

The trail into Lake Estelle avoids almost all the adjoining creeks or springs, so carry in enough water. Black bears occasionally are seen in the area; keep a clean camp.

Options: Nearby Gem Lake makes a good, moderately difficult hike in itself, starting from the trailhead near the intersection of Lightning Creek Road and Moose Creek Road 1022. The hike on Trail 554 is 2.5 miles round trip, gaining a hefty lung-burning 1,200 feet in elevation. Campsites are available.

• Make a 6-mile loop following the Lake Estelle Trail, doing the cross-country link to Gem Lake, and then hiking out the Gem Lake Trail. It's easily done as a day hike, with a 2-mile shuttle between trailheads that can be done by car or bicycle.

• See Hike 53 for directions to Char Falls.

55 | BEE TOP RIDGE

Location: Lake Pend Oreille
Status: Unprotected
Distance: Up to 19 miles round trip
Hiking time: Up to 9 hours or overnight
Difficulty: Moderately difficult
Season: Mid-June through early October
Maps: USGS Clark Fork, Trestle Peak
Information: Idaho Panhandle National Forests,
Sandpoint District

A destination high-ridge day-hiking area north of Lake Pend Oreille lends itself equally well to a one-day outing or to a midway car camp and two days of exploration. The limitation is water, which is not easily accessible. Maybe that sped up the process for Native Americans who once considered the high vistas overlooking Lake Pend Oreille important in communicating with spirits. As a rite of passage, a Native youth would climb up to a high point and stay there until he received a vision from a spirit. A rock cairn was built to mark the spot where the vision was received. These cairns are fairly common in the Bee Top area.

In the mid-1990s, private property owners blocked access to a traditional trailhead to the Bee Top–Round Top Divide at the south end of Trail 120 just north of Clark Fork. Forest plans call for establishing another trailhead there someday. Problems with a bridge on Road 419 (Lightning Creek Road) just out of Clark Fork have prevented easy access to other trailheads near Bee Top Mountain. But the hike, with its views of Lake Pend Oreille and fields of beargrass, is definitely worth scouting alternatives, such as the following.

From Sandpoint, Idaho, drive east toward Clark Fork on State Highway

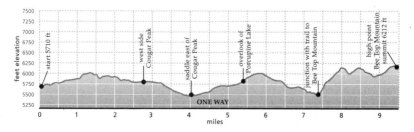

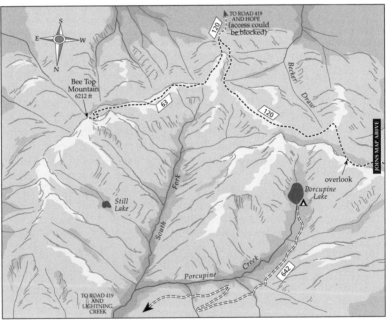

200 about 12 miles. Just east of milepost 42, turn left (north) on Road 275 (Trestle Creek). Drive about 13 miles (passing a small campground at 4.4 miles and the turn to Lunch Peak Road 1091 at about 12 miles) to the north terminus for Trail 120 at a sharp turn in the road. This section of trail is worth exploring. But to reach the heart of the ridge, continue left, driving down into the next drainage. Turn right (south) on Road 419 (Lightning Creek) and drive about 5 miles. Turn right on Road 489 and go a long, tedious 9 miles

to a camping spot and Trail 120.

From this trailhead, it's a short hike north to the top of Round Top Mountain, elev. 6,153. This is a pleasant enough trip for many people. The best route for serious hikers, however, heads south on Trail 120, along Cougar Peak. If you're up for a round trip of up to 19 miles (shorten to any desired length), follow the divide past the headwaters of Porcupine Lake to the junction with Trail 63 to Bee Top Mountain, elev. 6,212 feet. The 2-mile trail to Bee Top isn't always maintained to a high standard, but offers good views. The remains of a lookout burned by the Forest Service in 1966 can be found. From here, backtrack and, perhaps, be thankful that the closure of the south trailhead prevents any thought of plunging down the 47 switchbacks to the valley below.

Bee Top Mountain
(photo by Don Mattoon)

Water is scarce in summer in this high trail system. Take several full water bottles.

Options: From the Trail 120 Trailhead at the end of Road 489, the Bee Top Ridge Trail goes north 8 miles. This would be a good second day of hiking.

56 | SCOTCHMAN PEAK

Location: Lake Pend Oreille
Status: Proposed wilderness
Distance: 7 miles round trip
Hiking time: 4–6 hours
Difficulty: Moderately difficult
Season: Late June through mid-October
Maps: USGS Scotchman Peak, Clark Fork
Information: Idaho Panhandle National Forests,
    Sandpoint District

Hikers have to think a bit like a mountain goat to enjoy this hike. The trail is scotch with relief as it leads relentlessly uphill, but the reward is one of

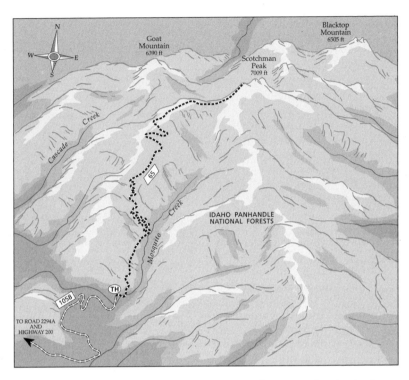

the best vistas in the area, formerly the site of a Forest Service lookout. During the 30 years the lookout was used, two of its watchmen were struck and killed by lightning in separate incidents. The peak lies within a region that has been proposed for wilderness.

From Sandpoint, Idaho, take State Highway 200 to Clark Fork, Idaho. Turn left (north) on Main Street, which is marked as a national forest entrance.

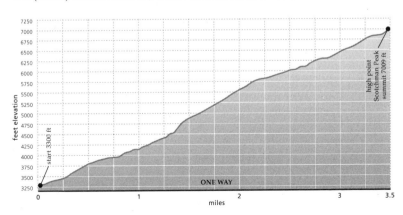

Lake Pend Oreille from near the top of Scotchman Peak
(photo by Jerry Pavia)

Follow this street, which becomes Forest Road 276, for slightly more than 2.5 miles. At the fork, turn right on a logging road following the signs toward Trail 65. Continue 1 mile and turn left on Road 2294A. Drive just less than 0.5 mile and turn left again on Road 1058. This road winds its way through a logging area and clearcuts ascending two major hills with switchbacks for about 2 miles. Turn left again and drive 0.1 mile to the trailhead. The roads are suitable for passenger vehicles with good clearance.

Scotchman Peak Trail 65 is periodically maintained by the Forest Service and is open to both hikers and horsemen. The route is direct, gaining 3,730 feet in 4 miles. (Hiking down portions of this trail can be more painful than going up, especially if boots are a shade too short.) Drink a quart of water on the way to the trailhead and take plenty more along, since no dependable sources are available. The trail ascends heartlessly out of the logged valley for the first mile, then it eases to a more humane grade, but it still proceeds steadily uphill. Long switchbacks start cutting through the alpine forest and beargrass slopes below the top of Scotchman Peak. The trail passes through south-facing meadows that are dappled with colorful wildflowers in spring and splashed with red and orange in the fall. The Clark Fork River Delta spreads out below. Then the trail intercepts the rocky west ridge, goes through the snags of a small 1994 lightning fire, and continues over the rubble of platter-size rocks to the summit.

Remains of the old lookout abandoned in the 1950s are evident at the top where there are views of the Selkirk Mountains and Lake Pend Oreille along with Cabinet Mountains peaks such as "A" Peak and Snowshoe Peak. Hikers have stacked large flat rocks to make a small wind hut just below the old lookout site. The peak's name comes from its resemblance to a Scotchman, complete with a ruffled shirt and tam-o'-shanter.

57 | GREEN MONARCH RIDGE

Location: Lake Pend Oreille
Status: Unprotected
Distance: Round trip 6 miles
Hiking time: 3–5 hours
Difficulty: Moderately difficult
Season: Mid-June through early October
Map: USGS Packsaddle Mountain
Information: Idaho Panhandle National Forests,
   Sandpoint District

This undulating ridge hike leads to a breathtaking view down an almost vertical cliff 3,000 feet above scenic Lake Pend Oreille. Big sailboats and cabin cruisers look like specks below. The town of Hope is a smudge in the distance surrounded by peaks in the Selkirk and Cabinet Mountains. Beware: cumulative elevation gain for this hike is 1,650 feet.

From Sandpoint, Idaho, drive 25 miles northeast on State Highway 200

Lake Pend Oreille from Green Monarch Ridge

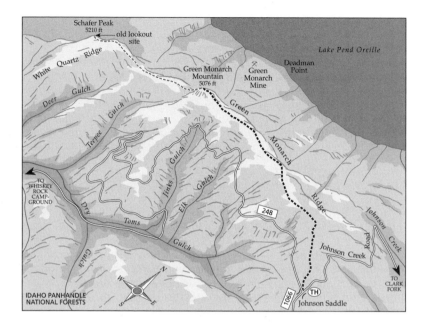

to Clark Fork, Idaho. Go through town and turn right at the forest access sign toward Johnson Creek Road. Cross the Clark Fork River and turn right on Johnson Creek Road toward Lakeview. Drive 2.6 miles and bear left at a Y onto Lakeview Road 278 toward Johnson Saddle. Go another 7.1 miles and bear right at a Y a short way to a parking area.

The trail starts at an old skid road at elev. 4,700 feet. After 0.2 mile, the road splits. Take the left trail, and head up the side of a hill. Near the top, the trail bears left into the timber. It undulates up and down several humps (hills?) in the ridge, offering only brief looks at the lake to the right. Finally, just before the top of 5,076-foot Green Monarch Mountain, a spectacular view develops over the northeast arm of the lake.

It's a short way farther up the trail to the top of the mountain and another scenic view. This is the turnaround for this hike, but the trail continues 1.5 miles to 5,210-foot Schafer Peak. The old Schafer fire lookout was sold to a Clark Fork farmer and removed in 1976.

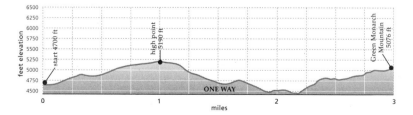

ST. JOE DISTRICT

58 | GRANDFATHER MOUNTAIN

Location: St. Maries River
Status: Proposed wilderness
Distance: 8 miles round trip
Hiking time: 4–5 hours or overnight
Difficulty: Moderate
Season: Early July through September
Map: USGS Grandmother Mountain
Information: Idaho Panhandle National Forests,
 St. Joe District, St. Maries Office

There's nothing geriatric about the hike to Grandmother and Grandfather Mountains. The trail rocks hikers to sleep with gentle ridge-top terrain before bringing out the creaks in their legs with steeper sections to the summits. Grandmother, at elev. 6,369 feet, and Grandfather, at 6,306 feet, have stood for generations above one of the few roadless areas remaining in northern Idaho. The Forest Service and Bureau of Land Management have designated this area for roadless, non-motorized use, but abuses by ORVs are evident.

The Grandfather Mountain trail leaves what was the Old Montana Trail, formerly a route used by Native Americans, beside Marks Butte. The Marble

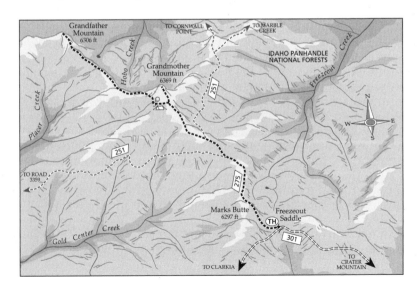

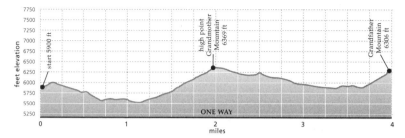

Creek drainage to the north was logged between 1916 and 1932. At one time it was said to contain the largest stand of uncut white pine in the country. But no more. Disease took its toll among the trees and the evidence of early-day logging is everywhere. Skeletons of steam engines, logging camps, flumes, trestles, and log chutes abound.

From St. Maries, Idaho, drive south on State Highway 3 toward Bovill. Turn left into Clarkia and drive to the southeast side of town. Head east on Forest Road 301, climbing steeply 12.3 miles to the trailhead at Freezeout Saddle. (The last 3 miles are rough.)

The trail heads north from an extra-wide turnout in the beargrass country at the saddle. Hike 1 mile on a gentle downgrade on Trail 275 off Marks Butte and follow an open ridge nearly 2 miles to Grandmother Mountain. Along this ridge, halfway between Marks Butte and Grandmother Mountain, is an intersection with Trail 251 coming up the ridge above Gold Center Creek from the Marble Creek drainage. A short way farther up Trail 275 is another junction at which Trail 251 heads north around the east side of

Hiking toward Freezeout Saddle, Grandmother Mountain in background

Grandmother to the Cornwall Creek drainage. Continue left on Trail 275. Enjoy good views of the Freezeout Creek drainage to the east and Gold Center Creek to the west, despite the occasional clearcut. Huckleberries in August will help keep your mind off the dusty trail.

A short spur trail heads through old hemlocks to good views at the summit of Grandmother Mountain. To continue the hike, drop back down the spur trail and continue right on Trail 275, descending to a spring and nice campsite before continuing 2.5 miles on a ridge through thick, twisted timber. The last 0.2 mile up Grandfather Mountain is steep, but the 360-degree summit view of the Marble Creek drainage and Clarkia is worth the effort.

Options: Continue driving east from Freezeout Saddle to the trailhead for the steep 0.5-mile hike down to Crater Lake, which might hold a fishing surprise.

59 SNOW PEAK

Location: Little North Fork Clearwater River
Status: Unprotected
Distance: 9.6 miles round trip
Hiking time: 6 hours or overnight
Difficulty: Moderately difficult
Season: July through September
Maps: USGS Bathtub Mountain, Montana Peak
Information: Idaho Panhandle National Forests,
St. Joe District, Avery Office

Big-game animals have left their mark on all the country sampled by this hike, which offers not only good views of the wilderness-quality Mallard-Larkins Pioneer Area but also the chance to see elk and a notorious band of mountain goats. The trail, along with others in this region, attracts large numbers of hunters in the fall, but usually it is lightly used in summer.

Take the St. Regis, Montana exit off Interstate 90. Head northwest on Camel Hump Road just north of the freeway about 0.8 mile and turn south, crossing over I-90, on Little Joe Road. Drive about 29 miles (the gravel road turns to pavement when it enters Idaho) to the St. Joe River and turn left

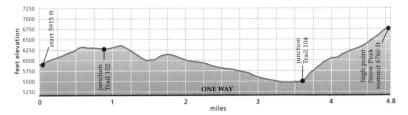

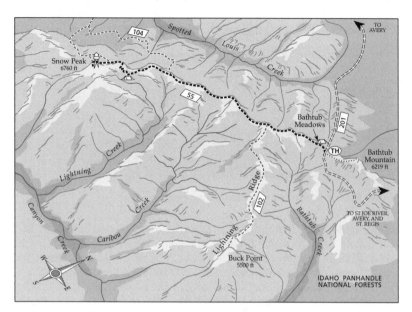

on Forest Road 218 toward Red Ives. Drive 8 miles to Beaver Creek Campground. Turn right at the campground onto Road 303 and cross the St. Joe River. Drive about 8.2 miles on the dirt road to the junction with Road 201 and continue straight toward Pineapple Saddle. Go another 8 miles to the trailhead on the south side of the road at the junction with the route up to Bathtub Mountain. A campsite and spring are a few hundred feet to the west. This area also is accessible via Avery, Idaho, as well as from Road 509 (Bluff Creek Road), which runs from the St. Joe River to near Pineapple Peak. It's a better road, but check on logging traffic, which can be dangerous on weekdays.

Trail 55 is a lovely walk through forest for nearly 4 miles before breaking uphill out of the trees the last long mile or so to the summit of Snow Peak. The trail roller-coasters along a ridge, gaining and losing considerable elevation in some cases but offering occasional glimpses of the peaks to the east into Montana as well as the Hoodoo Range to the west. About 1 mile from the trailhead, a spur trail along Lightning Ridge takes off to the south. (This trail dead-ends south of Buck Peak after 3 miles.) Walk a few hundred yards farther on Trail 55 for a good look at Snow Peak, distinguished from surrounding mountains by its tall granite face. At about 3.6 miles, the trail breaks into an open area on a saddle for another dramatic view of the peak and its lookout tower. Spotted Louis Trail 104 branches off to the northwest at this saddle, but this trail is primitive and is a challenge to follow down to the Little North Fork of the Clearwater River. A trail also branches off to the south from the opening, heading to a meadow below the rocky north face of the peak. This area makes a good campsite, although the only dependable

Snow Peak and lookout (Photo by Tony Dolphin)

water would come from two boggy lakes. This area also is a choice spot for a stand from which to watch for mountain goats that roam the cliffs. To continue up the ridge to the lookout atop Snow Peak, bear right at the fork in the trail. The last push to the summit gains 1,240 feet, but the view is worth it.

The mountain goats can be curious and almost tame one day and elusive and shy the next, but evidence of their presence is abundant. Please take care not to disturb them. This is *not* a hike on which the family dog should join the group. The Idaho Fish and Game Department has trapped goats from the Snow Peak group for relocation in other parts of the state.

Options: Two possible side trips are the Lightning Ridge spur, and a short 1.5-mile round-trip hike to Bathtub Mountain along the route beginning across from the Snow Peak Trailhead.

60 | MALLARD–LARKINS LOOP

Location: Little North Fork Clearwater River
Status: Proposed wilderness
Distance: 25 miles round trip
Hiking time: 3–4 days
Difficulty: Difficult
Season: July through September
Maps: USGS Mallard Peak, Buzzard Roost, Bathtub
Mountain, Montana Peak
Information: Idaho Panhandle National Forests,
St. Joe District, Avery Office

Hikers who have the time and enthusiasm to explore great hiking and fishing areas will find this trip to be one of the best in northern Idaho. The route is rugged, climbing to high ridges and plunging deep into river valleys, with

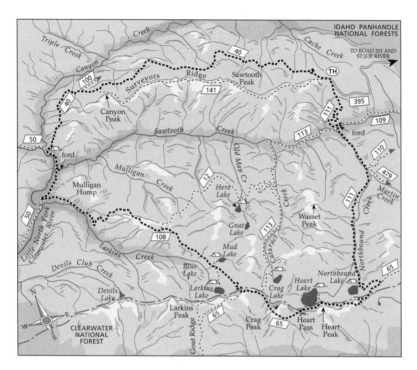

some trail sections less than lavishly maintained. But behold! This is Idaho!

Take the St. Regis, Montana exit off Interstate 90. Head northwest on Camel Hump Road just north of the freeway about 0.8 mile and turn south, crossing over I-90, on Little Joe Road. Drive about 29 miles (the gravel road turns to pavement when it enters Idaho) to the St. Joe River and turn left (south) on Forest Road 218 toward Red Ives. (This area is also accessible via St. Maries or Avery, Idaho.) Drive 8 miles to Beaver Creek Campground. Turn right (west) at the campground onto Forest Road 303 and cross the St. Joe River. Drive about 8 miles on the dirt road to the junction with Forest Road 201. Turn left (south) and drive 13 miles to the parking area at Sawtooth Saddle. The road is primitive and rough in spots; vehicles with low clearance could have trouble. Note: Nearby Surveyor Peak Lookout is available for rent through the Avery Forest Service office.

The route begins on Northbound Creek Trail 111 at elev. 5,420 feet and immediately drops 1,400 feet in the first 2 miles to Sawtooth Creek. Ford the creek and head up the Northbound Creek drainage. The trail is marshy in places. About 4 miles farther and 1,400 feet higher, come to Northbound Lake at elev. 5,436 feet. Several campsites can be found around the lake.

From Northbound Lake, Trail 111 switchbacks 0.5 mile up to the top of the ridge where it intersects Heart Pass Trail 65 at elev. 5,670 feet. Go right on this well-maintained trail following the ridge toward Heart Lake. The trail junction to Heart Lake, stocked with rainbows, is about 0.5 mile up the ridge; it is another 0.5 mile down this trail to Heart Lake, which is larger than Northbound Lake (stocked with cutthroats), but campsites are more concentrated because Heart is surrounded on three sides by steep cirque walls.

The high point on the trip, Heart Pass at 6,541 feet, is 0.5 mile beyond the junction to Heart Lake on the Heart Pass Trail. (Snow often covers the trail in the cirque above Heart Lake until early August.) Breathtaking views of the lake and mountains are visible along this stretch of trail. From Heart Pass, the trail is easy walking as it leads gently downhill. Walk 0.8 mile and pass the junction of Trail 13, which heads steeply down to Crag Lake. Go 0.2 mile to another trail junction and bear right on Larkins Lake Trail 108. Larkins Lake can be seen tucked beneath Larkins Peak to the left of this trail. Walk another mile to where the trail branches in three directions. Downhill and to the left is Larkins Lake. Uphill and to the right is Mud Lake, stocked with rainbows. Both have campsites. Most years, Mud Lake is a picturesque mountain lake nestled in a cirque. It earns its name during drought years.

From Mud Lake junction, follow Larkins Creek Trail 108 downhill. Trail 12 detours east, contouring 2.5 miles and dropping into Hero Lake (stocked with cutthroats) for a nice side trip and camp spot, but to continue the loop, drop down on Trail 108 toward the Little North Fork Clearwater River. It's downhill all the way, losing 3,000 feet in 5 brushy miles, sometimes hard to find depending on maintenance schedule. (Always seems longer.) The slope is gentle initially and the trail leads through a stand of giant cedars. Most of this area was burned in the Great Burn forest fire of 1910, with only a few pockets of trees such as these surviving.

After the cedar grove, the trail begins to lose elevation sharply while following the Larkins Creek drainage. As you approach the Little North Fork, the trail crosses an open slope high above the creek. At this point, about 4.5 miles past Mud Lake, it intersects Clearwater Trail 50. Go right,

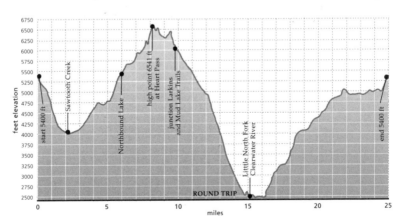

up a short distance to get over the base of Mulligan Hump, and then down 0.5 mile to Sawtooth Creek. Again, the creek must be forded. It's another 0.5 mile from the creek to Surveyors Ridge Trail 40.

Just beyond this intersection, the Clearwater Trail drops down to the mouth of Canyon Creek, which empties into the Little North Fork. A meadow suitable for camping and remains of an old trapper cabin can be found here. Unfortunately, like Northbound Lake, this spot has been abused; signs of people abound. The Little North Fork is a native cutthroat trout stream.

The last day is a somewhat arduous uphill hike up Surveyors Ridge Trail to Sawtooth Saddle. Even though the trail gains 2,000 feet,

Mountain goats, Mallard–Larkins proposed wilderness

packs should be light by now and the grade is evenly spread over the entire 8.5 miles. Water is available along the trail, which crosses many small drainages. But it is best to do this section in the morning, before the heat of the day.

61 | MALLARD–FAWN LAKES

Location: Little North Fork Clearwater River
Status: Proposed wilderness
Distance: 14 miles round trip
Hiking time: 6–10 hours or overnight
Difficulty: Moderate
Season: Late June through September
Maps: USGS Pole Mountain, Mallard Peak
Information: Idaho Panhandle National Forests, St. Joe District, Avery Office

A gentle hike with no demanding ups or downs brings hikers to a secluded lake off the paths beaten regularly to the more popular lakes in the Mallard-Larkins Pioneer Area. Mallard and Fawn Lakes are just two of numerous pleasant sites in an area that's been just one Congressional step from wilderness status for decades. The area is home for a large elk herd, which is why hunters stream in during fall.

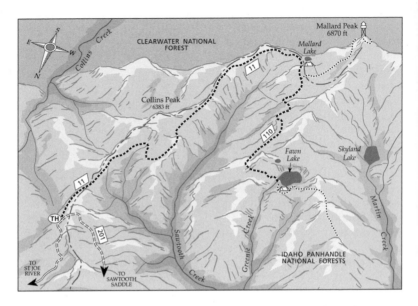

Take the St. Regis, Montana exit off Interstate 90. Head northwest on Camel Hump Road just north of the freeway 0.8 mile and turn south, crossing over I-90, on Little Joe Road. Drive about 29 miles (the gravel road turns to pavement when it enters Idaho) to the St. Joe River and turn left on Forest Road 218 toward Red Ives. (This area is also accessible via Avery, Idaho.) Drive 8 miles to Beaver Creek Campground. Turn right at the campground onto Forest Road 303 and cross the St. Joe River. Drive about 7.5 miles on the dirt road to the junction with Forest Road 201 and turn left. Drive 7.8 slow, rough miles to the signed trailhead, with turnouts for two or three vehicles. Parking and camping are also available 0.2 mile before the trailhead at Table Camp Meadow.

Trail 11 roller-coasters gently as it contours the headwaters bowl of Sawtooth Creek for 5 miles to the junction with the trail to Mallard Lake. Mallard is 0.1 mile south of Trail 11. To get to Fawn Lake, stay on Trail 11 and walk just past the Mallard Lake turnoff before bearing north on Trail 110. From here it is less than 2 miles on a pleasant pathway to Fawn Lake, which has several well-used campsites. The lake is periodically stocked with cutthroat trout.

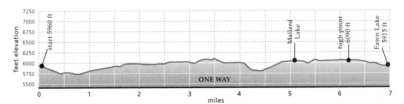

Picking huckleberries between Mallard Lake and Peak, Mallard-Larkins proposed wilderness

Options: Mallard and Fawn Lakes are good bases for huckleberry picking or a day hike 2 miles up from Mallard Lake to haunts of mountain goats and the refurbished fire lookout on nearby Mallard Peak, elev. 6,870 feet. The ground-level lookout, which is on the National Register of Historic Places, was restored in the early 1980s by lookout buff Ray Kresek of Spokane. Its fate lies largely in the hands of volunteers.

62 | BEAN–BACON LOOP

Location: St. Joe River
Status: Proposed wilderness
Distance: 24 miles round trip
Hiking time: 2–4 days
Difficulty: Difficult
Season: July through September
Maps: USGS Bacon Peak, Sherlock Peak, Chamberlain
　　　Mountain, Red Ives Peak
Information: Idaho Panhandle National Forests,
　　　St. Joe District, Avery Office

This loop, with a name that suggests heartburn, has many rewards for backpackers up to the test of a few steep grades, river fords, and a little

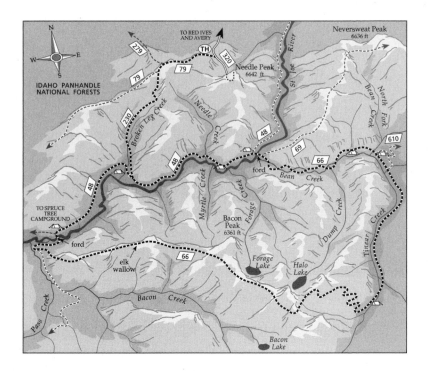

bushwhacking to reach off-trail lakes. The route crosses the pristine waters of the St. Joe River, along with several of its tributaries, and runs high into one of the more remote areas of the proposed Mallard–Larkins Wilderness. The alpine lakes are high and secluded and stocked with trout. Consider carrying wading shoes to ford the St. Joe.

Take the St. Regis, Montana exit off Interstate 90. Head northwest on Camel Hump Road just north of the freeway about 0.8 mile and turn south, crossing over I-90, on Little Joe Road. Drive about 29 miles (the gravel road turns to pavement at the pass when it enters Idaho) to the St. Joe River and turn left on Forest Road 218 toward Red Ives. (This area is also accessible via Avery, Idaho.) Drive almost 10 miles to Red Ives Ranger Station, cross Red Ives Creek, and turn left on Road 320. Follow this rough, rocky road 7 miles (low-clearance vehicles could have trouble; see "Options" below) and take a nearly 180-degree right turn toward Needle Peak. The trailhead is 1 mile farther on the right, with a slight widening in the road offering parking for three vehicles. Go another 300 yards to the end of the road for more parking and a turnaround area. (Follow the trail from this parking area 0.5 mile to the old Needle Peak lookout site for a view across the St. Joe drainage to the Bacon Peak area described below.)

Begin walking down Trail 79. Go about 1 mile to the junction with Trail 279 and turn left, continuing on Trail 79 for 0.2 mile to another junction.

Bear left on Broken Leg Trail 230 and walk down 3 miles to St. Joe River Trail 48. Water is abundant and three large campsites are available near this junction. Nearby is the rotted foundation of a ranger station built in 1911, one of the first in what was originally called the St. Joe National Forest. Broken Leg Creek was named for the Forest Service workers who fell off a structure while building a two-story ranger cabin. Apparently, the plans were changed to a one-story building after the accident.

Continue the loop by turning left on Trail 48, which soon begins to hug the shore of the St. Joe River. Go 2.8 miles upstream and turn right at Bean Creek onto Bacon Loop Trail 66. (Historical accounts indicate that Bean and Bacon Creeks were named by hungry prospectors.) Walk 0.2 mile to a large campsite and ford the St. Joe River. This leg-numbing ford can be foolish in late June and difficult in early July, depending on runoff. Wading shoes and a wading staff are recommended.

From the river, it's about 7 miles to Halo Lake. The trail is maintained every three years or so. Expect it to be hard to follow in some spots if it's the third year of the rotation. The first 5 miles of Trail 66 follow Bean and Tinear Creeks up the valley bottom, fording Bean Creek several times. Good campsites and plenty of water are found in this stretch. The observant hiker can spot evidence of turn-of-the-century mining, such as hand-placed rocks along the stream. Decades ago at a large meadow called Mule Camp, an old-timer stuck a gold pan in a small pine which has since grown up around the pan. The last good campsite and the last water source other than the lakes is near the Tinear Creek crossing just before the steep trail climbs up the last 1.5 miles to the ridge above Halo Lake. The trail can be vague in this area. The lake cannot be seen from the trail; you must scramble up from the last switchback and look over the ridge. No trail leads to the lake and it is a steep bushwhack down to the very limited camping area near the outlet.

The trail becomes faint as it contours around the ridge south of Halo Lake, stocked with cutthroats. You can continue along the ridge to the steep cliffs that plunge down to Forage Lake on the right. The trail is easy to pick up in the saddle south of Forage Lake as it begins to head up Bacon Ridge. From here it is a 0.5-mile bushwhack south to cutthroat fishing at Bacon Lake, which cannot be seen from the trail. You must walk farther on the trail to

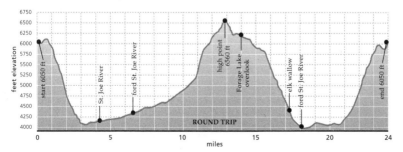

drop safely into the outlet end of Forage Lake, formerly stocked with golden trout, more recently with grayling. Again, few campsites are available.

No dependable water sources are along the scenic Bacon Ridge Trail 66 as it leads gently back 5 miles to the St. Joe River. About 1 mile above the river, the trail runs through a huge elk wallow. This is a dirt patch, rank with elk urine, the size of two volleyball courts, where elk come to dust and lick the ground for minerals—a very likely area to see elk. Trail 66 is the small and brushy track exiting on the downhill side of the wallow. Keep an eye out for the trail blazes, since the elk trails often look more substantial.

After fording the St. Joe River, bear left through the packers' campsite onto a trail that leads 0.2 mile to St. Joe River Trail 48. From here it is about 1.5 miles back to the mouth of Broken Leg Creek to complete the loop plus another 4 miles back up to the trailhead.

Options: To remove a rough stretch of driving and reduce the elevation gain/loss of the loop, start from Spruce Tree Campground and hike up Trail 48 paralleling the St. Joe River to the upstream junction for Bacon Creek Loop Trail 66 at Bean Creek. This adds 16 miles, making the round trip 36 miles, but anglers could easily justify an extra night or two along this premier cutthroat trout section of the St. Joe. On the downside, the river trail is heavily used by hikers, anglers, and pack strings for the first 5 miles upstream from the campground.

The St. Joe, a federally designated Wild and Scenic River, is the highest navigable river in the country, according to the Forest Service. The name St. Joe is a shortened version of St. Joseph, the name given to the stream in 1842 by Jesuit missionary Father Peter DeSmet. The river is 133 miles long from its origin at St. Joe Lake (see Hike 63) to its mouth at Lake Coeur d'Alene. The trail that begins at Spruce Tree Campground runs 17 miles along the roadless upper river to Heller Creek Campground.

Forage Lake on Bean-Bacon Loop, Mallard-Larkins proposed wilderness area

63 | ST. JOE LAKE

Location: St. Joe River
Status: Wild and Scenic River
Distance: 11 miles round trip
Hiking time: 6 hours or overnight
Difficulty: Moderate
Season: Late June through September
Maps: USGS Illinois Peak, Sherlock Peak
Information: Idaho Panhandle National Forests,
St. Joe District, Avery Office

St. Joe Lake, headwaters of Idaho's beautiful St. Joe River, is in an alpine area surrounded by steep ridges with snowfields, even in summer. This trail follows the river—a small stream at this point—to the lake, which holds cutthroat trout. Open ridges above beckon hikers to explore miles of additional trails on the Idaho-Montana border. Native Americans once called the lake Swallowing Lake. Legend has it that an Indian once disregarded a tradition of not drinking from the lake. He was subsequently chased up to the Bitterroot Divide and swallowed by the waters. The lake was renamed St. Joseph by a Jesuit priest, Father Peter DeSmet.

From St. Maries, Idaho, drive west of town 0.5 mile and take St. Joe River Road about 50 miles to Avery. Continue to Red Ives. Immediately after crossing the Red Ives Creek Bridge, turn left on Forest Road 320. (See Hike

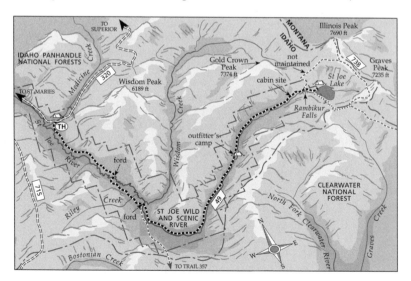

St. Joe Lake, headwaters of the St. Joe River
(photo by Don Hutchings)

62 for directions from Interstate 90 and St. Regis, Montana.) This is a slow, rough road not suitable for vehicles with low clearance. Drive up and past Heller Creek Campground to Medicine Creek. The trailhead is just across the Medicine Creek Bridge. (Eight established Forest Service campgrounds are scattered along the St. Joe River east of Avery.)

From Superior, Montana, drive 1 mile east on Diamond Road (State Highway 257) paralleling Interstate 90. Turn right on Road 320 up Cedar Creek. Drive 28 miles to the state line, where Road 320 then becomes rougher and drops down along Medicine Creek. As the road approaches the St. Joe River, it bends right and crosses Medicine Creek. The trailhead is just before the Medicine Creek Bridge.

From the trailhead, where water and campsites are available, follow St. Joe River Trail 49. For several miles the trail follows an old roadbed that winds through a valley of grassy meadows. The trail crosses the St. Joe River twice. During high water, which can last until the end of June, you will have to wade the river. Later in the year, you can jump across at narrow spots.

After the first crossing, look beyond a wide meadow for a diamond marker on a tree. The trail begins to gain elevation approximately 0.2 mile above Wisdom Creek Trail. Pass the junction of the trail to Bostonian Creek. Continue upriver about 2 miles, passing an outfitter camp used primarily by hunters during fall, as the trail opens into a high valley resplendent with wildflowers. Remnants of early-day mining activity can be seen along the trail. Several hand-dug water diversion ditches cross the area around

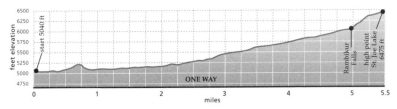

Wisdom Creek, but are overgrown. Rambikur Falls highlights the features at the head of the valley. Above the falls are remains of a log cabin. From the cabin site, the trail climbs steeply for 0.2 mile to the lake. If you become confused at any point, simply remember that the trail generally follows the river all the way to the lake.

A number of campsites can be found on the northwest side of the lake, as well as on the bench above the lake's east side at a spring and a pond where the St. Joe River originates. Snowfields below Graves Peak often linger well into summer.

Options: Hiking the ridge above the cirque of the lake provides a vista into Montana and additional trails to Illinois Peak, highest named peak on the Idaho Panhandle, elev. 7,690 feet (unnamed Fisher Ridge in the Selkirk Mountains is higher), and other nearby peaks. On the divide, you will find Stateline National Recreation Trail 738, which leads to more adventure. Trail 49 continues vaguely up to the Stateline Trail at Illinois Peak. Scramblers can reach the state line as easily by climbing southward from St. Joe Lake and turning east at the saddle. (Stateline Trail is also accessible from the Cedar Creek-Medicine Creek Road, which it crosses.)

• Additional side trips or extended backpacking destinations from the Stateline Trail include Missoula Lake and the Oregon Lakes, both on the Montana side of the divide.

64 | FIVE LAKES BUTTE

Location: St. Joe River
Status: Proposed wilderness
Distance: 6.4 miles round trip
Hiking time: 4–5 hours or overnight
Difficulty: Moderate
Season: July through September
Maps: USGS Bacon Peak, Chamberlain Mountain
Information: Clearwater National Forest,
    North Fork District

Vehicles gain most of the elevation on this trip, bringing hikers to a trail that leads to a high rocky butte pocked with five lakes and a view overlooking the St. Joe River drainage. It is an outstanding route for those who like off-trail exploring in high alpine areas and fishing and camping near small, secluded lakes.

From Interstate 90, exit at Superior, Montana, and head east on Diamond Road (State Highway 257), which runs parallel to the south side of I-90. From Superior, drive about 36 miles, over Hoodoo Pass, and turn right on Forest Road 720/5425. Cross the North Fork of the Clearwater River at

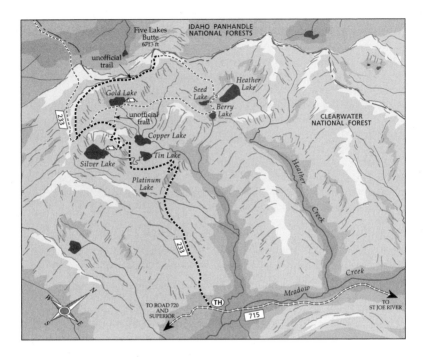

Cedars Campground and drive 10.5 miles on Road 720 toward Fly Hill. Turn right on Road 715, which can be blocked by snowdrifts into late July some years, and drive 7.5 miles to the trailhead and well-used camping area. (Note: Come equipped with Lolo and Clearwater National Forests maps, which show the road access to this hike. Trails coming in from the north are shown on the Idaho Panhandle National Forests' St. Joe District maps.)

Trail 233 begins at elev. 5,150 feet as an old road heading west, climbing to a large open meadow. The trail starts up again, crossing a trickling waterfall covered with moss and ferns. Look up to see slabs of schist, a metamorphic rock full of mica flakes that glisten in the sun, looking at times like lingering snowfields in the slopes above.

The trail leads to tiny Tin Lake with Copper Lake tucked behind a small knoll a few hundred yards beyond. Copper Lake is known to have a few

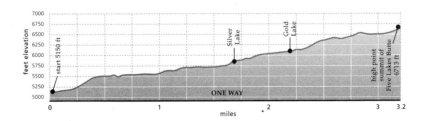

Five Lakes Basin

resident moose. Both lakes are periodically planted with cutthroat trout (but Silver and Heather Lakes are deeper and more dependable for fishing). The area has plenty of openings, but the ground is marshy and not the best for camping except at the south end of the meadow. Expect clouds of mosquitoes during summer. Continue on the trail another 0.2 mile, gaining 200 vertical feet up a rocky slope to Silver Lake, which holds cutthroat. This lake has good campsites away from the shoreline. The trail leads up another 0.5 mile to Gold Lake, a shallow lake with more campsites, and cutthroats, depending on potential winter-kill. Complete the hike by heading south up the trail, and then leaving the trail to go up the ridge, through the heather, for a 900-vertical-foot scramble to the summit of Five Lakes Butte, elev. 6,713 feet. Here you will find the best view in the area. This is a good place to hunker and watch for moose, deer, or elk in early morning or late evening.

Options: Off-trail hikers can contour gradually up and north 1 mile to the pass between two rocky buttresses and follow up a draw to Heather Lake nestled under a rocky cliff. (Heather and Platinum Lakes hold brook trout.) To make a loop, go up to a small pothole and head southwest above timberline back to Gold Lake.

• Explore westward by staying on the trail heading west from Gold Lake and following a route that roller-coasters for miles along the divide.

CLEARWATER NATIONAL FOREST

65 | GOOSE LAKE/STATELINE TRAIL

Location: Idaho-Montana Divide
Status: Proposed wilderness
Distance: 13 miles round trip
Hiking time: 6 hours or overnight
Difficulty: Moderate
Season: Late June through October
Maps: USGS Bruin Hill, Osier Ridge, Straight Peak
Information: Clearwater National Forest,
    North Fork District

Goose Lake is the hub of many possibilities for hikers with a yen to explore the proposed Great Burn Wilderness. This is the easiest of the four routes into this high-meadow setting on the Montana-Idaho border, but it can be extended into multi-day trips to savor views on the ridge-running Stateline National Recreation Trail.

From Interstate 90, take Exit 47 at Superior, Montana, and head east on Diamond Road (State Highway 257), which parallels the south side of I-90.

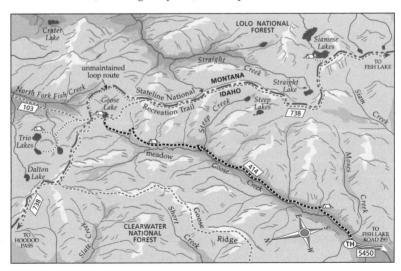

Lingering snow at Straight Lake below Stateline Trail

The pavement eventually ends and becomes Forest Road 250 (Trout Creek). From I-90, drive a total of nearly 35 miles, crossing over Hoodoo Pass, and turn left (east) up Lake Creek Road 295. Go 4.8 miles and turn left on Goose Creek Road 5450. Go 1 mile to the trailhead, which is a gate across the closed road just before Road 5450 makes a sharp right turn. (Note: Old maps don't show the reconstructed Trail 414, which stays on the east side of Goose Creek the entire 6.5 miles to the lake.)

Trail 414 begins as a closed logging road for more than a mile to a fork and a possible campsite. (Don't take the left fork, which drops a short way and crosses the creek.) Continue straight up Trail 414 as it gradually fades into a single track so pleasant, the miles seem to melt away. Ferns, thimbleberry, huckleberry, and wildflowers border the route. In wet conditions, portions of the trail can be quite muddy. Otherwise, it's sweet. Most of the tracks in the soft dirt are made by deer, elk, and moose. (You might notice a rugged and unauthorized trail in this area that heads up to Steep Lakes.) Soon the sound of roaring water from Goose Creek Falls is heard near the confluence with Steep Creek.

The trail climbs past Steep Creek and levels before entering a huge meadow area heavily trafficked by big game, and sometimes by wolves reintroduced to the region in the 1990s. Carpets of wild strawberry roll out from the trail into lush forage. After passing through the first big meadow opening, note a good campsite in scattered timber left of the trail. Soon the trail heads into the woods again, climbs, and then angles over a ridge above Goose Creek to Goose Lake outlet and the junction with Stateline Trail 738. Cross the outlet to campsites in the timber on the north side of the lake. Watch for moose.

Options: Stateline Trail 738 is the backbone for numerous hiking opportunities. Another excellent route starts at Hoodoo Pass and runs 8 high-but-exposed miles southeast on Trail 738 to Goose Lake. Groups with two vehicles can link this route with the one described above for a 14.5-mile hike from Hoodoo Pass, elev. 5,990 feet, to Goose Lake, elev. 5,165, and then

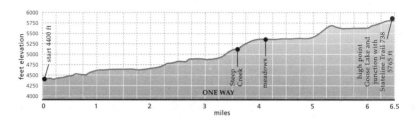

to a vehicle at Goose Creek Trailhead, elev. 4,400 feet. Vehicle shuttle distance would be 16.5 miles, mostly on paved road.

• Scenic day trips of variable lengths are easy to create from Goose Lake in either direction on Stateline Trail 738.

• Many topo maps show a trail that follows ridges around Goose Lake and joins with Stateline Trail 738 to form a 5-mile loop. The trail isn't officially maintained, and it fades away in many places, but it's well worth exploring. Serious scramblers can take off from the loop route and follow a ridge up to 7,663-foot Crater Mountain.

• Visit Trio Lakes by hiking north on Trail 738 and dropping down North Fork Fish Creek Trail 103. About 0.5 mile down, watch for an unmarked junction on the left. The unauthorized trail leads in with three forks leading to the three lakes.

About the Stateline Trail: Native Americans and the trappers and forest rangers who followed them took the high way when traveling the length of the Bitterroot Mountains. The Bitterroot Divide was relatively open and gradual compared with the steep, dark canyons below. Nowadays, Stateline Trail 738, a National Recreation Trail, traverses the same route to give recreationists a scenic advantage along the Montana-Idaho border and its jewelry of cirque lakes.

The trail follows the crest of the Bitterroots and skirts a line of 7,000-foot peaks for nearly 70 miles, although 26 miles are unmaintained, or rarely cleared, for a primitive experience in the heart of the proposed Great Burn Wilderness. Generally the route runs from Little Joe Mountain south to Granite Pass near U.S. Highway 12 at Lolo Pass. It overlooks the headwaters of major trout streams, such as the St. Joe River, and a stunning landscape shaped by the horrific forest fires of 1910. Most of the lakes, including Heart, Dalton, Crater, Siamese, and Straight, are stocked with cutthroat trout on a rotation of 7 to 10 years. Lower Steep Lake has the last non-native but self-sustaining population of golden trout in the region. Fish Lake, the largest in the region, has naturally spawning cutthroat trout. Check with Idaho Fish and Game Department for special fishing regulations on some of these waters.

The easiest access to the trail is on the Lolo National Forest south from Interstate 90 in the area near Superior, Montana. On the Idaho side, access is possible from the Clearwater National Forest and the Panhandle National Forests' St. Joe District.

Keep two things in mind when planning a route on the Stateline Trail: (1) It looks easy on a map, but it involves a considerable amount of elevation gain and loss. (2) Much of the trail is open and exposed to weather that can change dramatically. Thunderstorms or high winds can be hellish on the divide.

Three sections of Stateline Trail 738 have dramatically different characters:

• The 18-mile stretch from Little Joe Mountain south to Hoodoo Pass is open to motorcycle use as well as to horses and hikers. The 2 miles north from Hoodoo Pass are road. However, the route passes a dozen small lakes, most of which require a bushwack to reach, leaving motorcycles behind. These lakes and the Stateline Trail are also accessible by short trails and roads on the Montana side.

• The 28-mile middle section from Hoodoo Pass to the junction with Schley Mountain Trail near Kidd Lake is prime real estate for trail hikers. It snakes above two dozen lakes, although only Goose, Upper Siamese, Fish, Mud, Cedar Log, and Kidd Lakes have easy access trails leading down from the crest. The route is maintained every five years or so with a tread that can fade away for short stretches on heathered ridges, yet annual maintenance is not needed in this alpine and subalpine environment. All-terrain vehicles are allowed into Fish Lake, but stopped short of the Stateline Trail.

• About 10 miles of the route south of Kidd Lake is virtually unmanaged, an opportunity for cross-country hikers to use topo maps and thrill at the discovery in the wildest section of the proposed Great Burn Wilderness. While trails run through about 80 percent of the proposed wilderness, this section of the Bitterroot Divide is the most pristine.

• The 16 miles from Cache Saddle south to Granite Pass is maintained only rarely. Its route through the rugged, undulating terrain seems to climb or drop a thousand feet every few miles.

Topographical maps needed for the Stateline Trail from north to south include: Sherlock Peak, Illinois Peak, Hoodoo Pass, Straight Peak, Osier Ridge, Bruin Hill, Schley Mountain, Toboggan Ridge, Rhodes Peak, Granite Pass, Indian Post Office, Cayuse Junction, and Rocky Point.

66 | GOAT LAKE-RHODES PEAK

Location: North Fork Clearwater River
Status: Proposed wilderness
Distance: 7 miles round trip
Hiking time: 3–4 hours or overnight
Difficulty: Moderate
Season: July through September
Map: USGS Rhodes Peak
Information: Clearwater National Forest, Powell District

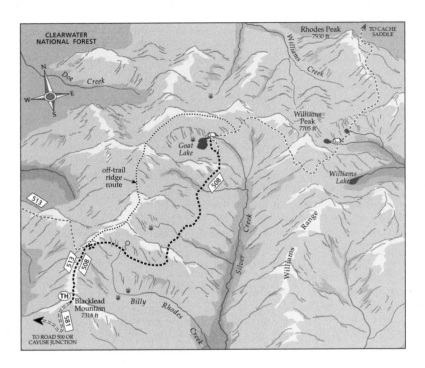

Goat Lake is a surprisingly scenic, pristine, and lightly used alpine lake surrounded by steep, open cliffs and slopes that retain many of the characteristics observed by the Lewis and Clark Expedition, which traversed nearby across the Bitterroot Mountains. It offers good campsites and fishing. Elk, deer, and mountain goats can be seen in this area early or late in the day, although the goats tend to stay in the craggy areas of Williams Creek to the north. Hike that direction as a side trip, and possibly climb the talus to Rhodes Peak, the highest mountain in roughly 124,000 acres proposed for the Great Burn Wilderness.

From Missoula, Montana, drive south on U.S. Highway 93 to Lolo. Turn right onto US 12 toward Lewiston, Idaho. Drive 45 miles (over Lolo Pass and into Idaho) and turn right onto Parachute Hill Road 569. (This turn is 0.2 mile before the turn to Lochsa Lodge and Powell Ranger Station.) From this junction, drive 7 miles to Papoose Saddle. Stay on the main road; don't turn off on the many spur roads. (Also note that the road number changes to 500 just before Papoose Saddle at Powell Junction. This is the "Lolo Motorway" that follows a portion of the Lewis and Clark Trail.) From Papoose Saddle, drive 11.5 miles to Cayuse Junction. Turn right onto Road 581 and drive 8 miles to a road junction marked by a sign reading "Deer Creek Trail 513." Turn right onto this rough road and drive 1 mile up to Blacklead Mountain, where the hike starts at elev. 7,270 feet.

If driving to the area from west of Missoula, see travel directions for Hike 67. Then, from the Cayuse Creek Bridge, drive 17.3 miles on Road 581 up Toboggan Ridge to the turnoff toward Deer Creek Trail 513 and Blacklead Mountain.

From the top of Blacklead Mountain, begin hiking north along a jeep road down the open ridge for 0.5 mile, where the road ends in a saddle. Trail numbers on maps and signs have not always matched. Trail 513 branches left and heads down Deer Creek to the Hanson Meadows area of Kelly Creek (see Hike 68). However, follow Trail 508, the main route heading off the ridge to the east, switchbacking down the steep slope. Soon the trail levels off. An abandoned trail forks off to the right down Billy Rhodes and Silver Creeks toward Cayuse Creek. Trail 508 contours around through timber, cirque basins, and open slopes about 3 miles to camping spots at Goat Lake, which has naturally reproducing cutthroat trout. The landscape, still semi-open from the Great Burn of 1910, is particularly beautiful in autumn colors.

Options: For hikers who aren't opposed to a little cross-country walking, an excellent loop trip can be made by following the ridges to Goat Lake. From the end of the jeep road north of Blacklead Mountain, a trail can be seen heading straight up the ridge to the northeast. This tread leads up to an unnamed 7,514-foot peak. From here, stay to the left of the ridge, crossing talus and heading up a slope of scattered timber to another unnamed peak, elev. 7,497 feet, for an overlook of the lake and several tarns above it. Rock cliffs make it tricky to go straight down to the lake. The best route is to follow the ridge farther, swinging east and down another ridge just north of the lake and coming down a grassy slope to the outlet. Return via Trails 508/513 to complete the loop.

• Continue from Goat Lake northeast on Trail 508, climbing more than 900 feet to the Williams Peak ridge and dropping into mountain-goat

Goat Lake, proposed Great Burn Wilderness

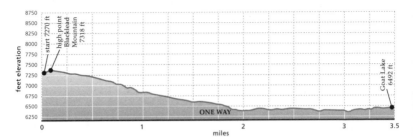

country worth exploring around the three Williams Lakes. From here, it's difficult to resist the temptation to go up again on the trail for a scramble to the 7,930-foot summit of Rhodes Peak. The trail fades beyond the peak, but hikers adept at off-trail map and compass navigation can have a ball north to Cache Saddle and along the Idaho-Montana border. Rhodes Peak was named for Billy Rhodes, a prospector who was particularly competent in making his home in the wilderness. His grave is near Blacklead Mountain.

• Don't overlook the many opportunities to immerse in the history of the Lolo Trail and the Lewis and Clark Expedition from Road 500 (Lolo Motorway). Interpretive signs and entire books are devoted to this Native American route over the Bitterroot Mountains, which caused desperation and inspired unforgettable entries in the expedition journals in 1805 and 1806. It's notable that while the expedition nearly starved as it traveled through this area, the region is now filled with elk that weren't to be found here a century ago. For a particularly pleasant hike, stop on Road 500 about 3.8 miles west of Papoose Saddle and trek a moderate 6 miles round trip to Lost Lakes, which hold cutthroat trout.

67 | CAYUSE CREEK

Location: North Fork Clearwater River
Status: Unprotected
Distance: 8 miles round trip
Hiking time: 3–6 hours or overnight
Difficulty: Moderate
Season: July through September
Map: USGS Gorman Hill
Information: Clearwater National Forest,
    North Fork District

Hikers who never like to be far from a clear mountain stream will enjoy this hike, the darling of fly fishers interested in decent trout waters away from the crowds. The trail runs along Cayuse Creek, a catch-and-release native cutthroat stream and tributary to another famous trout stream, Kelly

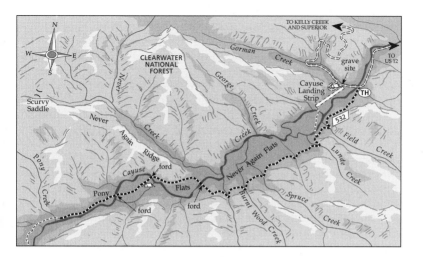

Creek (see Hike 68). The hike leads to good camping areas near Pony Flats, a perfect base camp for day hiking and fishing (although the creek can get low in late summer and deeper pools are found downstream). The hike is easy, except for three fords of Cayuse Creek, which can be tricky as late as mid-July. Cayuse Creek was named by two trappers in 1887 when they dropped into the drainage and found a pony, or cayuse, that had wintered there.

From Interstate 90, exit at Superior, Montana, and head east on Diamond Road (State Highway 257), which runs parallel to the south side of I-90. The pavement eventually ends and the highway becomes Forest Road 250 (Trout Creek) and goes 20 miles to Hoodoo Pass. From the beginning of the pavement on the Idaho side of the pass, drive 14.5 miles to the junction of Roads 250 and 255. Turn left onto Road 255 at a sign that says "Pierce, Idaho, via Kelly Creek." (If you miss this junction, you will continue down the North Fork of the Clearwater toward Hidden Creek Campground.) Follow this road to Deception Saddle, continuing on Road 255 south down Independence Creek and Moose Creek to the junction with Road 581 at Kelly Creek. From here it is 8.8 miles to the Cayuse Creek Trailhead. Turn left on Road 581 and cross Kelly Creek. Bear left at

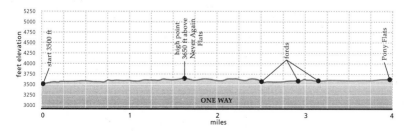

the Y and head up, over East Saddle and down to the Cayuse aircraft landing field. The trailhead is just across the Cayuse Creek Bridge and to the right. (This road can be rough, but usually it is navigable by passenger cars with good clearance. When muddy, however, it can be passable only to four-wheel-drives.) Several good car-camping areas are scattered around the landing field area. Don't camp on the airstrip! (This area is also accessible via forest roads from Orofino, Idaho, or the Lolo Pass area off U.S. Highway 12 southwest of Missoula, Montana. See Hike 66.)

Hike southwest on Trail 532 paralleling Cayuse Creek. At 1 mile, deteriorating Field Creek Trail 532 heads up to the left toward Lunde Peak. Continue on Trail 532, which is well maintained for 2.5 miles to the first crossing of Cayuse Creek. From here, you might have to follow a faint tread, blazes, and cut logs to keep on the trail. The route crosses the creek two more times before all but disappearing near Pony Flats, a large, gravelly burned area. The route passes several good campsites and, of course, water is plentiful.

Although relatively small numbers of people visit Cayuse Creek each year, fly fishers from across the nation have helped thwart proposed timber sales and even mining plans that could destroy part of this hiking trail or seriously threaten the fish-producing water quality of Cayuse and Kelly Creeks. Thanks to the cast of thousands who cared.

Cayuse Creek

68 KELLY CREEK

Location: North Fork Clearwater River
Status: Proposed wilderness
Distance: 20 miles round trip
Hiking time: 2–3 days
Difficulty: Moderate
Season: June through October
Maps: USGS Gorman Hill, Toboggan Ridge
Information: Clearwater National Forest,
North Fork District

Fishing rods generally are in the hands of people hiking this trail into a roadless area that's part of the Great Burn Wilderness proposal. Kelly Creek, named after a prospector, is nationally known because of its excellent fly fishing for native cutthroat trout. It has special regulations requiring anglers to use single, barbless hooks and release all fish caught. The trail is gentle, leading into country full of deer, elk, moose, and black bear.

From Interstate 90, exit at Superior, Montana, and head east on Diamond

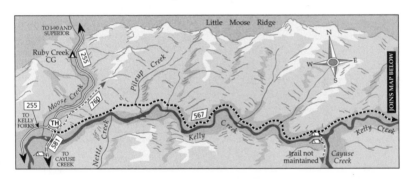

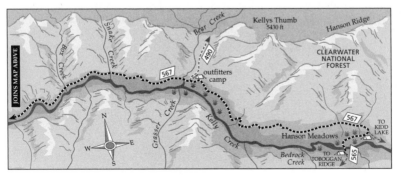

Kelly Creek, proposed Great Burn Wilderness

Road (State Highway 257), which runs parallel to the south side of I-90. The pavement eventually ends and the highway becomes Forest Road 250 (Trout Creek) and goes 20 miles to Hoodoo Pass. From the beginning of the pavement on the Idaho side of the pass, drive 14.5 miles to the junction of Roads 250 and 255. Turn left onto Road 255 at a sign that says "Pierce, Idaho, via Kelly Creek." (If you miss this junction, you will continue down the North Fork of the Clearwater toward Hidden Creek Campground.) Follow this road to Deception Saddle, continuing on Road 255 south down Independence Creek and Moose Creek to the junction with Road 581 at Kelly Creek. (Look up the hill to the left: the large bare area is a mineral lick, where deer and elk come to eat dirt for nutrients required in their diets.) The trailhead is just left of the road junction. (You can also reach this area via forest roads from Orofino and Pierce, Idaho. See Hike 66.)

Kelly Creek Trail 567 follows up the north side of the creek, often ranging high above it. The first 3.5 miles of trail to the confluence with Cayuse Creek are gentle with a good view of the creek. The trail is on an open, unshaded south-facing slope that can be hot during midday. The creek is broad with occasional deep holes and there are a few places to camp along gravel bars in this section. The Cayuse Creek-Kelly Creek confluence campsite is heavily used. The trail heading up Cayuse Creek is not maintained, but you can ford to the south side of Kelly Creek to a campsite along Cayuse Creek.

Soon after the confluence with the Cayuse, the Kelly Creek Trail climbs into a forested canyon, with occasional views of the creek's tumbling falls

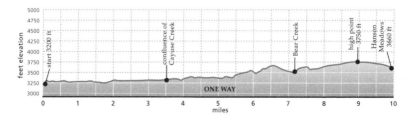

and boulder gardens below. It leads 3.7 miles before heading down to camping areas and an outfitter's base at Bear Creek and Bear Creek Meadow. Natural mineral licks attract moose to this area. The trail again retreats from the creek for another 2 miles to camping areas at Hanson Meadows, where elk are often seen. The trail in this section is through light forest with abundant huckleberries, and the bears they nourish.

Options: Long-distance hikers can continue up Kelly Creek Trail 567 all the way to alpine lakes along Stateline National Recreation Trail 738 on the Idaho-Montana border.

69 | PETE OTT LAKE– COLD SPRINGS PEAK

Location: North Fork Clearwater River
Status: Unprotected
Distance: 3.5 miles round trip
Hiking time: 3–4 hours or overnight
Difficulty: Moderate
Season: July through September
Map: USGS Elizabeth Lake
Information: Clearwater National Forest,
    North Fork District

This is a pleasant hike—or at least it has been—to several lakes host to brook trout and cutthroats. In the late 1990s, ATV groups started targeting the area, especially on group-outing weekends. Portions of a once subtle trail soon began resembling an arterial for elephant traffic. Come September 16, when the bull elk are bugling, a gate is locked to prevent vehicle traffic on the last short stretch of road to the trailhead, restoring this to the sanctuary it once was.

The access road is suitable only for vehicles with good clearance. Only four-wheel-drives might be able to make it the last mile to the trailhead. Nearby lakes are nestled in trees below rounded, timbered mountains. Pete Ott Lake is named after a former Forest Service trail foreman who died in 1921. The hike offers a ridge trip extension to Cold Springs Peak fire lookout cabin, which is available for rent through the Clearwater National Forest's North Fork District in Orofino.

From Interstate 90, exit at Superior, Montana, and head east on Diamond Road (State Highway 257), which runs parallel to the south side of I-90. The pavement eventually ends and the route becomes Road 250 (Trout Creek). From Superior, drive 53 miles—over Hoodoo Pass and through the North Fork of the Clearwater River's Black Canyon—to the Kelly Forks intersection. (Serious fishermen should allow an extra day or two to drive

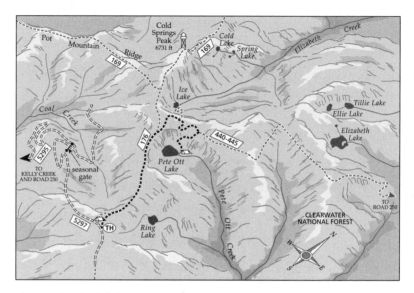

this road, which follows the North Fork's excellent cutthroat and rainbow fishery for more than 15 miles, with good car-camping sites.) Turn right at the junction, continuing past the Kelly Creek Ranger Station on Road 250 and drive 2.2 miles to Cold Springs work center. (You can also reach this area via forest roads from Orofino and Pierce, Idaho.) Turn right toward Mush Saddle on Road 711. Drive 1.7 miles and turn right on Ice Creek Road 5295. Drive 5.6 miles, noting the road number changes to 5297 on a switchback to the right. At the last switchback to the right, there's a gate scheduled to be open from when the snow clears in July through September 15. From here the road can be rough, with deep water bars for 1.6 miles. If the gate is closed, the road is an enjoyable walk. The road levels at the saddle where the trail begins on the left.

From the trampled campsite, follow the good footpath that eventually melts into the eyesore of a trail "improved" by men for their machines. Follow Trail 176 for about 1 mile up and down along a ridge to the Pete Ott-Cold Springs Peak junction. Turn right down Trail 440-455 and go 0.2 mile to another junction. A trail leads to the left and switchbacks down to

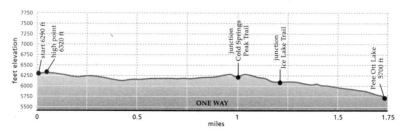

Ice Lake, near Pete Ott Lake

Ice Lake, which has several small campsites, but they can be boggy and buggy. Continue on a trail leading to the right and down 0.3 mile to Pete Ott Lake, which has a large campsite and naturally reproducing cutthroats. No water is available along the trail.

Options: Continue from Pete Ott Lake area on the trail toward Elizabeth Lake. Getting down to the lake, a destination for determined cutthroat anglers, requires a rugged bushwhack. Other cutthroat lakes in the area include Ellie, Tillie, Ice, and Ring. Cold Lakes are fishless.

• Continue on Trail 176 from the Pete Ott trail junction to Cold Springs Peak where there's a lookout cabin for rent and a good view of the area for free.

70 | SELWAY CRAGS-COVE LAKES

Location: Selway River
Status: Selway-Bitterroot Wilderness
Distance: 13 miles round trip
Hiking time: 2 days minimum
Difficulty: Difficult
Season: Mid-July through September
Maps: USGS Fenn Mountain, Fog Mountain
Information: Nez Perce National Forest, Moose Creek
District, Fenn Ranger Station

This rugged but rewarding hike roller-coasters into one of the most scenic—and popular—areas of the 1.8-million acre Selway-Bitterroot Wilderness. The Crags, as you might guess, is an alpine area of sky-scratching
peaks pocked with lakes. This trip is but an introduction to faint trails that
offer many extensions into the heart of the wilderness. The area is fragile
and off-limits to pack animals. Hikers, too, must respect the area by camping away from the fragile lakeshores.

From Lewiston, Idaho, drive east on U.S. Highway 12 about 95 miles to
Lowell, a small resort area situated where the Selway and Lochsa Rivers
meet to form the Middle Fork of the Clearwater. Turn southeast, cross the
bridge over the Clearwater, and follow the road upstream for about 18
miles, keeping to the left of the Selway River, where sandy beaches make a
tempting post-hike place to freshen up. (Information is available from the
historic Fenn Ranger Station, on the left side of the road about 7 miles up
from the Clearwater Bridge.) After crossing Gedney Creek, turn left onto
Fog Mountain Road. This road switches back steeply up ridges and slopes

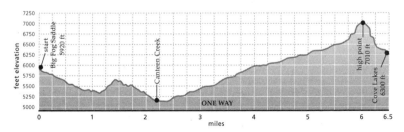

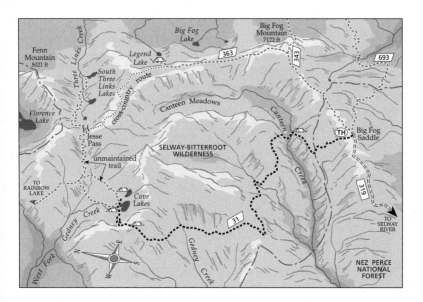

for about 12 miles, gaining 4,100 feet, to the trailhead at Big Fog Saddle. The road is rocky, rutted, and slow, even for vehicles with good clearance. Vehicles with low clearance probably can make it, but at a snail's pace. It is especially hazardous when wet. Big Fog Saddle offers the highest elevation vehicle access to the Selway Crags.

From the saddle, take the westernmost Trail 31 toward Cove Lakes. Beginning at 5,920 feet, the trail heads northwest through trees and brush, dipping just under elev. 5,200 feet as it crosses two forks of Canteen Creek. It then climbs brushy slopes along less-than-perfect trail. These few miles are the most difficult en route to Cove Lakes. The trail tops out at 7,010 feet in a pleasant subalpine meadow with wildflowers and trickles of water. After traversing the meadow, the trail drops to a ledge that looks north to the central part of the Crags with the two Cove Lakes below. From here, the trail drops quickly to several campsites near the lakes.

Cove Lakes are a good introduction to the Crags, although it's a tough pull out of the lakes to get into the South Three Links area and the base of beautiful Fenn Mountain. Some hikers make this excursion as a day trip from Cove Lakes. The Forest Service treats this as a primitive area with few trails. The trail to Chimney Rock near Rainbow Lake is maintained occasionally, but other routes to the ridge over Jesse Pass are purely user trails.

During the Pleistocene, these mountains were covered with a small ice cap that sent short valley glaciers radiating outward in all directions. Glacial activity has carved numerous subalpine basins, cirque lakes, horns, and arêtes into granite bedrock of the Idaho Batholith. Cove Lakes sit at the southern edge of this rugged and rocky area. Fenn Mountain, at elev. 8,021

Smoky skies above Three Links Lakes in the Selway Crags

feet, is the highest point. Huckleberries are abundant and moose, elk, deer, and other wildlife can be seen in this relatively remote area. Some of the lakes in the Crags are stuffed with brook trout; a few have been stocked with cutthroats. The area north of Cove Lakes is managed as a pristine area, which means trails are not maintained and signs are not posted. Use those topo maps!

Options: Hikers willing to search through faint trail sections and navigate trailless stretches over talus can make a classic loop starting at Big Fog Saddle, but heading northeast over Big Fog Mountain and continuing on a faint ridge trail to camp at Legend Lake (a good trip in itself). From there, a faint trail gets you started on a cross-country trek heading west above Canteen Meadows. Go up through an unnamed pass and then down a ridge to Jesse Pass. Hike the faint trail down to Three Links Lakes to the east or find the even fainter trail heading west from Jesse Pass down to Trail 3, which can be followed to Cove Lakes and the relatively simple return to Big Fog Saddle.

KOOTENAI NATIONAL FOREST

71 | TEN LAKES LOOP

Location: Tobacco River
Status: Proposed wilderness
Distance: 10.5 miles round trip
Hiking time: 8 hours or overnight
Difficulty: Moderate
Season: July through early September
Maps: USGS Ksanka Peak, Stahl Peak
Information: Kootenai National Forest, Fortine District,
     Murphy Lake Ranger Station

In 1977, Congress identified about 33,000 acres to be studied for possible wilderness designation in the vicinity of the 7,000-acre Ten Lakes Scenic Area. In 1987, an enhanced wilderness package totaling roughly 40,000 acres was proposed by the Kootenai National Forest management plan.

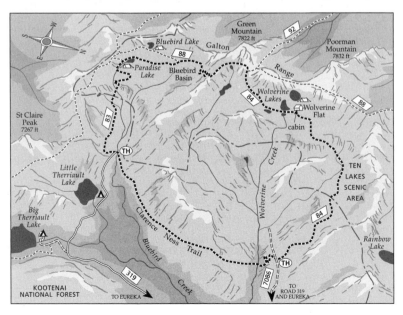

Nothing official has ensued, but the area remains unspoiled and the route from Little Therriault Lake to Wolverine Lakes, 4.5 miles one way, remains a beautiful hike through a high alpine area that's sinfully easy to reach. From Bluebird Basin to Wolverine Lakes, the route goes through forests and alpine meadows dappled with wildflowers. The peaks and ridges forming the high country around the alpine lakes are impressive, and this hike just skirts the edge of the protected area. Other opportunities range from day hikes and huckleberry picking to extended trips.

From Eureka, Montana, travel south on U.S. Highway 93 for 9 miles and turn left onto Forest Road 114 (Graves Creek), which is marked by a sign for Therriault Lakes/Ten Lakes Scenic Area. Or, from Whitefish, Montana, travel north on US 93 for 42.5 miles and turn right onto Graves Creek Road (milepost 170.4). This is grizzly bear country and food storage rules are in effect. Stop for information at Murphy Lake Ranger Station off US 93 at milepost 165 south of Eureka.

Graves Creek Road is a paved two-laner that narrows after a short distance to a single-lane paved logging road with turnouts. Be on guard for logging trucks, especially on weekdays. From US 93, drive 11 miles and bear right at the junction, continuing on Road 114, which becomes gravel. At milepost 14.2 (note that the mileposts are about 4.5 miles less than the mileage from the highway), continue straight onto Road 319 (Therriault Lakes). At milepost 25.5, go past the turnoff for Road 7091 to Wolverine Lakes Trailhead. Continue to milepost 28 and turn right toward

Little Therriault Lake, Ten Lakes Scenic Area
(photo by Ida Rowe Dolphin)

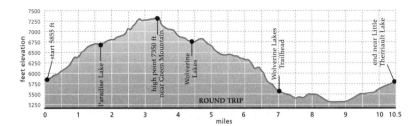

Little Therriault Lake. Pass the campground and go 1.8 miles farther to the end of the road and the trailhead for Bluebird Basin Trail 83. Both Therriault Lakes have campgrounds and small cutthroat trout.

Bluebird Basin Trail 83 begins at 5,855 feet and heads gradually uphill through the forest for the first 0.5 mile. The grade increases and gains 800 feet in the next mile to Paradise Lake at 6,720 feet. (At a fork in the trail, go left to Bluebird Lake or right to the campsites at the north end of Paradise Lake.) From this fork, heading left toward shallow Bluebird Lake, walk up a slope to a junction with Trail 88. Turn right and walk a short way toward Green Mountain to Bluebird Lake, which has several campsites. (Bluebird Cabin, which still appears on some maps, burned down years ago.) From the lake, continue north. The trail switchbacks up a steep grade and contours around Green Mountain to elev. 7,350 feet. (Green Mountain's summit is elev. 7,822 feet, but the highest peak in the Ten Lakes area is nearby 7,832-foot Poorman Mountain.) At the junction with Trail 84, go right, dropping down a slope to Wolverine Lakes.

An historic but deteriorating cabin formerly used by the Border Patrol has been available at Wolverine Lakes on a first-come, first-served basis. The future of the cabin has been undetermined. The lakes hold small cutthroat trout and there's ample room for camping.

From here, return by the same 4.5-mile route. Or continue 2.5 miles to the Wolverine Lakes Trailhead, where a shuttle vehicle could be left. To complete the loop of 10.5 miles, leave the Wolverine Trailhead and hike 3.5 miles on the Clarence Ness Trail (named for a stalwart among the Backcountry Horsemen) back to the start at the Bluebird Trailhead.

Hiking parties with more than one vehicle could leave a car at the end of Trail 84. To drive to this trailhead, follow the previous road directions to milepost 25.4 and turn right onto Forest Road 7091 (Wolverine Lakes). Drive about 2.5 miles to a fork. Turn left onto Road 7086 and drive 0.3 mile to the trailhead.

Options: Trail 88, at the junction with Bluebird Lake Trail 83, continues southeast 6 miles to Therriault Pass. Continue to Stahl Peak or drop down to Big Therriault Lake. A lookout tower on Stahl Peak is open to the public for overnight use on a first-come, first-served basis.

• Ambitious? Take Trail 335, a high scenic ridge-trail south from Therriault Pass 3.5 miles to Mount Gibralter.

• From Wolverine Lakes, hike Trail 84 to Green Mountain and north-west on Trail 92 through an area of mining history. Better yet, hike Trail 88 from Green Mountain north to Poorman Mountain and beyond.

• Hike the short trails around Big and Little Therriault Lakes.

72 | CEDAR LAKES–SCENERY MOUNTAIN

Location: Cabinet Mountains
Status: Cabinet Mountains Wilderness
Distance: 11 miles round trip
Hiking time: 5–7 hours or overnight
Difficulty: Moderately difficult
Season: Mid-June through early October
Maps: USGS Scenery Mountain, Treasure Mountain,
          Kootenai Falls
Information: Kootenai National Forest, Libby District

Hikers who don't mind the likelihood of skipping over a few horse muf-fins consider this one of the prettiest hikes in the Cabinet Mountains Wil-derness. Cedar Lakes are nestled in the midst of towering peaks. A short climb from the lakes puts hikers in position to see Kootenai Falls on the Kootenai River and a distant look into Glacier National Park. Ambitious hikers tack on a scramble of Dome Mountain or extend this trip into a multi-day loop.

From Libby, Montana, head west on U.S. Highway 2 about 3 miles and

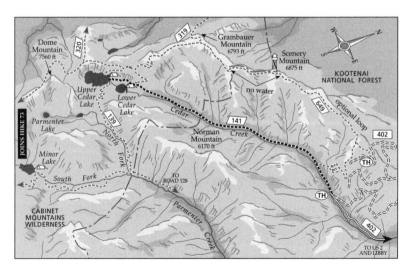

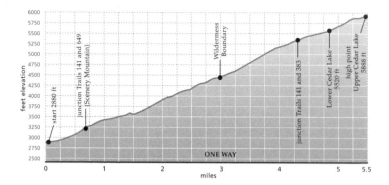

turn south at milepost 27.7 onto Road 402 (Cedar Creek). Drive nearly 3 miles, staying on the main road, to the trailhead parking area.

Trail 141 climbs steadily up Cedar Creek, passing the Scenery Mountain trail junction at 0.7 mile (keep this in mind for the loop "Options" discussed below) and enters the Cabinet Mountains Wilderness at nearly 4 miles. Continuing up, with a few steep pitches, it reaches Lower Cedar Lake, elev. 5,520 feet, at 5 miles. The upper lake, the larger of the two, is 0.5 mile farther at elev. 5,888 feet. A major forest fire started between the two lakes in 1998. The trail is well maintained and is an authorized horse trail as well as a hiking trail. According to Forest Service statistics, this trail gets the heaviest stock use of any trail in the wilderness. The thick forest leaves no doubt about the origin of the name Cedar Creek.

Campsites are available at both lakes and fishing in either lake can often provide enough small rainbow trout for a meal. This is bear country; keep a clean camp.

Options: Day hike up Trail 360 on the west side of Upper Cedar Lake and turn up onto one of Dome Mountain's two south ridges for a scramble to the broad twin summits,

Upper Cedar Lake, Cabinet Mountains Wilderness

elev. 7,560 feet. See hidden lakes as well as the numerous peaks surrounding the area.

• Here's a roundabout return from Cedar Lakes that makes a fabulous high-reaching loop, although there's no water available. From just below Lower Cedar Lake, turn north onto Trail 383 and hike 2.5 miles up to Grambauer Mountain, elev. 6,793 feet and then hike Ridge Trail 319 east 2 miles to the 6,875-foot summit of Scenery Mountain, where there's a fire lookout and magnificent views to the south. Trail 649 drops down 3.3 miles to a trail heading to an upper trailhead where a shuttle car could be waiting. Otherwise, continue another 2 switchbacking miles to Cedar Creek Trail 141 and the last 0.7 mile to the lower trailhead. The elevation drop from Scenery Mountain is 4,100 feet through various habitats in 6 miles.

• The Cedar Lakes Trailhead could be the starting point for another loop option described in Hike 73.

73 | SKY LAKES–HANGING VALLEY

Location: Cabinet Mountains
Status: Cabinet Mountains Wilderness
Distance: 13 miles round trip
Hiking time: 8 hours or overnight
Difficulty: Moderate
Season: Mid-June through early October
Map: USGS Treasure Mountain
Information: Kootenai National Forest, Libby District

A pair of pretty mountain lakes at the base of an unnamed 7,700-foot peak near Sugarloaf Mountain attracts more than a thousand visitors a year to this part of the Cabinet Mountains Wilderness. The trail to Sky Lakes is popular among both hikers and equestrians, although it passes a rugged spur option heading up with no mercy to a significantly quieter little Shangri-la.

From Libby, Montana, drive 1.2 miles from the City Center sign southeast

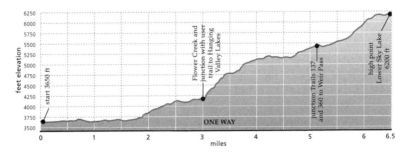

on U.S. Highway 2 and turn right (milepost 33.4) onto Shaugnessy Road. Drive up 0.8 mile to a three-way intersection at the top of the hill. Bear left. Drive 0.5 mile and turn right (west) onto Road 618 (Granite Creek). Drive 0.8 mile to Road 128. Bear right and follow this main Flower Creek Road 5 miles to the trailhead parking area for three trails. The Flower Creek-Sky Lakes Trailhead is about 50 yards south of the parking area.

Trail 137 starts gently before starting to climb, passing the wilderness boundary, to a campsite about 3 miles in at the junction with the primitive trail heading left and up to the Hanging Valley. This lightly maintained anglers' trail heads up a sometimes brutally steep and tractionless slope 2.3 miles to a pair of lakes worth visiting briefly or overnight. It holds undernourished rainbows.

For hikers continuing up Trail 137 to Sky Lakes, the Hanging Valley trail junction and creek crossing is a good spot to resupply with water. The trail continues through timber and huckleberries in and out of meadows with head-high brush. You might see bears in this area in late July and August. The trail breaks into an open meadow at nearly 6 miles and turns to the left at the base of Sugarloaf Mountain for the last ascent to Sky Lakes. It's the last 2 miles that tend to make the trail seem longer than it is. The lower lake is surrounded by timber and brush, but anglers find a way to cast for cutthroats. It has several campsites east of the outlet. A faint footpath leads from the outlet up the east-side ridge to fishless Upper Sky Lake.

Options: The Sky Lakes Trail is the beginning for a classic 27- or 31-mile loop that treats hikers to some of the best scenery—high and low—in the Cabinets. Although it can be done in a weekend by bypassing Sky Lakes, here's a more leisurely itinerary: Day 1: Hike to Sky Lakes as described above. Day 2: Backtrack and head northwest on Trail 360, past Sugarloaf Pond. Older maps don't show that the trail has been rerouted to the north side of the pond. This is critical, since it's the last reliable water source on the 8.5 spectacular miles of the Cabinet Divide to Upper Cedar Lake. Day

Upper Hanging Valley Lake, Cabinet Mountains Wilderness

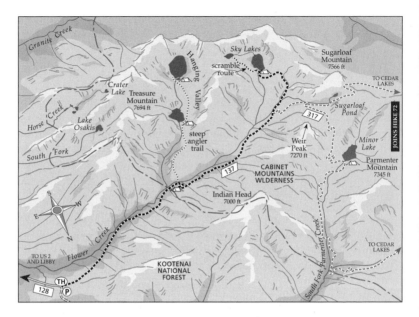

3: Leave Cedar Lakes and drop 2,100 feet in elevation in 3 miles on Trail 139/140 into the North Fork of Parmenter Creek. At a confluence, ford the North Fork and look for Trail 317 heading up the west side of the creek. This trail can be brushy and isn't maintained to the standard of other more popular trails. It gains 1,300 feet in 2 miles from the confluence to Minor Lake. Day 4: Climb another 1,050 feet in 1.7 miles to Weir Pass and soon to the junction with Trail 360. Turn left and hike out 5.5 miles to the Flower Creek Trailhead.

74 | GRANITE LAKE

Location: Cabinet Mountains
Status: Cabinet Mountains Wilderness
Distance: 12 miles round trip
Hiking time: 6–8 hours or overnight
Difficulty: Moderate
Season: Late June through early October
Maps: USGS Little Hoodoo Mountain, Treasure Mountain, Snowshoe Peak
Information: Kootenai National Forest, Libby District

Granite Lake is but one of many "destinations" along this route. Just 2 miles up the trail, hikers can enjoy scenic Granite Falls. The trail winds through

Granite Lake, Cabinet Mountains Wilderness (photo by Tom Horne)

heavy timber of the Cabinet Mountains Wilderness for the first 4.5 miles before breaking into open, brushy country and spectacular views of "A" Peak. This route is a longer but gentler approach than most hikes into the wilderness core, offering good camping and alternatives for further exploration. Beware, however, that Granite is low in elevation compared with other lakes in the Cabinets and the "brush zone" is thick for those with a yen for reaching the high country. Expect plenty of mosquitoes in late June and July.

From Libby, Montana, drive 1.2 miles from the City Center sign southeast on U.S. Highway 2 and turn right (milepost 33.4) onto Shaugnessy Road. Drive up 0.8 mile to a three-way intersection at the top of the hill. Bear left. Drive 0.5 mile and turn right (west) onto Road 618 (Granite Creek). Follow Road 618 about 8 miles to the trailhead parking area, which is about 0.3 mile past a parking area for trailers. Use the first parking area if you do not have four-wheel drive.

Trail 136 is well-marked and well-traveled, following Granite Creek 6 miles to Granite Lake. The trail crosses the creek at four points where you must ford or cross using deadfall. These crossings require extra care early in the hiking season during high water. Dense brush makes off-trail hiking unpleasant; few campsites are available between the trailhead and the area just down from the lake. "A" Peak to the south dominates the scenery. The main feed for Granite Lake is melt from the Blackwell Glacier that comes

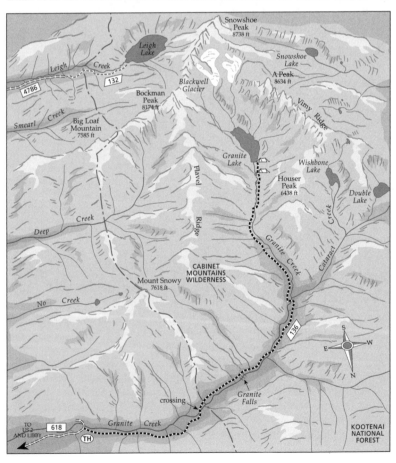

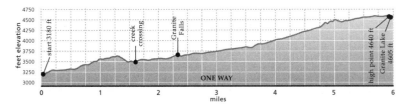

1,500 feet down an almost solid black slab of rock to the south of "A" Peak, which has had several names over the years. The 1897 General Land Office plat for the State of Montana shows it as Summit Peak. The 1914 Kootenai National Forest map labels it Craig Peak. From 1922 onward, the Forest Service has called it "A" Peak, partly for its shape and also as a shorter version for Apex Peak, as it was called on the 1927 Lincoln County map.

Options: For a side trip, consider a brushy but rewarding bushwhack up to Vimy Ridge, west of the lake. Going up the forested slope, you will find snarls of deadfall along with acres of huckleberries, which usually are prime in late July and early August.

75 | LEIGH LAKE

Location: Cabinet Mountains
Status: Cabinet Mountains Wilderness
Distance: 3 miles round trip
Hiking time: 3 hours or overnight
Difficulty: Moderate
Season: Mid-June through early October
Map: USGS Snowshoe Peak
Information: Kootenai National Forest, Libby District

It's almost sinful that such a stunning area is so easy to reach. Leigh Lake is a spectacular alpine area accessible to virtually anyone who can negotiate a 20 percent uphill grade for nearly 1.5 miles. Problem is, this quick access has made this granite basin the most popular area in the Cabinet Mountains Wilderness. In July and August, this is not always a place of solitude. To help protect the fragile shores of the lake from admirers, the Forest Service has banned stock use and prohibits camping within 300 feet of the water. This leaves only a few bivouac sites suitable for sleeping, and they're on the rock benches above the lake to the north. Check with the Kootenai National Forest for updates on restrictions.

From Libby, Montana, head south on U.S. Highway 2 about 7 miles to milepost 40.4 and turn right (west) onto Forest Road 278 (Bear Creek). Drive nearly 3 miles and turn right off the pavement onto Road 867 (Cherry Creek). Then drive 4.3 miles and turn right onto unimproved Road 4786 (Leigh

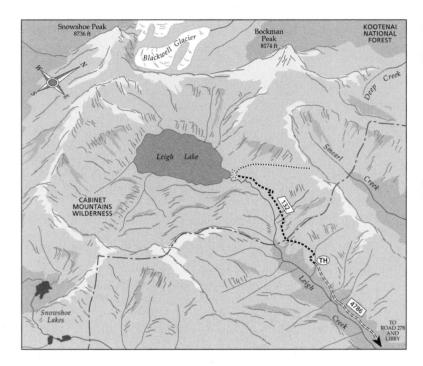

Creek). (If you pass over the Leigh Creek Bridge, you have driven 100 yards or so too far.) Drive this rough, narrow road nearly 2 miles to the trailhead.

The hike on Trail 132 is a moderate-to-steep switchbacking climb into the wilderness up Leigh Creek, which is distinguished by many small waterfalls. About 1 mile from the trailhead, the well-maintained trail crosses a creek and heads up more switchbacks to the second largest lake in the wilderness. Snowshoe Peak, elev. 8,736 feet, the tallest mountain in the wilderness, looms above. Leigh Lake also holds some rainbows and brook trout and is the starting point for one approach to the summit of Snowshoe Peak, a climb that's best left for those with routefinding and mountaineering experience. Faint, unmaintained routes lead up the north side of the lake toward ridges between Bockman and Snowshoe Peaks. Binoculars are helpful in watching for mountain goats, bears, and mule deer common to this area.

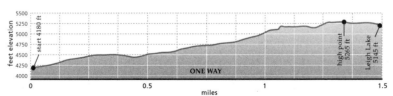

Leigh Lake, Cabinet Mountains Wilderness (photo by Steve Weinberger)

76 | ROCK LAKE

Location: Cabinet Mountains
Status: Cabinet Mountains Wilderness
Distance: 8–10 miles round trip
Hiking time: 5–6 hours or overnight
Difficulty: Moderate
Season: Mid-June through mid-October
Map: USGS Elephant Peak
Information: Kootenai National Forest, Cabinet District

Rock Lake offers a relatively easy access to a remote and scenic high alpine mountain lake just inside the border of the Cabinet Mountains Wilderness. Most of the trail is outside the wilderness and subject to intrusion from a proposed mine.

From State Highway 200 about 1.8 miles east of the turnoff to Noxon, Montana, and just east of the railroad overpass (milepost 17.1), turn north onto Rock Creek Road. Drive 0.3 mile and bear right under the powerlines onto Forest Road 150 along Rock Creek. Follow the road as it deteriorates for 5.3 miles and bear right onto Road 150A (East Fork Rock Creek). Mileages start here for hikers who don't have four-wheel-drives or vehicles with high clearance. Otherwise, go uphill about 1 mile to a gate, where

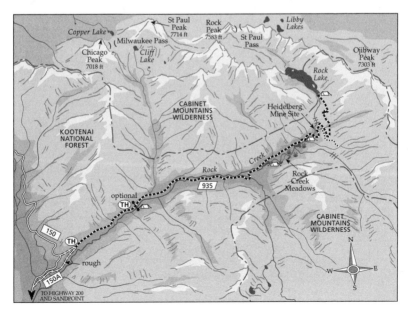

Rock Lake, Cabinet Mountains Wilderness (photo by John Roskelley)

there's room for parking and camping and subtract 1 mile each way from the descriptions.

The first part of the hike continues up this old mining road, passing a campsite at 3 miles and a larger campsite with a pit toilet at 3.5 miles. (Since there is only one campsite at Rock Lake itself, these group campsites are recommended, leaving only a day hike of less than 2 miles up to the lake.) At about 4 miles, the trail is posted with a Trail 935 sign. The trail then leads to an abandoned mine and Rock Creek waterfall before leaving the old road grade and heading to the right and uphill. The trail to Rock Lake (labeled "Main Trail") forks to the right about 100 feet before reaching the Heidelberg Mine. Camping at the lake is limited to one designated site to the right of the outlet stream, although a makeshift campsite is available to the left of the outlet. Water is frequently available along the trail. The lake is bordered mostly by steep rockslides high above timberline and offers scramblers access to several peaks.

While the history of mineral exploration is intriguing in this area, the consequences of a proposed modern mining operation could have dramatic impacts on the aesthetics of the Rock Lake area.

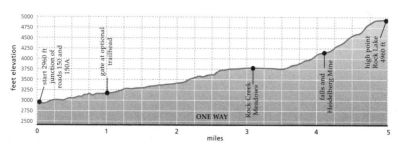

71 | WANLESS LAKE

Location: Cabinet Mountains
Status: Cabinet Mountains Wilderness
Distance: 18 miles round trip
Hiking time: 2 days minimum
Difficulty: Moderately difficult
Season: July through September
Maps: USGS Howard Lake, Goat Peak, Noxon Rapids Dam
Information: Kootenai National Forest, Cabinet District

Hikers who simply want to get quickly to a mountain lake won't appreciate this hike. Many other lakes in the Cabinet Mountains Wilderness are easier to reach. But this trip is worth the effort, with lofty views, cutthroat trout, and a little less competition for a campsite than the more accessible areas. The area does, however, attract quite a few horse packers. Signs warn

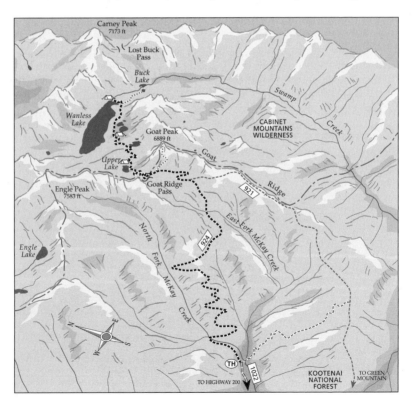

that stock is not allowed to come right into Wanless Lake, but sometimes the signs mysteriously disappear. The trail gradually gains 3,500 feet to Goat Peak Ridge before snaking down to a series of lakes leading to Wanless, the largest lake in the wilderness.

From Sandpoint, Idaho, drive east on State Highway 200 into Montana. From the Clark Fork River Bridge that leads to Noxon, continue 3 more miles on Highway 200 and turn left onto McKay Creek Road 1022. (Noxon Dam Road is on the right.) Drive north about 4 miles to the trailhead at the end of the road.

Trail 924 begins at 2,900 feet, where it might be cool and damp in the morning. But be sure to begin with full water bottles, since the next dependable water source is 6.6 miles up the trail at Upper Lake. From the trailhead, the route is a long series of switchbacks 5 miles uphill to the Cabinet Mountains Wilderness boundary just west of Goat Peak. The first 3-plus miles are through coniferous forest before the

Outlet at Wanless Lake, Cabinet Mountains Wilderness

trail breaks into beautiful high alpine country for the remaining 2-plus miles to the boundary. The trail reaches its high point, both physically and visually, here at elev. 6,380 feet. The trail then descends from the pass on a dozen switchbacks 0.8 mile to Upper Lake, at 5,900 feet. Fit hikers can make it here in about 4 hours. Some might choose to camp here or at other sites just down the trail and day hike the remaining 2.5 miles to Wanless Lake.

The trail continues on from Upper Lake past three smaller unnamed lakes. It's downhill from here to Wanless Lake, at 5,090 feet, but plan on about 1.5 hours of hiking. The lake is visible several times, but the trail takes its time getting there. Just before dropping to the east end of Wanless, the trail traverses a spot where the earth seems to have broken off into the classic glacial valley of Swamp Creek. Look down to Buck Lake and across the valley to the trail switchbacking up to Lost Buck Pass on the Cabinet Divide (see Hike 78). Wanless has campsites and naturally reproducing cutthroat trout, although fishing without a float tube is possible from only

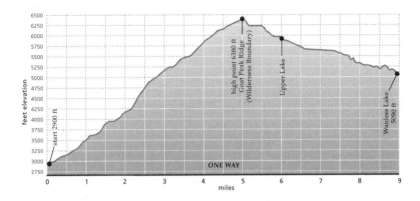

a tiny percentage of the steep shoreline. Remember, however, this is bear country. Prudent hikers will keep a clean camp.

Options: Drop down the trailless Swamp Creek headwall, over talus to Buck Lake. Then make your mother even prouder by hiking Trail 912 up to Lost Buck Pass.

• From the pass on Goat Peak Ridge south of Upper Lake, scramble up the talus to Goat Peak.

• Make the trip into a loop on the return to the trailhead by branching left onto Trail 921 south of Goat Peak. This is a neat, little-traveled walk through tons of huckleberries along Goat Ridge. The last leg on Trail 923, however, drops steeply, and ends in old clearcuts.

78 | GEIGER LAKES–CABINET DIVIDE

Location: Cabinet Mountains
Status: Cabinet Mountains Wilderness
Distance: 6.8 miles round trip
Hiking time: 4–5 hours or overnight
Difficulty: Easy
Season: Mid-June through early October
Map: USGS Howard Lake
Information: Kootenai National Forest, Libby District

This is a popular and painless introduction to an alpine scenic area in the Cabinet Mountains Wilderness. As might be expected, easy access to a lake framed by stunning granite walls is likely to attract plenty of company.

From Libby, Montana, head east on U.S. Highway 2 for 24 miles and turn right at milepost 56.8 onto Forest Road 231 (Geiger–West Fisher Creek). Follow this road for 5.5 miles and turn left on Road 2332. Go 0.5 mile to the

Lower Geiger Lake sign and turn left onto Road 1054. (Continuing straight leads to Lake Creek Campground.) Follow Road 1054 for 1.8 miles to the trailhead parking area.

Lake Creek Trail 656 leads hikers over 2 miles of gentle uphill to Lower Geiger Lake, a pretty spot surrounded by rocky slopes. Continue up the trail 1.4 slightly steeper miles to the upper lake. Campsites are available at both lakes, but check for campfire restrictions.

Options: Continue day hiking beyond the upper lake 1.2 miles and 600 feet in elevation on a less-frequently maintained trail to Lost Buck Pass for a stunning view across Swamp Creek drainage. (A short trail extends north toward Carney Peak but fades away.) Hike south on the Cabinet Divide along Trail 360 for some of the best ridge-trail hiking in the wilderness.

Moose near Geiger Lakes, Cabinet Mountains Wilderness (photo by Steve Weinberger)

• Carry your pack up from Geiger Lakes and south on the Cabinet Divide to make a full 15-mile loop. Drop down (east) from Cabinet Divide Trail 360 to camp in the Bear Lakes area. (See Hike 81.) Continue north on

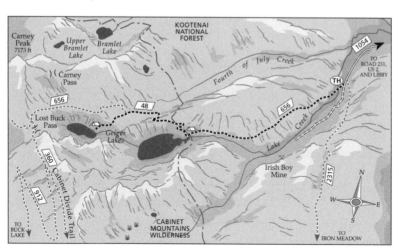

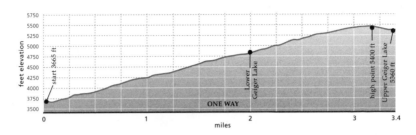

Divide Cutoff Trail 63 through logged but decent areas outside the wilderness through Iron Meadow and eventually connect with a 1-mile-long portion of road to the Lake Creek-Geiger Trailhead.

79 | CHICAGO PEAK–CLIFF LAKE

Location: Cabinet Mountains
Status: Cabinet Mountains Wilderness
Distance: 2–3 miles round trip
Hiking time: 1–3 hours or overnight
Difficulty: Easy
Season: Mid-July through September
Map: USGS Elephant Peak
Information: Kootenai National Forest, Cabinet District

Few hikes can match this trip as an introduction to wilderness backpacking for families and novices, that is, as long as they have a vehicle with enough clearance to negotiate poor stretches of the road. The route, which hasn't even been shown on official maps, offers a short and fairly easy walk to an alpine lake perched at elev. 6,700 feet on a cliff where mountain goats hang out. On the way, the trail passes a peak that resembles a city skyline. All of this, and some hikers might not even break a sweat getting here, unless it's to change a tire.

From State Highway 200 about 1.8 miles east of the turnoff to Noxon, Montana, and just east of the railroad overpass (milepost 17.1), turn north onto Rock Creek Road. Drive 0.2 mile and bear right under the powerlines onto Forest Road 150. (Do not go left on Road 150 or you'll drive 24 miles to reach the trailhead instead of 14 miles.) Go 5.3 miles along Rock Creek and bear left at a Y. Continue 2.5 miles on Road 150. Turn right onto Road 2741, which goes into a series of switchbacks and deteriorates in the next 6 miles to the trailhead. The road might be too rough in places for low-clearance vehicles.

The trail heads uphill, climbing briefly over a ridge and into the Cabinet Mountains Wilderness. The trail gently drops down the north side of the

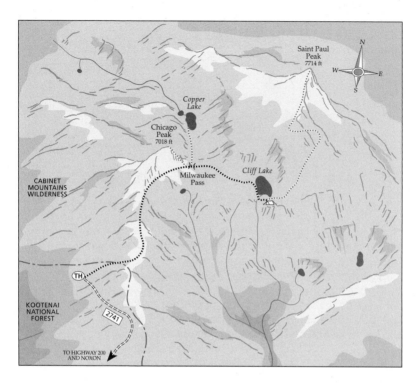

ridge and traverses the east side of Chicago Peak on a rock bench liberally moistened with tarns. After about 1 mile, the trail forks. The left fork drops down through Milwaukee Pass into the talus surrounding Copper Lake. The right fork crosses an opening before winding through upper reaches of timberline and contouring to Cliff Lake. Keep track of youngsters here. There really are cliffs. Tent sites are scattered throughout the area, so please don't camp near the fragile shores. Keep a clean camp as a measure against potential bear visits and to prevent mountain goats from becoming too bold. Wood is scarce at this elevation. Hikers sensitive to this special place will forgo the campfire and welcome the stars.

Names in this area stem from the full name of the Chicago, Milwaukee, St. Paul and Pacific Railroad, which was key to the economic development of the region in the early 1900s. The checkerboard pattern of land grants

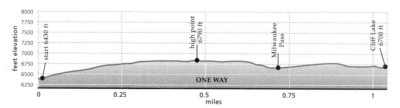

Chicago Peak behind Cliff Lake, Cabinet Mountains Wilderness

the federal government gave as an incentive to the railroads later was a blueprint for abusive logging practices that affected national forests.

This area is directly over an ore deposit Sterling Mining Company has proposed to extract from tunnels that start outside the wilderness borders.

Options: Follow the faint trail up the ridge on the east side of Cliff Lake for a scramble route to the summit of St. Paul Peak, elev. 7,714 feet. From here you'll see numerous other destinations for future trips. Look below to the northeast and make a plan to hike up the lovely trail through the old growth in the East Fork Bull River to St. Paul Lake.

• Chicago Peak, elev. 7,018 feet, is a long ridge of rock with gaps that look like missing teeth in the lower half of a hockey player's smile. Before sunset from Cliff Lake, the ridge looks like a city skyline. The peak can be climbed from the northeast ridge, but be careful near the top for loose rock that can be dislodged and sent whistling downslope where it could seriously injure following hikers.

80 | ENGLE LAKE

Location: Cabinet Mountains
Status: Cabinet Mountains Wilderness
Distance: 6 miles round trip
Hiking time: 4–6 hours or overnight
Difficulty: Moderately difficult
Season: Late June through early October
Map: USGS Elephant Peak
Information: Kootenai National Forest, Cabinet District

Get a high start from the road and take this hike even higher on a lightly used trail that eventually follows a ridge. Savor good views of 7,000-foot

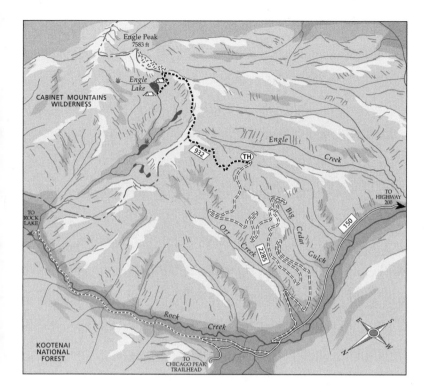

peaks before dropping to campsites at a mountain lake just inside the Cabinet Mountains Wilderness. Engle Lake holds cutthroat trout and the surrounding landscape offers wildflowers and huckleberries and the option for a relatively easy sky-scraping hike extension.

From State Highway 200 about 1.8 miles east of the turnoff to Noxon, Montana, and just east of the railroad overpass (milepost 17.1), turn north onto Rock Creek Road. Drive 0.2 mile and bear right under the powerlines onto Forest Road 150. Go about 4.5 miles and turn right onto Road 2285. Drive uphill about 7.3 miles to the trailhead.

Stock up with water before setting out, since no water sources are found on the hike until the trail drops into Engle Lake basin. Some snow could be found along the trail into early July.

Trail 932 starts at 4,920 feet and climbs steadily on a fairly steep grade—about 1,100 feet in the first mile. Have faith. The grade moderates as the trail skirts a ridge and the boundary of the 94,360-acre wilderness. Ascend another steep hump and enjoy the best views. Look for mountain penstemon in the rocks at your feet, unnamed lakes at the base of the cliff, and then look farther north toward a crop of 7,000-foot peaks. Can you see Chicago, St. Paul, Rock, Ojibway, Lost Horse, and Flat Top Peaks?

Scrambling up Engle Peak above Engle Lake, Cabinet Mountains Wilderness

Drop into the timber, then follow the trail as it traverses a talus slope. Climb gradually to a ridge and a trail junction. The left fork drops down and switchbacks more than 500 feet in 0.7 mile to Engle Lake. Campsites are on both sides of the outlet. This is grizzly country; camp accordingly.

Options: Several routes lead to the summit of 7,583-foot Engle Peak, which looms above and offers spectacular views of the area, including Wanless Lake basin and Lost Buck Pass (see Hike 77). The most direct route is on a decent trail that continues up the talus ridge from where the trail drops down to the lake. USGS map Howard Lake is helpful for exploring this area.

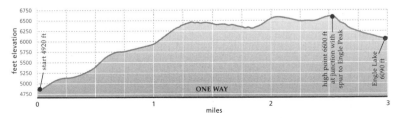

81 | Bear–Baree Lakes Loop

Location: Cabinet Mountains
Status: Cabinet Mountains Wilderness
Distance: 8 miles round trip
Hiking time: 5–7 hours or overnight
Difficulty: Moderately difficult
Season: Late June through early October
Maps: USGS Goat Peak, Silver Butte Pass
Information: Kootenai National Forest, Libby District

For the effort in gaining 2,700 feet in elevation, hikers are handsomely rewarded on this hike. The mileage is low enough to make it suitable for a day hike, yet several mountain lakes and a wide-open stretch on the Cabinet Divide make this worthy of dallying with a backpack for a few nights.

From Libby, Montana, head east on U.S. Highway 2 about 27 miles and turn right at milepost 60.6 onto Forest Road 148 (Silver Butte). Follow this road for 9 miles and turn right on the spur road that leads up to the Bear Lake Trailhead at the powerline. A vehicle or bike can be shuttled up Road 148 another mile to the Baree Lake Trailhead if desired. (This area is also accessible from the south, heading into the forest east of Trout Creek, Montana, on Road 154 and connecting with a deteriorating section of Road 148 over Silver Butte Pass.)

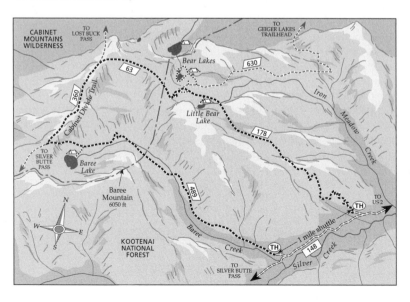

Trail 178 wastes no time gaining altitude from elev. 3,780 feet, switchbacking up a ridge before taking a gentler sidehill approach to the high country. After 2.5 miles, note an unofficial trail heading left a short way into Little Bear Lake, which is unnamed on maps and left out of the wilderness because it was previously owned by Plum Creek Timber Company. (The Forest Service purchased section 31 with Little Bear Lake from the company in the late 1990s.) Check it out, then continue up Trail 178 another short way. At the junction with a shortcut trail, continue straight in order to reach the other Bear Lakes. Then turn right at a T to a connection with the Cabinet Divide Cutoff Trail 630 and an overlook of Middle Bear Lake. Continue down on Trail 630 and look for an old outfitter trail branching left to a campsite near the lake. From here, you can hike the open talus slope along the lake and northward down to Big Bear Lake, where there's camping at the outlet. All the lakes are periodically stocked with trout. (Bear Lakes don't start out in the same drainages, but they all eventually flow into the Fisher River.)

The best part of the hike begins back at the T junction, as Trail 63 heads south to a pass and then west into the heart of the Cabinet Mountains Wilderness. The trail goes past a craggy ridge to the high point of the route at 6,380 feet and breaks into an open sidehill. From here, the trail contours and the walking is difficult only because there's so much to gawk at, scanning down into the expansive Baree Creek basin. At a pass, connect with Cabinet Divide Trail 360, and the scenery suddenly gets even better. You could head north on the divide for more adventure (see Hike 78). To continue this hike, however, follow the divide trail as it contours south along the west side of a rocky ridge. Scramblers will want to head directly up and over the rocky ridge to gain another great vantage from elev. 6,320 feet. Angle west at any time to pick up the trail, which contours along the ridge for about 1.6 miles to the junction with Trail 489.

In good weather, you are justified in being reluctant to leave the divide (see "Options" below) as Trail 489 drops quickly, past huckleberries that ripen in August, 0.5 mile to the junction with the spur that heads right to campsites at Baree Lake. The rest is all downhill 2.6 miles, making two hopover crossings of Baree Creek, to the trailhead. From here, Road 148 contours 1 mile back to the spur that leads up to Bear Lakes Trailhead.

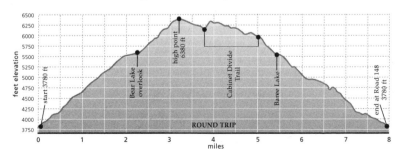

On the Cabinet Divide to Baree Lake, Cabinet Mountains Wilderness

Options: To extend the hike on the Cabinet Divide, or to make a great day trip from camp at Baree Lake, continue south on Trail 360, which runs another 6.5 miles from the junction with Baree Lake Trail 489 to the rough powerline road at Silver Butte Pass.

82 | TUCANNON RIVER– DIAMOND PEAK LOOP

Location: Blue Mountains
Status: Wenaha-Tucannon Wilderness
Distance: 21 miles round trip
Hiking time: 2 days minimum
Difficulty: Moderately difficult
Season: June through October
Maps: USGS Stentz Spring, Diamond Peak, Panjab Creek
Information: Umatilla National Forest, Pomeroy District

This loop provides a vigorous two-day, or a more leisurely two-and-a-half-day, backpacking trip with a good option for a shorter loop. Because of the scenic vistas, it's a fine introduction to the Wenaha-Tucannon Wilderness, a land of rocky canyons. Elk hunting season, which opens in late October, tends to be the busiest time in this area.

From U.S. Highway 12 about 4 miles west of Pomeroy, Washington, (or 8 miles east of the junction with State Highway 127) turn south on Tatman Mountain Road. Follow the signs for Camp Wooten, joining the Tucannon River Road after 9 miles. (Note: Hikers coming from points farther west should get on the Tucannon River Road at Dayton.) Turn south on Tucannon River Road and drive about 13 miles, passing Camp Wooten, to the Tucannon River Bridge at the junction with Panjab Creek. Numerous

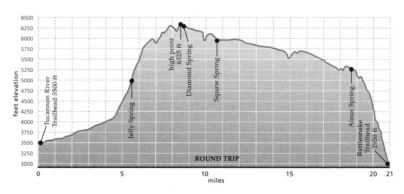

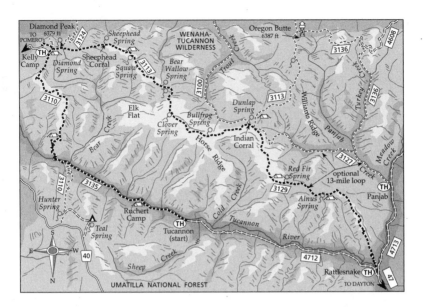

camping areas are available along the Tucannon River. Just before the bridge, turn left onto Forest Road 4712 and parallel the Tucannon River east 4.5 miles to the Tucannon River Trailhead at the end of the road. To make the loop easier, shuttle a car (or leave a bicycle) back at the Rattlesnake Trailhead at the Tucannon River-Panjab Creek junction.

From the trailhead, follow Trail 3135 about 4.2 miles along the Tucannon River to the confluence with Bear Creek. This is an easy walk that passes several good campsites. This section of trail is not inside the Wenaha-Tucannon Wilderness boundaries, but has remained relatively undisturbed, and conservationists would like to see the forest north of here added to the wilderness. Beyond the Tucannon River crossing, 0.2 mile above Bear Creek, the route becomes Trail 3110 and gains a whopping 1,000 feet of elevation in 1 mile. The ridge near Jelly Spring (a reliable water source and a good campsite) is reached at 5.2 miles from the trailhead. You get your first scenic vistas here. Similar wide-angle views are available frequently for the rest of this loop hike.

At 8.5 miles, Trail 3110 joins with Trail 3124 at elev. 6,100 feet near Diamond Peak. Here you must decide whether to camp or to continue west on Trail 3113 to an excellent campsite at Squaw Spring 2.2 easy miles away. Check on water quality in Diamond Spring, about 200 yards south of the trail junction before making the decision. (Reaching Sheephead Spring, between Squaw Spring and Diamond Spring, may involve crashing through stinging nettles, dense alder, and muddy elk wallows.)

From Squaw Spring, continue west on Trail 3113 (Mount Misery Trail) to the junction with Rattlesnake Trail 3129, which is 7.2 miles west of Diamond

Peak. Nearby Dunlap Spring is a reliable water source and a good campsite. At the junction with Trail 3129, turn right, heading north on Trail 3129. Pass campsites at Red Fir and Alnus Spring at 2 and 3 miles, respectively, from the open expanse of Indian Corral. (Alder, which surrounds the spring, is in the genus Alnus.) The trail between Diamond Peak and Alnus Spring is easy, straying little from an elevation of about 5,500 feet. After Alnus Spring, the trail descends steeply, dropping 2,300 feet in the last 2 miles to the Rattlesnake Trailhead and road at the confluence of the Tucannon River and Panjab Creek.

Options: A shorter 13-mile loop (includes 2.4 miles of Road 4713) to explore this northwest corner of the wilderness also ends at this Rattlesnake Trailhead, but it starts 2.4 miles up Road 4713 at Panjab Trailhead and heads into the wilderness on Trail 3127. You miss the Tucannon River on this loop, but the route is blessed with pleasant little waterfalls in the canyon section en route to the Indian Corral-Dunlap Spring area. Consider camping in this area and taking a day to explore the ridge trail south toward Oregon Butte Lookout (see Hike 83) and even more impressive views into the bowels of the wilderness. Loop back past springs and campsites on Trail 3129 to the Rattlesnake Trailhead near the confluence of Panjab Creek and Tucannon River.

Mule deer, Wenaha-Tucannon Wilderness

83 | OREGON BUTTE

Location: Blue Mountains
Status: Wenaha-Tucannon Wilderness
Distance: 6 miles round trip
Hiking time: 3 hours or overnight
Difficulty: Easy
Season: Early June through October
Map: USGS Oregon Butte
Information: Umatilla National Forest, Pomeroy District

A relatively easy out-and-back hike for impressive views of the Wenaha-Tucannon Wilderness, this trek can be extended different directions into an overnighter. Oregon Butte, a Forest Service lookout site, offers a high vantage over the rugged Wenaha River drainage. The 14-by-14-foot lookout cabin, built in 1931, still stands and is often staffed by volunteers.

From U.S. Highway 12 about 4 miles west of Pomeroy, Washington, (or 8 miles east of the junction with State Highway 127) turn south on Tatman Mountain Road. Follow the signs for Camp Wooten, joining the Tucannon River Road after 9 miles. (Note: Hikers coming from points farther west should get on the Tucannon River Road at Dayton.) Turn south on

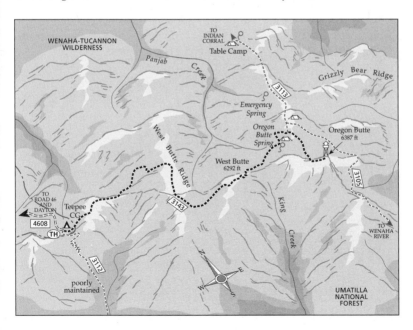

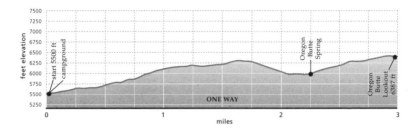

Tucannon River Road and drive nearly 2 miles past Camp Wooten and turn right on Forest Road 4620. Drive 4 miles and turn left on Road 46 (Skyline Road). Continue south on Skyline Road for about 11 miles and turn left on Road 4608 at the Godman Spring Guard Station. Continue east 6 miles to the end of the road at Teepee Campground, elev. 5,500 feet.

Follow Trail 3143 uphill for a little more than 1 mile to the first open meadow and a trail junction. Trail 3143 continues to the left and is the newer, shadier, and most direct route to Oregon Butte Spring. The right fork, likely to be left unmaintained, is the higher route that goes past West Butte, connecting with Trail 3143 just before Oregon Butte Spring. Water is piped from the spring to a trough on the trail, with campsites up the hillside 50 yards. More exposed tent sites, offering a spectacular sunrise view of the northern part of the wilderness area, can be found 400 yards beyond the spring and above the junction with Trail 3113. At this junction, bear right to continue the hike up the scenic ridge to Oregon Butte Lookout, elev. 6,387 feet.

Options: From Oregon Butte, Trail 3105 angles south and down past Danger Point toward Weller Butte. The first 2 miles are open and studded with numerous springs, wildflowers, and huckleberries.

Oregon Butte Lookout, Wenaha-Tucannon Wilderness

• Hiking parties with more than one vehicle can shuttle a car to the Rattlesnake Trailhead at the confluence of Panjab Creek and the Tucannon River on Forest Road 47, where they will end up after a delightful hike that drops 3,200 feet in elevation in about 8 miles. From Oregon Butte Spring, head north on Trail 3113, following ridges about 3 miles to the junction at Indian Corral (about 5.5 miles from Teepee Campground and a good day hike in itself). There's a good campsite at nearby Dunlap Spring, a short way down Trail 3100. From the Indian Corral junction, head north, descending on Trail 3129 past good campsites at Red Fir Spring (1.5 miles from Indian Corral) and Alnus Spring (3 miles from Indian Corral) to the trailhead.

84 SQUAW SPRING

Location: Blue Mountains
Status: Wenaha-Tucannon Wilderness
Distance: About 3.5 miles one way
Hiking time: 3–4 hours or overnight
Difficulty: Easy
Season: Early June through October
Map: USGS Diamond Peak
Information: Umatilla National Forest, Pomeroy District

Avoid the radical ups and downs of other routes into the rugged Wenaha-Tucannon Wilderness with this uncommonly easy hike suitable for families. It can be done as a day trip or as an overnighter and has several options for side trips.

From U.S. Highway 12 in Pomeroy, Washington, turn south on 15th Street. Continue south out of town 15 miles. (The road becomes Mountain Road.) The pavement ends at the national forest boundary. Continue straight on Forest Road 40 for 15 miles and turn right on Road 4030. Go 4 miles to the Misery Spring-Kelly Camp Trailhead.

Hike west on Trail 3113 into the wilderness. The trail climbs fairly steadily for the first mile to an overlook near an old trailhead. Continue west along the north side of Diamond Peak. Near junctions with trails that head north to the Tucannon River and south toward the Wenaha River, take

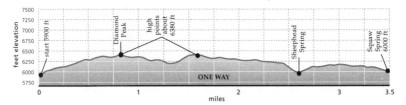

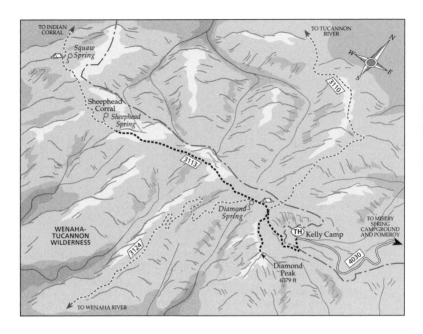

a side trip up to the top of Diamond Peak, elev. 6,379 feet. Then come back down and continue west—over a butte that's as high as Diamond Peak—to Sheephead Corral. This could be a good campsite, except that its access to water may not be easy. Go farther to Squaw Spring, a total of about 3.5 miles from the trailhead, which has a good wind-sheltered campsite with clear-flowing water, although it should be purified for drinking.

Rocky Mountain elk, Wenaha-Tucannon Wilderness

Options: Trail 3110 north from Diamond Peak offers good views of the upper Tucannon River drainage, and Trail 3124, heading south from Diamond Spring, offers a good overlook of the Melton Creek drainage from its first switchback.

• An excellent long-distance trek—25 miles round trip from the Misery Spring-Kelly Camp Trailhead—follows the high country from Squaw Spring on to the open expanse of Indian Corral and south to Oregon Butte. Several campsites are along the route at springs near Indian Corral and at Oregon Butte Spring.

85 | TWIN BUTTES–WENAHA RIVER LOOP

Location: Blue Mountains
Status: Wenaha-Tucannon Wilderness
Distance: 18.5 miles round trip
Hiking time: 2–3 days
Difficulty: Moderately difficult
Season: Early June through October
Maps: USGS Godman Springs, Wenaha Forks, Elbow Creek,
    Oregon Butte
Information: Umatilla National Forest, Pomeroy District

The fit hiker who has only two or three days in which to see the best of the Wenaha-Tucannon Wilderness will find this trip ideal. Typical of this vertical country, hikers will encounter some steep trail sections up and down the canyons, where the heat can bear down on hot summer days. But the Wenaha River will refresh your spirit.

From U.S. Highway 12 about 4 miles west of Pomeroy, Washington, (or 8 miles east of the junction with State Highway 127) turn south on Tatman Mountain Road. Follow the signs for Camp Wooten, joining the Tucannon River Road after 9 miles. (Note: Hikers coming from points farther west

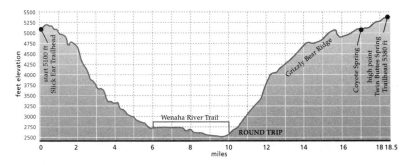

False hellebore blooming in ponderosa parkland of Grizzly Bear Ridge

should get on the Tucannon River Road at Dayton, Washington.) Turn south on Tucannon River Road. Pass Camp Wooten, drive about 2 miles, and turn right onto Forest Road 4620. Drive 4 miles and turn left on Road 46 (Skyline Road). Go south on Skyline Road, passing Godman Spring Guard Station, for a total of about 16 miles before turning left onto Road 300. Drive about 5 miles and bear left at a Y (may not be marked) to the trailhead and camping area at Twin Buttes Spring. This is where the trip ends. Leave a shuttle car or stash a bike here or plan on adding 2 miles to the end of the hike. Backtrack to the Y and take a sharp left onto Road 301. Go south 1.3 miles and bear left, passing some private cabins just before the Slick Ear Trailhead and parking area. The private inholdings, which predate the Wilderness Act, are the reason these access roads poke like a fork into the wilderness boundary.

Slick Ear Trail 3104 meanders down to a fairly open ridge before dropping 2,300 feet to the Wenaha River, 6 miles from the trailhead. At the river, turn left onto Trail 3106. Camp here if you're allowing three or more days for the trip (fishing for rainbow trout can be good in the river; an Oregon fishing license is required), otherwise follow the river 4.7 miles downstream to Rock Creek and the junction with Trail 3103. Camp at any one of several sites just past this junction.

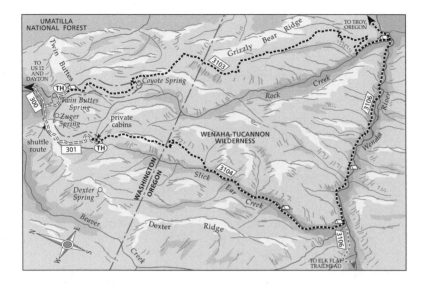

To complete the loop, load up with water and ascend Trail 3103, known as the Grizzly Bear Ridge Trail even though no grizzlies exist in the Wenaha-Tucannon Wilderness. After 1 mile, the trail reaches the ridge. Here, with wind-whipped fir snags in the foreground and miles of Wenaha River leading the eye to distant gorge walls, is one of the best photographic viewpoints in the area. Soon the trail enters a grassy parkland of scattered ponderosa pines, an ecosystem as unique as it is striking in its beauty. Along with the eastern slopes of Smooth Ridge (10 miles to the east), this is one of few virgin ponderosa pine–grass parklands to escape the chain saws in Washington. The grasslands here serve as summer home to numerous birds, including two of the Northwest's most colorful: the Audubon warbler and the western tanager. Prepare to miss a heartbeat or two when a blue grouse explodes into flight along the trail.

The trail continues at a more gradual incline up Grizzly Bear Ridge, generally in the shade of towering firs and pines and often past the large conspicuously leafy-stemmed false hellebore, which blooms with spectacular "trees" of densely clustered yellowish-green (and poisonous) flowers. If the trail disappears in occasional pockets of downfall, look for cut logs indicating short rerouted sections. It is 8 miles from the Wenaha River to Twin Buttes Spring with no dependable water sources in between. Coyote Spring is a source of water for desperate hikers with a water filter. Check the map and look for lush growth in a stand of timber and a partially exposed culvert that goes under the trail just after the trail begins to follow an old road bed. Bushwhack down to where water forms small pools. From the spring, it's 1.5 miles to the Twin Buttes Trailhead.

86 | WENAHA RIVER

Location: Blue Mountains
Status: Wenaha-Tucannon Wilderness
Distance: Up to 22 miles one way
Hiking time: 2–4 days
Difficulty: Moderate
Season: May through early November
Maps: USGS Eden, Elbow Creek, Wenaha Forks
Information: Umatilla National Forest, Pomeroy District

A trail runs along the Wenaha River for nearly 30 miles, making an excellent hike for anglers and river lovers through a variety of terrains, from meadows to lush vegetation to dry rocky canyon lands. The river trail can be reached several ways, the easiest of which is simply in and out from the east trailhead just outside of Troy, Oregon. No river crossings are required from Troy, making it a good choice for hikers eager to get on the trail in May, when the river is still swollen with runoff. Later in the year, groups of hikers can use car shuttles to make adventurous trips that don't require backtracking.

From Asotin County Road 100 on the northeast edge of tiny Troy, Oregon, turn north on the road toward Pomeroy and the Wenaha State Wildlife Area. Go 0.3 mile to the trailhead at a sharp bend.

Upper Wenaha River, Wenaha-Tucannon Wilderness

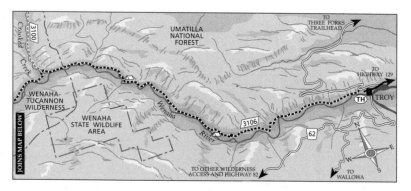

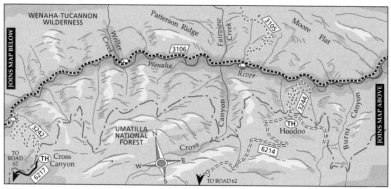

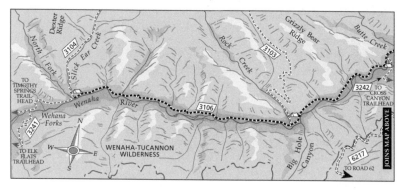

This trip can be tailored to virtually any group's ability. The trail rarely goes more than 3 miles or so before offering a camping opportunity. The trail undulates up from the river along the canyon walls and back down, but the climbs are never prolonged. Bighorn sheep could be seen anywhere in the canyon, and rattlesnakes are well entrenched. From July into September, the fishing can be good for rainbow trout. An Oregon fishing license is required.

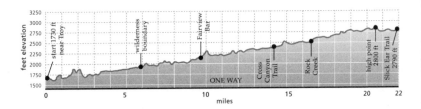

The terrain is arid in the lower reaches of the river and gets greener and more vegetated as the trail progresses upstream. Sometimes the vegetation can be so thick (particularly noticeable on dewy mornings or wet days), the trail almost disappears. Despite the long hiking season here, the river trail is lightly traveled. Most of the use comes during the fall hunting seasons.

From the start, Trail 3106 follows the north shore of the river through grasslands and ponderosa pines, climbing the canyon wall for a stretch and dropping to the river again just inside the national forest boundary at 3 miles. At almost 6 miles, the trail enters the Wenaha-Tucannon Wilderness and then comes to the junction with Trail 3100 at the mouth of Crooked Creek canyon. The trail passes a junction with Trail 3244, which would re-quire a river ford (advisable only in low water) if you were to branch south and climb up from the river to the Hoodoo Ridge Trailhead (see "Options").

Just after Trail 3105 forks north toward Weller Butte, bracken ferns sweep the air along the Wenaha River Trail 9.5 miles upstream where the river braids into several channels at Fairview Bar. Good upriver views en-tice you to continue. At 14.2 miles, another route branches off to the south, fording the river, to climb up from the Wenaha to the Cross Canyon Trailhead. If you want to make just one special day hike up from the Wenaha, save your energy until you get to mile 16.5 and the trail junction at Rock Creek. Find a campsite and day hike 3 or 4 miles up Trail 3103 to the unique ponderosa parklands halfway up Grizzly Bear Ridge (see Hike 85). At 21.2 miles up the Wenaha, campsites near the junction with Slick Ear Trail 3104 make another logical turnaround point. Depending on main-tenance, the trail tends to fade from here upstream.

Options: Late in the summer or early fall, when river flows are low, hik-ing groups can shuttle vehicles to one of two trailheads at the end of roads that spur off Road 62 west of Troy, Oregon. Start an excellent downstream hike by driving 21 miles west from Troy to the Elk Flats Trailhead. Drop down 2,800 feet in 5 miles from Elk Flats, ford the Wenaha River (wading shoes recommended), and hike the river trail downstream. For a 16-mile trip, cross back to the south side of the river on Trail 3242 and hike up to a vehicle waiting at the Cross Canyon Trailhead. For a 25-mile trip, exit the Wenaha canyon via Hoodoo Ridge Trail 3244, which switchbacks more than a dozen times to gain 1,800 feet in 3.2 miles to the trailhead on the canyon rim.

WALLOWA-WHITMAN NATIONAL FOREST

87 | ICE LAKE

Location: Wallowa Mountains
Status: Eagle Cap Wilderness
Distance: 16 miles round trip
Hiking time: 2 days minimum
Difficulty: Moderately difficult
Season: Early July through September
Maps: USGS Eagle Cap, Aneroid Mt., Joseph
Information: Wallowa Mountains Visitor Center

Ice Lake is a popular destination in the Eagle Cap Wilderness even though many hikers might be discouraged by a long series of switchbacks to its perch in the granite slopes of the Hurwal Divide. The lake is at timberline below Sacajawea and Matterhorn, the two highest peaks in the Wallowas.

From Enterprise, Oregon, drive south on State Highway 82 to Joseph. Follow the signs through Joseph to Wallowa Lake. At the south end of the lake, bear left and drive 1 mile through a concentration of tourist facilities to the trailhead at the end of the road by a power substation. (Bearing right at the fork leads to Wallowa Lake State Park, where overnight camping accommodations and hot showers are available during the summer season. See Appendix C.) Pitching tents at the trailhead is not permitted. No, those are not fake mule deer lounging around the buildings.

Register at the trailhead and follow the signs onto West Fork Wallowa

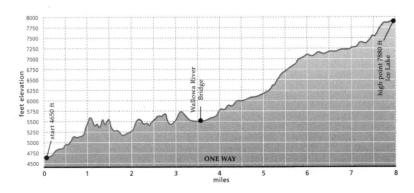

River Trail 1820 toward the Lakes Basin. This is one of the most popular trails in the wilderness, beginning at elev. 4,650 feet. Hike 2.8 miles and turn at the junction onto Trail 1808 heading uphill to the west toward Ice Lake. From here, much of the horse and foot traffic continues south toward the heavily used Lakes Basin (see Hikes 89 and 90), but there's no shortage of diehards willing to head up to eye-pleasing Ice Lake. Cross a bridge and be prepared to start heading steadily up; make sure you have plenty of water. The well-graded trail makes 37 switchbacks in 5.2 miles to the lake. This is the steepest part of the hike, but it's also the most beautiful. Look

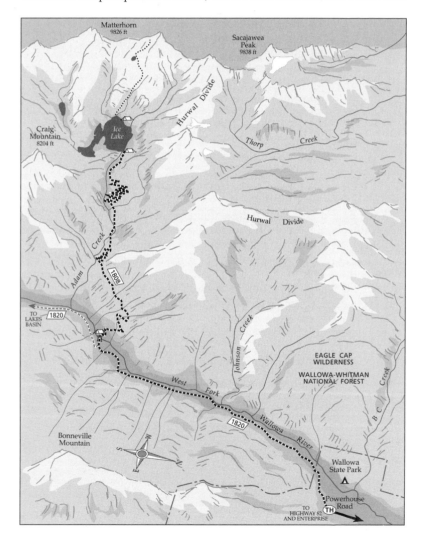

Ice Lake below peaks on the Hurwal Divide, Eagle Cap Wilderness
(photo by Terri Janek)

for a good lunch stop near a breathtaking view of a waterfall between switchbacks 22 and 23.

Ice Lake is a cold, refreshing, blue-green lake with several good campsites to the right (north) of the trail as it approaches the lake.

Options: It is possible to scramble to the top of Matterhorn (note the limestone above the granite around the summit) and Sacajawea Peak following a trail that starts from the far west end of the lake near the inlet stream. Be wary of changing weather.

88 | SWAMP LAKE

Location: Wallowa Mountains
Status: Eagle Cap Wilderness
Distance: 19 miles round trip
Hiking time: 2 days minimum
Difficulty: Moderately difficult
Season: July through September
Maps: USGS Eagle Cap, Steamboat Lake
Information: Wallowa Mountains Visitor Center

Swamp Lake is a small, picturesque lake in the Eagle Cap Wilderness off the beaten track of the more popular Lakes Basin. It is not swampy in the sense of a shallow lake. Instead, one end of the lake is dotted with tiny grass islands in shapes that have the appearance of a finely arranged Japanese garden.

From Enterprise, Oregon, drive northwest 10 miles on State Highway 82 to Lostine. As the highway through town bends right, turn left onto Lostine Canyon Road 8210 toward Lostine River Campground and proceed south about 17 miles (road eventually gets narrow and rocky) to Two Pan Campground.

Register at the trailhead, then follow the route to the left for 0.2 mile to a

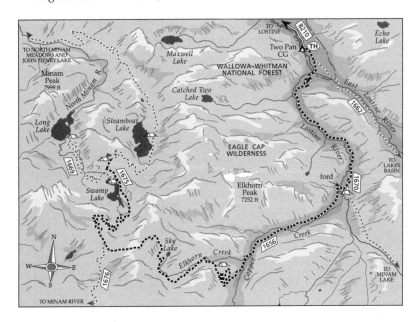

junction and head right onto West Lostine River Trail 1670. Signs may refer to Copper Creek without mentioning Swamp Lake. This trail, the main route to Minam Lake, climbs gradually beside the (West) Lostine River through dense forest. Hike 2.6 miles and head right on Copper Creek Trail 1656, crossing the Lostine River. The trail crosses at a shallow spot, but there is no bridge. Fallen logs often can be found spanning the stream. The trail follows the north side of Copper Creek. The several crossings of Copper Creek and Elkhorn Creek can be treacherous often through July. The trail heads up moderately through forest that thins into open meadows about 3 miles from the turnoff. This is a trail that fools you into thinking the lake is "just over the next ridge." The trail continues by Copper Creek through some rocky meadows that are filled with flowers during much of the hiking season. Several good campsites can be found in this area. When the creek starts to peter out, fill water bottles because this is the last water until reaching the lake.

At a high rocky plateau with beautiful views into the Minam River valley and beyond, Swamp Lake eventually comes into view below to the right, nestled in a picturesque basin. The trail traverses the plateau up to 8,610 feet, then meets a junction with Trail 1676 to Upper Minam River at 5 miles past the Copper Creek turnoff. Continuing toward Swamp Lake, the trail descends a steep embankment via switchbacks to the south end of the lake and closeup views of the "Japanese garden." Follow the trail a short way past the north end of the lake to the junction of the trails to Long and Steamboat Lakes. Since campsites must be 100 feet from lakes, an example of a good place to camp is reached by following the Steamboat Lake Trail for a short distance to the pass between the lakes. Here you will find a pond with good views.

It is an easy 1.7 miles down to lovely Steamboat Lake at 7,837 feet. The lake's terrain is similar to Swamp Lake and takes its name from a rock island

Swamp Lake, Eagle Cap Wilderness (photo by Mary Weathers)

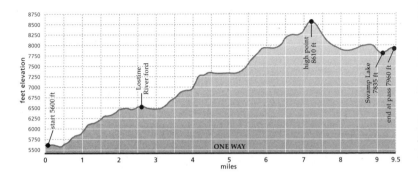

in the center. The 1.5-mile trail to Long Lake descends in a steep, rough path. Long Lake is surrounded by trees with plenty of campsites. Both of these lakes, which hold brook trout, make good side trips. Swamp is one of the last lakes in the wilderness to hold a fragile self-sustaining fishery of golden trout, which are no longer being stocked. If they still exist, any that are caught should be released.

Options: Expand the trip into a 25-mile loop by heading north from Steamboat Lake and back to the Lostine River Road via Wilson Pass. Camp in the John Henry Lake area. A side trip to the Hobo Lake area is recommended, adding another 4 to 5 miles to the loop. The road shuttle from Bowman Trailhead to Two Pan Campground is about 4 miles.

89 | MIRROR LAKE

Location: Wallowa Mountains
Status: Eagle Cap Wilderness
Distance: 15 miles round trip
Hiking time: 2 days
Difficulty: Moderate
Season: July through early October
Maps: USGS Eagle Cap, Aneroid Mt., Joseph
Information: Wallowa Mountains Visitor Center

Join the crowd and hike the most direct and popular route into the heart of Eagle Cap Wilderness to a lake that often reflects the stunning image of 9,572-foot Eagle Cap Peak.

From Enterprise, Oregon, drive northwest 10 miles on State Highway 82 to Lostine. As the highway through town bends right, turn left onto Lostine Canyon Road 8210 toward Lostine River Campground and proceed south about 17 miles (road eventually gets narrow and rocky) to Two Pan Campground, elev. 5,600 feet.

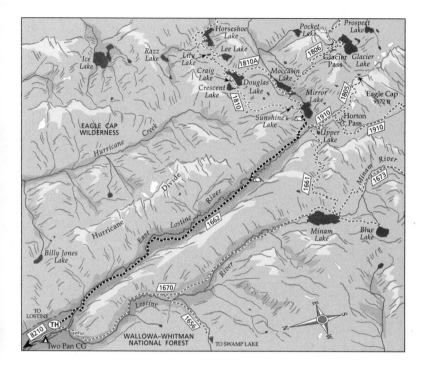

Register at the trailhead and follow the trail to the left for 0.2 mile to a junction and bear left onto East Lostine River Trail 1662. The first 2 miles or so are fairly steep, switchbacking through boulders and tall stands of spruce and fir. The trail gradually straightens and continues to climb for about 1 mile before entering a big meadow, which marks the beginning of the upper valley. Water is plentiful en route. The next 2 miles of trail are fairly gradual through a classic U-shaped glacier valley. The trail meanders through small open stands of timber and boulder fields. The mystical half-dome shape of Eagle Cap Peak looms at the head of the valley. The trail reverts once again to a series of short steep switchbacks up to the rim above Mirror Lake. As the lake begins to come into view, there is a junction where a trail heads off to Horton Pass. Bear left and hike a short way to Mirror Lake, elev. 7,595 feet. Outcrops of brilliant marble-like granite hang above the lake. Talus slopes and steep granite slabs meet the south shore of the lake and drop to invisible depths. Campsites can be found on the benches above the north shore. Be sure to keep a minimum of 100 feet from the water.

Options: There's no shortage of day hiking options or loop extensions from a base camp near Mirror Lake.

• Scramble to the summit of Eagle Cap by loading up with water and backtracking to the trail junction and heading south toward Horton Pass on

Mirror Lake, Eagle Cap Wilderness

Trail 1910. A trail branches off to the left (east) and heads steeply up to the summit. Another summit trail heads up from Horton Pass. From the summit, enjoy sweeping views of Hurricane Canyon, the towering white Matterhorn, Lostine Canyon, Glacier Lake to the southeast, and much more.

• Walk the loops to visit eight lakes to the east of Mirror, or make the scenic trek over Glacier Pass to Glacier Lake.

• Convert the hike to an excellent 18- or 24-mile multi-day loop by heading west to Minam Lake area via Carper Pass, or longer and better yet, over Horton and Frazier Passes, and return to the trailhead via the (West) Lostine River Trail.

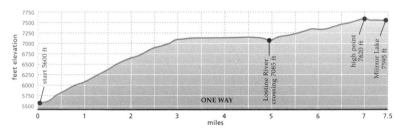

90 | LAKES BASIN LOOP

Location: Wallowa Mountains
Status: Eagle Cap Wilderness
Distance: At least 38 miles round trip
Hiking time: 4–7 days
Difficulty: Moderately difficult
Season: Early July through early September
Maps: USGS Eagle Cap, Cornucopia Aneroid Mt., Joseph,
    Krag Peak
Information: Wallowa Mountains Visitor Center

This classic multi-day loop trip—with tempting side trips that could easily stretch the mileage to 50-plus—weaves below, around, and through the sky-scraping peaks of Oregon's Eagle Cap Wilderness. The route leads through deep valleys, along sparkling streams, and near dozens of alpine lakes, a concentration of which is known as the Lakes Basin in the shadow

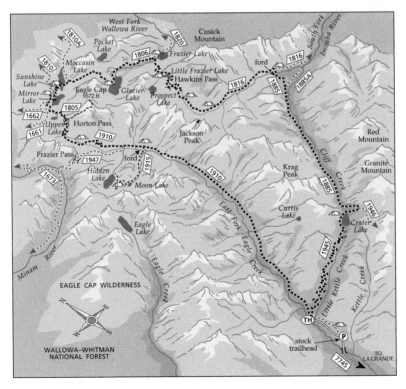

of 9,572-foot Eagle Cap Peak. Cumulative elevation gain is about 7,000 feet, as the trip scales three mountain passes for a top-to-bottom wilderness experience.

This is a "backdoor" route that avoids the most popular accesses to the popular high-lakes area. For ease in identification, many of the recommended camping areas described below are near lakes. Please be aware the Forest Service enforces a regulation that prohibits camping within 100 feet of any lake within the wilderness and restricts campfires at the most popular lakes. Do your share in minimizing the heavy impact around these fragile lakes by considering the many choice campsites along creeks and ridges.

From La Grande, Oregon, the winding 63-mile, 2-hour drive to the trailhead is as follows: Drive south on State Highway 30/203 to Union. Continue south on 203 about 20 miles to a spot on the map called Medical Springs. Bear left toward Boulder Park. Go 1.7 miles and bear left onto Forest Road 67 toward Eagle Creek. Go 14 miles and continue straight onto Forest Road 77 (toward Richland). Go 6.5 miles, passing Tamarack Campground, and turn left onto Road 7745 (East Fork Eagle Creek). Drive 6 miles to the trailhead for large vehicles and trailers or continue to the more limited parking area a short way farther at the main trailhead.

Walk north on Trail 1910 up East Fork Eagle Creek through a deep valley once filled with a 13-mile long glacier. The trail gains 1,600 feet of elevation moderately but steadily in the 6.5 miles to the junction with Trail 1915 to Hidden Lake. Water is abundant, but campsites are few among the granite boulders strewn about the valley. Choice spots for a first night camp are in the hanging valley holding Moon and Hidden Lakes. But you have to be game for fording the East Fork and adding an additional 2 miles and 955 feet in elevation gain to reach Hidden Lake. (Note: Elevation profile does not include this spur.) Like many of the waters nestled in the bowls among the Wallowa Mountains, this lake can offer good trout fishing.

Hawkins Pass, Eagle Cap Wilderness

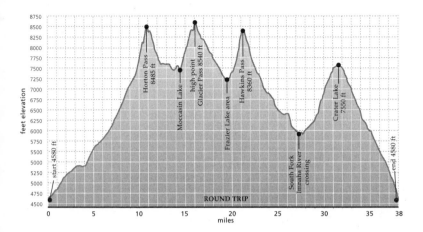

From this junction with the Hidden Lake Trail, it's still another 4.3 miles up the East Fork Eagle Creek Trail to Horton Pass, elev. 8,485 feet. A campsite can be found farther up Trail 1910 at the junction with Frazier Pass Trail 1947. Consider staying two days here and day hiking over Frazier Pass to Minam Lake and back. Several more campsites can be found up the East Fork Eagle Creek valley where the trail gets steeper as it makes the last push toward the rocky apex of Horton Pass. Depending on snow conditions, the Frazier Pass-Minam Lake route to the Lakes Basin could be the best option to avoid snowfields that can linger all summer long on the east side of Horton Pass. Horton Pass is the preferred route, however, for the views and because it offers convenient access to the summit of the wilderness namesake. A trail heads up from the pass and eventually intersects on the ridge with the main trail to the summit of Eagle Cap.

To continue the Lakes Basin Loop, drop down the east side of Horton Pass, taking precautions to avoid slipping if there are snowfields, and head into the Lostine River Valley. Continue past the junction with Trail 1805, the main route to the top of Eagle Cap. After nearly 1.5 miles from Horton Pass, bear right onto Lakes Basin Trail 1810 and drop into the area around Upper, Mirror, and Moccasin Lakes. The Lakes Basin is a 2-by-4-mile plateau dotted with lakes, tarns, and countless campsites, including many good ones that are away from the main lakes. It's a perfect area for a layover day, exploratory hikes, or another crack at the summit of Eagle Cap (see "Options" in Hike 89). A dozen lakes could be explored in a long day. Moccasin and Mirror are the most popular, but others are scenic and less congested.

To continue the loop, follow Trail 1806 southeast from Moccasin Lake, elev. 7,473 feet. The trail heads 3 miles to Glacier Lake and into the West Fork Wallowa River drainage. But first, the trail goes over the highest point of the loop, Glacier Pass, elev. 8,540 feet. Just south of the pass, Glacier Lake, elev. 8,166 feet, makes a stunning lunch stop with Glacier Peak looming above. It's also a good camp area in hospitable weather, but an exposed and nasty spot when wind and temperatures turn foul. From here, the trail goes another easy and scenic 3 miles to protected campsites at Frazier Lake, elev. 7,127 feet. While hiking between Glacier and Frazier Lakes, listen for a waterfall.

From Frazier Lake, head south on Trail 1820 and begin the 1,260-foot climb in 2.2 miles to Hawkins Pass, elev. 8,360 feet. The drop into the South Fork Imnaha Valley is one of the most spectacular on the loop, an observation you will find hard to believe during the first few days of the trip. A crystalline mountain on the shoulder of Hawkins Pass and a great glacier cirque filled with wildflowers in summer and ablaze with fall colors in September are sights to behold. Scramble up ridgelines from the pass for climbing options and even better views. Continue down the valley to clearings just north of the confluence of Cliff Creek and the South Fork, where you might call it quits for the day 7.5 miles from Frazier Lake. Beware of overly friendly deer.

From here, the route heads across the South Fork Imnaha River (the bridge has been known to wash out) and southwest on Trail 1885, which climbs 1,500 feet in the 4.5 miles to Crater Lake. The trail leads into deep woods of lodgepole pine and past a few giant larch along Cliff Creek, where camping spots are not so common. Good fishing might make it worthwhile to camp at Crater Lake, even though the lake was shored up decades ago by machinery for irrigation storage and is not pristine.

In hot summer weather, it's best to finish the loop in the cooler morning hours. Head west from the west side of Crater Lake on Trail 1945 and begin the 3,100-foot plunge down Little Kettle Creek. This dry, dusty 6.5-mile descent could be the most grueling part of the trip. After a numbing blur of switchbacks and about four distinct climate zones, the trail leads to the trailheads in familiar territory of the East Fork Eagle Creek valley.

91 | ECHO LAKE

Location: Wallowa Mountains
Status: Eagle Cap Wilderness
Distance: 10 miles round trip
Hiking time: 5 hours or overnight
Difficulty: Moderate
Season: Early July through September
Maps: USGS Bennet Peak, Steamboat Lake
Information: Wallowa Mountains Visitor Center

The climb into the rocky Echo Lake alpine basin only whets your appetite for further exploration into a less heavily used high-country area of the Eagle Cap Wilderness. Note that this is *not* the Echo Lake farther northeast

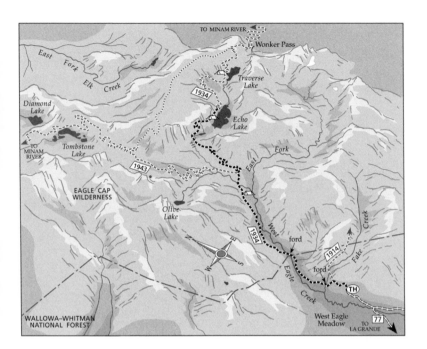

that is reached up from Hurricane Creek by one of the steepest trails in the wilderness.

From La Grande, Oregon, drive south on State Highway 30/203 to Union. Continue south on 203 about 14 miles and turn left (east) onto Forest Road 77 toward West Eagle Meadows. Go 15 winding miles to West Eagle Trailhead. The last 5 miles of Road 77 are rough and rocky, but usually passable for passenger vehicles at slow speeds.

The hike starts gently on Trail 1934, eventually going through old-growth and fording Fake Creek and West Eagle Creek—a potential problem early in the season. The trail improves at the wilderness boundary. Campsites are found around 2 miles, thoughtfully situated just before the trail starts the first of many switchbacks. Pass the junction with Trail 1943 (a branch worth exploring for a good view of what you'll soon hear) and

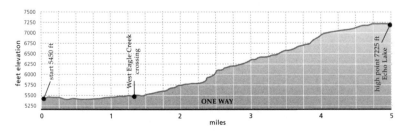

Traverse Lake from Echo Lake scrambling loop route

continue up through granite boulders. Listen for a hidden waterfall. Near the top of the 1,775-foot elevation gain to Echo Lake, follow the sound and walk over the rocks to see the creek just before it begins tumbling down the slope. From here, the trail leads a short way farther to campsites at Echo Lake.

Echo and its neighbor Traverse Lake are natural lakes that were shored up into larger irrigation reservoirs with dams built before the Eagle Cap was declared a wilderness in 1940. Traverse in particular has a decidedly man-made look as the water level draws down.

Options: No hiker with an ounce of energy left would come this far without continuing up the trail 1.7 miles, passing Traverse Lake, to Wonker Pass, elev. 8,500 feet, for a stunning view of the rugged Eagle Cap interior and the who's who of the wilderness peaks.

• Scramblers can follow just south of the ridge heading west from Wonker Pass to the bouldered summit of an unnamed 8,934-foot point that looms above Echo Lake. Backtrack or make a rugged but lovely 13-mile loop by boulder-hopping down from the summit's west side to Trail 1943 and making a mettle-testing trek down and back up to Echo Lake.

• For a 35-mile loop, backpack to Echo, over Wonker Pass, descend (passing yet another option for a loop in the Heart Lake area), and follow the Minam River downstream to Trail 1944, which leads up to Tombstone Lake. After climbing out of Tombstone's basin, it's a relatively easy, mostly downhill day full of switchbacks on Trail 1943 to West Eagle Trailhead.

92 | IMNAHA RIVER CANYON

Location: Snake River
Status: Hells Canyon National Recreation Area
Distance: 10 miles round trip
Hiking time: 5 hours or overnight
Difficulty: Easy
Season: Virtually year-round
Maps: USGS Cactus Mt., Deadhorse Ridge
Information: Wallowa Mountains Visitor Center

"Eureka!" say the hikers looking for a nifty early- or late-season hike. A trail along the lower Imnaha River leads 5 gentle miles through a narrow, rocky canyon to Eureka Bar on the Snake River. On this site in Hells Canyon, where gold miners once toiled, hikers might be wearing shorts (if only until sundown) and sniffing wildflowers as early as March.

From the city center of Joseph, Oregon, drive east 30 miles to the town of Imnaha. Cross the river and turn downstream on Lower Imnaha Road. After 6 miles, the pavement ends. Cross the river again and turn right onto Dug Bar Road 4260, which leads a rough and slow 14 miles downstream to the trailhead just before crossing Cow Creek Bridge. The surface is rock

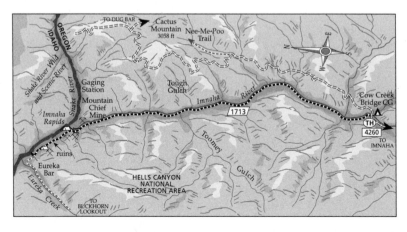

and clay, making the road best suited to four-wheel-drive vehicles, especially in rainy weather.

Drivers might have trouble taking their eyes off the road, but passengers should keep watch on the hillsides for critters such as chukar partridges, mule deer, elk, and bighorn sheep. Weather drives the activity here among wildlife and hikers alike. Virtually nothing moves once the sun bears down in the stifling heat of summer.

Trail 1713 follows the north side of the river downstream, starting at elev. 1,140 feet and easing into a narrowing slot of jagged rocks. The trail was blasted and built by the Civilian Conservation Corps in the 1930s. It stays pretty much at river level, except for a half dozen minor rises. Unruly blackberry vines might reach out to scratch passersby, and be alert for poison ivy. Expect to see a few steelhead anglers along the trail from late fall through early April. Rattlesnakes could be seen in warm weather.

Near the confluence of the Imnaha and the Snake, the openings of a few mine tunnels still stand agape. Across the Imnaha is an opening to the Mountain Chief Mine tunnel, which runs 740 feet through the ridge to an opening on the Snake River side. Townsend's big-eared bats winter in the tunnel.

The trail continues down the Snake on a broad open flat and ends 1 mile downstream at Eureka Bar, elev. 958 feet. In this area, you will see foundations remaining from a settlement, including a hotel and other buildings that supported the Eureka Bar Mine. The activity peaked around 1903 and went bust soon after. As with so many such ventures, investors realized mining the marginal deposits was not economically viable in this remote niche of wilderness. Valuable lumber from the buildings was scavenged by ranchers. Stone terraces of the mill foundation are still in the hillside. What was left of the mill beams was eventually taken by the Forest Service to build bridges.

Campsites are easy to find among the cheatgrass and prickly-pear cactus

Eureka Bar at mouth of Imnaha River in Hells Canyon

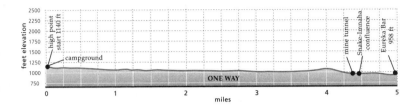

from the confluence downstream. Driftwood is sometimes available, but check wilderness rules for strict regulations regarding fires in Hells Canyon. Visitors obviously have been exploring portions of tunnels that haven't been sealed, but Forest Service officials make no official claim that the tunnels are safe.

Options: From the end of the trail, continue up Eureka Creek as far as your legs and lungs will allow, or all the way up 4,300 feet to the Buckhorn fire lookout site, elev. 5,330 feet.

•From the trailhead, cross Cow Creek Bridge over the Imnaha and continue on Dug Bar Road a few miles to the trailhead for the Nee-Me-Poo National Historic Trail. There's a spiritual sense to hiking this 5-mile route over Lone Pine Saddle and down to the Snake at Dug Bar, save for the cattle trails that make the route hard to find in places. Walk in the footsteps of Chief Joseph and about 700 Nez Perce as they began their 1,800-mile flight from the U.S. Army. About 400 Nez Perce men, women, and children safely crossed the Snake at Dug Bar during their journey, although many of their 1,000 horses and cattle perished.

93 | SNAKE RIVER–KIRKWOOD RANCH

Location: Snake River
Status: Hells Canyon National Recreation Area
Distance: 10.4 miles round trip
Hiking time: 5 hours or overnight
Difficulty: Moderate
Season: March through November
Maps: USGS Kirkwood Creek, Temperance Creek
Information: Hells Canyon National Recreation Area,
    Riggins Office

Especially in the premier months of April and May, no place in Hells Canyon of the Snake River packs so much great hiking, scenery, and history into a small package as Trail 102. The section of the trail featured here heads up the Idaho side of the Snake from Upper Pittsburg Landing to the Kirkwood Living History Ranch. But come prepared with water or means of purification. No potable water is available, not even at the trailhead camping area.

From Grangeville, Idaho, drive south on U.S. Highway 95. At 1.2 miles south of Whitebird Junction, turn west toward Hammer Creek Recreation Area. Cross the Salmon River and turn left toward Pittsburg Landing on Deer Creek Road 493. Drive nearly 17 slow, windy miles (chains recommended when snowy or icy; good brakes required any time of year) over Pittsburg Saddle and down to the Pittsburg Landing area on the Snake River. At the paved junction, turn left toward the Upper Landing and drive 1.7 miles, passing the stock trailhead, to the small campground and hiker trailhead at the end of the road. Read information here regarding strict regulations on campfires.

Trail 102 is a beautifully constructed National Recreation Trail shored up by rock walls and blasted in some places out of basalt cliffs. It runs along and above the Snake, sometimes twisting away into draws and over benches of hackberry trees and bunchgrass away from the roar of the river,

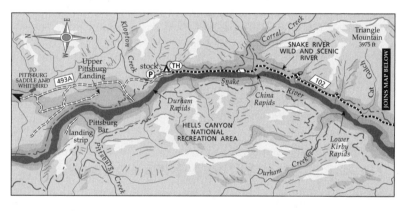

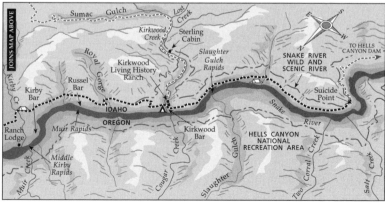

Snake River from Suicide Point in Hells Canyon

where the cascading calls of canyon wrens and other birds can be appreciated in breathless quiet.

Also listen for rattlesnakes, although your heart is more likely to get a jolt from the occasional surprise of flushing chukar partridges. Keep an eye out for poison ivy, especially in the draws. During winter and spring, poison ivy has no "leaves of three." However, clusters of small white berries on the bare woody vines give away its potential to inflict rashes even without its greenery.

The trail starts with a couple of fairly sharp ups and downs to test your leg strength and footwork (note a possible campsite when you get beyond the first cliff section, and check out China Rapids below after gaining some altitude), but from there on the climbs are brief or relatively gentle. The exception is the sharp switchbacking pitch about 5 miles into the hike down to Kirkwood Ranch historical site. Still, with an elevation loss of 300 feet, it's not *that* bad.

Walnut trees at the ranch are a testimony to the canyon's warm climate. Although snow falls here occasionally, it rarely stays long. In summer, the heat can be, well, hellish. Fall is a pleasant time here, sans the blooming balsamroot, shooting stars, phlox, wild hyacinth, prickly-pear cactus, serviceberry, and other flowers that bring joy to a hiker's heart in spring. But the firelike orange of the sumac and other autumn colors maintain the eye appeal.

The Kirkwood Campground extends for a couple hundred yards along

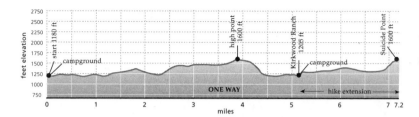

the river, complete with picnic tables and two flush toilets. The site's greenery and spaciousness makes it popular with visitors from jet boat tours to Boy Scout troops. But even the ranch hosts get their water from the creek and treat it for consumption.

At Kirkwood Ranch, formerly a home to cattle and sheep operations, check out:

• Kirkwood Creek, which could hold a few spawning steelhead for viewing from mid-April well into May.

• Jordan House, a ranch house built in 1925. An extension was added during the Depression by Leonard and Grace Jordan, who left the place in 1943 as Len went on to become Idaho's governor and later, a U.S. senator. The extension he built to the house included the first real bathtub in Hells Canyon. The place was purchased by the Forest Service in 1973 and is occupied year-round by Historic Ranch hosts and volunteers.

• Sterling Cabin, a beautifully constructed bunkhouse built in 1952, now serves as a museum with exhibits of prehistoric artifacts, plant specimens, photos, mining equipment, and more.

• Carson Mansion, just up the creek 0.7 mile, was once the finest in Hells Canyon. Now it's the decaying and fetid bastion of mice, bats, and packrats. Behind the outhouse is a pit into an ash deposit from the eruption of Mount Mazama (now Crater Lake, Oregon) some 6,700 years ago. The pit was first excavated by the homesteaders, who used the ash for various purposes, including whitewash for the ranchhouse kitchen.

Options: This hike can be extended another 21 miles upstream to Granite Creek.

• Numerous day hikes up creeks and along ridges can be made from the ranch. Ask hosts for tips on routes and archeological sites.

• The must-do extension continues about 2 miles upriver, gaining 300 feet in elevation to a tummy-churning overlook nearly that high above the river called Suicide Point. A legend tells of two lovers who came to this spot in despair as Native American versions of Romeo and Juliet. Forbidden from union because they were from different tribes, the story goes, the lovers tied their braids together and leaped off this cliff.

• Some groups book rides with Lewiston (Idaho)-based jet boat services from Lower Pittsburg Landing to the Kirkwood area so they can hike—or run—back to the trailhead. Jet boats can reach this area even when snow prevents road access over Pittsburg Saddle.

94

GWILLIM LAKES

Location: Slocan Lake
Status: Valhalla Provincial Park
Distance: 6.8 miles round trip
Hiking time: 5 hours or overnight
Difficulty: Moderate
Season: Late June to mid-October
Maps: Burton 82 F/13 or Slocan 82 F/NW
Information: British Columbia Parks, Nelson Office

For lovers of towering granite peaks and rock-gouging glaciers, this is a particularly scenic hike high into British Columbia's Valhalla Provincial Park. Hikers must see this place to believe it—124,000 acres with no roads and only six trails penetrating into the boundaries. This is grizzly country and no pets are allowed.

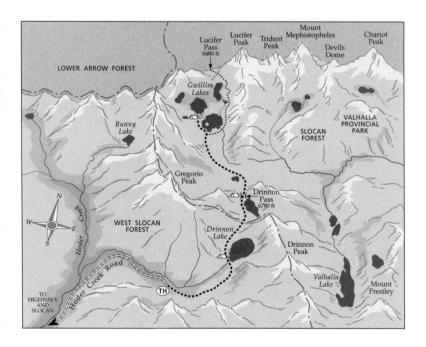

Drinnon Peak from Drinnon Pass,
Valhalla Provincial Park

From the Playmor junction with Highway 3A between Castlegar and Nelson, British Columbia, drive 27 miles north on Highway 6. About 0.3 mile south of the turnoff to Slocan, turn west at the street lamp onto Gravel Pit Road. (Note the kilometer marker at the first intersection on Gravel Pit Road is 2. Markers progress 1 kilometer at a time.) Cross the Slocan River; continue straight up the hill, crossing Gwillim Creek and stay left on the Little Slocan Forest Service Road. Pass Bannock Burn Road at K-marker 15 (see Hike 95). Just past K-marker 22, near the tiny campground at Upper Little Slocan Lake, bear right onto Hoder Creek Road, where the K-markers start at zero. (The route is marked with "Valhalla" signs, but sometimes the signs disappear at logging roads that sprout up here faster than knapweed in a meadow.) Near K-6, stay left at the fork. Near K-7, go straight, following the creek rather than any of the new logging roads going up the sides of the valley. Past K-10, bear right to the trailhead. The last portion of this road can be rough.

From elev. 5,300 feet, begin climbing the well-graded trail to Drinnon Lake. This alpine lake is above timberline and clearcuts and holds trout known to rise to a Royal Wulff or Black Gnat. Around the west or left side of Drinnon Lake the trail wanders, climbing somewhat to Drinnon Pass. A few small alpine tarns and campsites exist around the pass area and excellent vistas of the peaks behind Gwillim Lakes and Gregorio Peak to the west invite the mountaineer. This is some of the best scenery in North America. Beyond Drinnon Pass, the trail, which was first cut by the Kootenay Mountaineers in 1980, descends about 400 feet in elevation to a small lake set in a wet, green meadow. Snow can linger on the trail through July. After a short, relatively flat stretch, the trail begins an ascent toward the first of four Gwillim Lakes at elev. 7,150 feet. The surrounding valley of Gwillim Creek unfolds as all the peaks you might want to climb become sentinels on the horizon. Summits with names such as Black Prince, Lucifer, Devils Couch, Mount Bor, and Mephistopheles conjure up stories of ancient history.

Tread lightly around Gwillim Lakes as the area is fragile and footprints

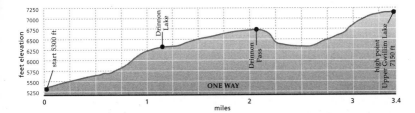

will be seen for years. No open fires are allowed in this area. Camping is limited to designated tent pads at Gwillim Lakes. Park rules require campers to use the separate cooking area and food caches at Drinnon and Gwillim Lakes to avoid attracting black bears and grizzlies.

Options: This is open alpine country. Continue up and beyond wherever your skills allow and your heart desires. An easy goal would be the upper Gwillim Lakes Basin. A tougher scramble for even better views continues up to the pass on the west side of Lucifer Peak.

95 | GIMLI RIDGE-MULVEY BASIN

Location: Slocan Lake
Status: Unprotected
Distance: 5 miles round trip
Hiking time: 4–7 hours or overnight
Difficulty: Moderately difficult
Season: Late June to mid-October
Maps: Burton 82 F/13 or Slocan 82 F/NW
Information: British Columbia Parks, Nelson Office

No pain, no elevation gain on this trail, which climbs 2,000 feet in about 2 miles to one of the most eye-pleasing alpine areas at the edge of Valhalla Provincial Park.

From the junction with Highway 3A between Castlegar and Nelson, British Columbia, drive 27 miles north on Highway 6. About 0.3 mile south

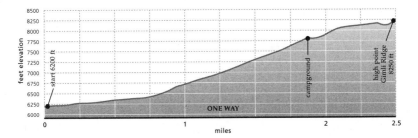

of the turnoff to Slocan, turn west at the street lamp onto Gravel Pit Road. (Note the marker at the first intersection on Gravel Pit Road is 2. Markers progress by kilometers.) Cross the Slocan River and continue straight up the hill; cross Gwillim Creek and stay left on Little Slocan Forest Service Road. Beware of logging trucks. At kilometer-marker 15 (7.8 miles), turn right onto Bannock Burn Road. (See Hike 94 for another nearby option.) Go 3 miles to a Y at K-marker 5 and bear right. The road gets steeper from here with waterbars that become progressively more severe. The road may be suitable only for vehicles with high clearance. At the first major switchback, continue straight. At nearly 7 miles, turn right and up at a switchback. At about 8 miles, turn left at a switchback and drive 0.2 mile toward the trailhead.

Look upward to the north at the towering granite wall of Mount Gimli, elev. 9,206 feet, or look west for impressive views of Mount Prestley and other alpine features of the 124,000-acre Valhalla Provincial Park. This is a

mere sampling of the eye candy that rewards hikers who endure a steep but good trail leading above tree line to haunts that marmots and climbers once had all to themselves. The trail, mostly completed in 1995, is one of the few maintained routes to the spine of the Valhalla Range in the Selkirk Mountains, although it's not officially within the park.

The hike begins around 6,200 feet in an old clearcut, crosses a footbridge, and then heads steadily uphill for more than a mile before breaking above tree line. Cairns mark the way toward the base of Gimli spire, along a treeless ridge, through an alpine meadow, and angling up and across a snowfield that can hold snow year-round. Be careful kicking steps. At the top of the snowfield is a broad gravelly area where campers can avoid impact on fragile alpine heather and plants. An unsheltered green latrine is on the west side of the ridge.

Snowfield playground below Gimli Peak

Continuing over to the ridge west of Gimli requires scrambling on loose rock. Walk up through the scree and angle toward the base of

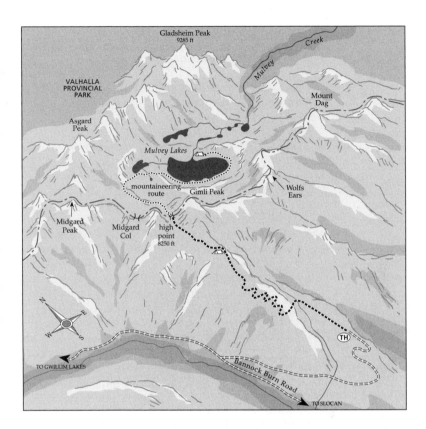

Gimli's vertical southwest face. A faint trail then leads up through talus to a col at elev. 8,250 feet on the west side of Gimli. Enjoy an impressive and precipitous view down 700 feet into Mulvey Basin, where ice can remain in lakes well into August.

Mulvey Lakes sit in an amphitheater below rock spires that tantalize climbers—Mount Dag, Wolfs Ears, Gimli, Midgard, and Asgard, all towering around 8,600 feet, plus Gladsheim, the park's tallest peak at 9,285 feet. Depending on the snow depth on the north side of the col, getting off the rocky ridge can be scary or downright risky, requiring an ice ax, rope, and perhaps crampons. With a lot of soft snow, it's sometimes possible to angle west off the ridge onto the snowfield and down to the lakes, although there could be a dangerous gap between the rock cliff and snow. Proceed only if you've practiced the skills.

Mosquitoes can be thick anywhere in Valhalla high-country, and the local horseflies are on steroids. This is grizzly country. Keep your camp clean and don't sleep near food or the cooking area. Check park rules. No dogs are allowed.

96

KOKANEE GLACIER

Location: Canadian Selkirk Mountains
Status: Kokanee Glacier Provincial Park
Distance: 12 miles round trip
Hiking time: 9 hours or overnight
Difficulty: Moderate
Season: July through early October
Maps: Slocan 82 F/14 and Kokanee Peak 82 F/11
Information: British Columbia Parks, Nelson Office

This is a must-do hike to become acquainted with the best of Kokanee Glacier Provincial Park, one of the oldest designated provincial parks in British Columbia. The following hike leads to historic Slocan Chief Cabin, the newer Kokanee Glacier Cabin, and camping sites in the grizzly bear country and alpine meadows near the park's namesake glacier. The popular area offers many side trips, including an easy climb to 8,500 feet above the glacier for those who bring in glacier-travel gear. Kokanee Peak and the park's highest mountain, Cond Peak, elev. 9,200 feet, loom above the glacier.

Porcupine alert: For some still unexplained reason, the porcupines at Kokanee Glacier Park trailheads, especially at Gibson Lake, have become notorious for gnawing on brake linings, electrical wiring, and even tires of parked vehicles. The nuisance is cyclical, becoming worse in some years, but it's been going on for decades with grim results for victims. Veteran Kokanee hikers bring a roll of chicken wire long enough to go completely around their vehicle for protection while it's parked—a small but wise investment.

From Nelson, head northeast on Highway 3A about 12 miles. After

Trail near Kokanee Lake (photo by Robert J. Shaer)

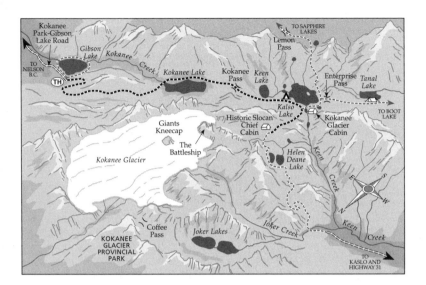

passing Redfish and Sandspit Campgrounds, watch for the sign indicating Kokanee Park/Gibson Lake Road, which makes a hairpin turn to the left. Follow this gravel road 9.5 miles to the parking area, where there's a 1.5-mile loop trail and picnic shelter at Gibson Lake, elev. 5,050 feet. No camping is allowed at Gibson Lake. Cutthroat or rainbow trout are stocked in lakes such as Gibson, Kaslo, Kokanee, and Helen Deane, although they tend to be small.

This trail up to Kokanee Glacier is the most heavily used in the park, even though the cumulative elevation gain is a lung-taxing 2,500 feet. It climbs steeply and crosses several creeks for the first mile. About 2 miles from the parking lot, the trail contours across a flower-filled open slope before reaching Kokanee Lake, which is nearly 300 feet deep. This is a photogenic and popular lunch stop. Follow the trail above the lake around its western shore and on up to 6,700-foot Kokanee Pass. Continue down and past Keen Lake to the designated camping area between Garland and Kaslo Lakes. Farther up the trail at the north end of Kaslo Lake is the Kokanee Glacier Cabin, built starting in 2002. During the summer season, up to 20 hikers can sleep in the cabin and use the propane cooking facilities on a first-come, first-served basis. The ranger's residence is nearby, and so are the designated camping sites. Bring Canadian currency to pay fees charged for the cabin and for camping. Other designated camping areas in the park core are at Sapphire and Tanal Lakes. Food caches for bear safety are installed at these sites.

To continue to the glacier, walk eastward from Kaslo Lake, up and over a low shoulder. After a short descent, the trail leads into the park core with its impressive view of Kokanee Glacier and the rocky spine known as the Battleship. Slocan Chief Cabin, built by miners in 1896, sits on a hump and is retired from decades of housing park visitors. It was transformed into a

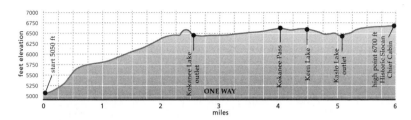

historic site in 2002, and camping here has been curtailed. Steep but short trails lead up to the glacier. The trek to nearby Helen Deane Lake is well worth the effort.

Options: Take the 0.5-mile side trip from the north end of Kaslo Lake to Enterprise Pass for another good view of the glacier.

• Hikers with an extra day can continue on the marked route from Enterprise Pass up to Lemon Pass and Sapphire Lakes, where snow can linger through July.

• An alternate and less-traveled route to Kokanee Glacier comes in from the north via Keen Creek and the Joker Mill site. This can be a shorter trail, 6 miles round trip, but steeper and less scenic. Elevation gain is 1,900 feet. Unfortunately, the road is prone to washouts, and it's likely that you would have to tag on another 4.5 miles of road walking (each way) starting at Desmond Creek in order to reach the trailhead. Also, this trail is closed from mid-August to early October because of grizzly bear activity. From Kaslo, British Columbia, drive 4.5 miles east on Highway 31A toward New Denver and turn left on South Fork Kaslo Creek Road. Bear left at a fork about 8 miles up.

• Kokanee Glacier is also accessible from the northwest via Highway 16 and Slocan City. Hike up Enterprise Creek Trail and past Tanal Lake about 6 miles to Slocan Chief Cabin.

97 | SILVER SPRAY-WOODBURY BASIN

Location: Canadian Selkirk Mountains
Status: Kokanee Glacier Provincial Park
Distance: 8, 10, or 14 miles round trip
Hiking time: 8 hours or overnight
Difficulty: Moderate to difficult
Season: Early July through early October
Maps: Slocan 82 F/NW or 82 F/14
Information: British Columbia Parks, Nelson Office

No getting around it, the hike to the historic Silver Spray Mine and hikers' cabin is a groaner that gains 3,400 feet in elevation in 4 miles. But the

Woodbury Glacier, Kokanee Glacier Provincial Park

roaming opportunities and views of jagged peaks in the Kokanee Glacier Provincial Park area of the Canadian Selkirks is worth the sweat. Besides, miners once made the trek laden with picks, shovels, and beans—and the beans weren't freeze-dried, either. Modern hikers have more time than the miners to appreciate the scenery, such as the scattered alpine larch that light up with gold needles in late September. The trailhead for this hike also offers three other options important to consider up front:

• Try a 3.5-mile round-trip hike to Sunset Lake (name sounds prettier than it is) from the Scranton Mine Road Trailhead, which is just before the Silver Spray-Woodbury Trailhead.

• Consider a slightly longer but easier hike and a little less elevation gain to Woodbury Cabin, with another scenic setting and one of the continent's best views from an outhouse.

• Link the Silver Spray and Woodbury Basin Trails with a high cross-country traverse to make a difficult but sensational hut-to-hut loop of nearly 15 miles.

From Nelson, British Columbia, follow Highway 3A northeast to Balfour, bearing north onto Highway 31 to Ainsworth Hot Springs, a total of nearly 29 miles. (The hot springs provide a soothing side trip after the hike, although the aquatic center in Nelson has an impressive pool, hot tubs, and water slide for a fraction of the cost.) From Ainsworth, continue 5.5 miles and turn west on the Woodbury Creek access road. This gravel road is steep at its beginning and can at times be dangerously icy or muddy. From the highway, drive 0.7 mile and stay left at a junction. Go another 0.8 mile to a three-way junction. Continue straight toward Kokanee Glacier

Park about 5.8 miles and turn right (left goes toward Sunset Lake). Park here, or go a rough 0.8 mile to the trailhead, elev. 4,400 feet. (See "Porcupine alert" in Hike 96.)

Start on a good path that was originally constructed in the 1920s to service lead and silver mines. Follow the trail nearly 1 mile to the remains of a miner's cabin and a junction. Bear left here to continue toward Woodbury Cabin or go right to Silver Spray Cabin.

Silver Spray: For a hike to remember, turn right (north) here and get into low gear for a steep climb. It takes about an hour to chug up 1 mile to another old cabin site and, just beyond, a crossing of Silver Spray Creek. This is a good place for a rest. In late August, a feast of huckleberries can be found. The trail soon breaks out of thick woods into an open, flower-covered subalpine forest, up past the remains of yet another old cabin site and into Clover Basin. Crossing open meadows, small brooks, and rock outcroppings below Sunrise Mountain, the trail continues up the ridge before topping the rise and terminating at Silver Spray Cabin, elev. 7,850 feet.

Silver Spray is a 1920-vintage high-elevation mine. Because of its backcountry location, little was salvaged from the mine when it closed. Unfortunately, visitors have absconded with a lot of the history, much of the theft occurring between 1980–2000. The original cabin was the bunkhouse for the Violet Mine, offering shelter to the miners who hacked away at the surrounding peaks. A new cabin for hikers was built in 1994, but the old stable continues to be used for storage. The area is open and ripe for scrambling. For a worthwhile side trip, follow the route up the rocky hillside above the cabin to the old mine site at the pass between Sunrise Mountain and Mount McQuarrie. The remains of the blacksmith shop are near the collapsed mine tunnel.

Woodbury Cabin: From the junction 1 mile in from the trailhead, the route leading to Woodbury Cabin is sometimes crude but gentler than the Silver Spray Trail, gaining more than 2,200 feet in 5 miles. Travel through a luxuriant forest cut by numerous open avalanche paths into the subalpine basin below Woodbury Glacier. The semi-open forest, with its abundance

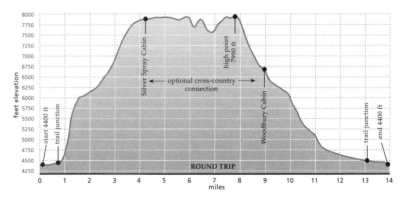

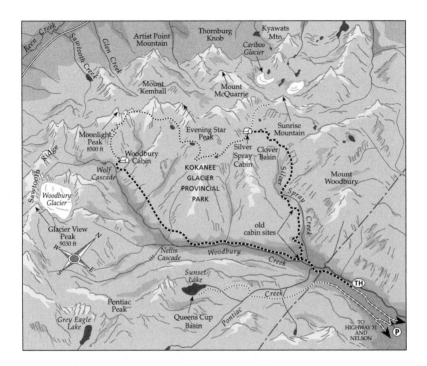

of food and cover, makes the valley an ideal refuge for both black and grizzly bears. In the first mile from the junction, the Woodbury Creek Trail is disrupted by muddy and rocky sections remaining from modern mining in the early 1970s. Depending on trail maintenance, this can be slow or a breeze. Beyond this poor section, the next 1.5 miles up the valley is pleasant. The last half of the route is somewhat steeper.

Woodbury Creek Basin nestles on the eastern flank of the rugged Sawtooth Ridge—watch for mountain goats—while the Woodbury Glacier sprawls down the side of Glacier View Peak to the south. Just below the basin, Wolf Cascade tumbles down the headwall. The trail continues above the basin to the Woodbury Cabin, a stone and wood-frame chalet built in 1985. Additional tent pads are situated around the cabin. Rambling from the cabin area is not as open and easy as from Silver Spray, but several unmaintained mining trails continue above the hut toward several summits, which offer spectacular views of Kokanee Glacier to the south and high peaks of the Selkirks and Purcells to the north and northeast. Only trained visitors with proper equipment—ropes, ice axes, and crampons—should attempt crossing Woodbury Glacier.

Cabins: British Columbia Parks maintains both cabins and a reasonable fee is charged for overnighters. Bring Canadian currency for the collection boxes. The Woodbury Cabin sleeps eight and the Silver Spray Cabin sleeps

10. Both are available on a first-come, first-served basis. A cabin register at the trailhead helps visitors gauge availability. Wood, rare and precious at this elevation, is provided for heating at Woodbury. Both cabins have propane cooking stoves and lights, but no cooking utensils. Sleeping mats may or may not be provided. Campfires and pets are not allowed beyond the trailhead.

Options: In good weather, hikers who know how to navigate with map and compass or GPS can traverse nearly 4 miles in either direction between the two cabins to make a loop. The route is almost entirely above tree line. An ice ax could be required for a few short stretches until mid-August. The route is penciled in on maps on the walls of each cabin. Roughly, here's how it goes:

From Woodbury Cabin, switchback up the basin behind the cabin on the miner's trail. Traverse north around the base of Moonlight Peak and follow the contours as they turn northeast at around elev. 8,000 feet. Drop down and around an alpine tarn, contouring southeast around a ridge. Drop down and along the north side of another tarn. Climb around the southeast ridge of Evening Star Peak and then around along tarns on the east face of Evening Star. Now head northeast along the east side of a ridge and work your way in that direction to Silver Spray Cabin.

98 | EARL GREY PASS TRAVERSE

Location: Purcell Mountains
Status: Purcell Wilderness Conservancy
Distance: 36.5 miles one way
Hiking time: 4–5 days
Difficulty: Difficult
Season: July through September
Maps: Lardeau, 82 K/SE or 82 K, plus 82 K/2, 82 K/7, 82 K/8
Information: British Columbia Parks, Nelson Office

A multi-day in-and-out hike to Earl Grey Pass will capture most of what this trail has to offer—and that's considerable. But hikers who can organize two groups coming from east and west to take the sting out of a long vehicle shuttle should consider the entire Earl Grey Pass Traverse, a centuries-old route over the glacier-laden Purcell Mountains. Either way, the trek covers some of the best Canada has to offer, from dark old-growth hemlock and cedar forest along Hamill Creek, past moose meadows and waterfalls, to ragged ice-capped peaks surrounding 7,500-foot Earl Grey Pass. Hand-operated cable cars help with five major stream crossings, but many smaller crossings must be forded or crossed on logs. The area has the region's richest concentration of grizzly bears.

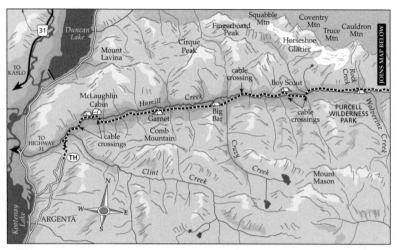

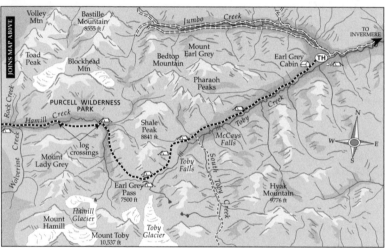

On a 1908 sightseeing visit to British Columbia, this Shuswap Indian route was used by Earl Grey, Canada's governor general from 1904 to 1911. Hikers approach Earl Grey Pass from both the Kaslo (west) and Invermere (east) sides, but few make the entire traverse because of the 287-mile shuttle between trailheads. In other words, roads over the Purcells are scarce. So are trails.

Canada topos 82 K/2, 82 K/7, 82 K/8 are helpful, although the trail along Hamill Creek may not be indicated. The trail is shown with limited accuracy on the less detailed 82 K/SE if you can find it, but not on the 82 K. Hike this trail in small groups, since most campsites in the mid-portion of

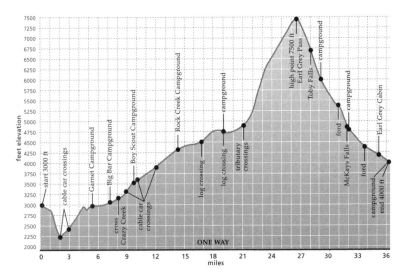

the route accommodate only one or two tents comfortably. At least three hikers are recommended for travel in grizzly country and assisting at creek crossings. Five is an ideal number.

West trailhead: This is the recommended side to start the traverse as well as for in-and-out hikes. (The ancient forest along lower Hamill Creek makes a good day hike even in spring and late fall when the high country is snowed in.) From Kaslo, British Columbia, head north on Highway 31. Pass through tiny Lardeau and drive 3.7 miles before turning right toward Argenta. Cross the bridge over Duncan River and turn right toward Argenta and Johnson's Landing. Go about 2.5 miles on gravel and turn left through the scattered village of Argenta (watch for a small Earl Grey Pass sign). Go by the post office, driving 2.6 miles to the trailhead at a sharp right turn in the logging road.

East trailhead: From Invermere, British Columbia, drive 11 miles to Panorama Ski Resort. Pass the resort on the right (north side) of Toby Creek, where the road turns to gravel, and drive about 12 miles toward the Mineral King mine site. Just past the road to Jumbo Pass (see Hike 99) and the bridge over Jumbo Creek, turn left into a primitive campsite and trailhead parking area at the confluence of Jumbo and Toby Creeks.

Starting from the west side, the trail descends about 700 feet and intersects an early 1900s mining road that headed a short way up the Hamill Creek drainage. Remnants of the log roadbed over bogs are still evident in places. Cross Clint Creek and walk to the first of five cable-car crossings over Hamill Creek. Fasten a pack to one bench, and sit on the other. Hiking partners help by pulling on the cables. Leave the car hanging free over the creek after use. (Planning tip: Bring leather gloves to protect hands from possible frayed cables.)

The route gains 5,300 feet in about 25 miles from this area to Earl Grey Pass. Walk by a compressor site for mining that ended in 1907. Pass the dilapidated McLaughlin's Cabin, a trapping base built in 1906. (Holes cut a few feet off the ground in large trees along the trail are marten trap sites.) Trail maintenance varies from here. The trail is easy to follow in timber. In avalanche chutes, where brush engulfs the trail, look for ribbons, cairns, and previously cut alder to find the way. Make a lot of noise and stay in a group when entering and walking through brushy areas to avoid surprising bears. Pepper spray is recommended. Finding ideal trees in an old-growth forest for hanging food away from bears can take some effort. But don't let down. (Planning tip: Bring lots of cord for hanging food, plus 50 feet of rope and a carabiner just in case you have to highline packs over a washed-out log crossing.)

The toughest trail section is the 12 or so miles from Rock Creek to Earl Grey Pass, where the route requires some effort to follow through avalanche paths and bogs. Expect encounters with devil's club and stinging nettles. Sometimes, spring runoff can sweep away the trees the park crews often topple across the streams for budget bridges. The trail heads up steeply in the last 7 miles to the pass, with no opportunity to camp. Small, fragile campsites can be found at the pass, but good low-impact campsites are just over the pass and down several switchbacks in the vast open area on the moraine at the base of Toby Glacier. Watch for toads on the way down.

Horses are prohibited on the wilder west side of the pass, but allowed on the east side. The trail is easy to follow on the east side in the Toby Creek drainage, but creek crossings can still be tricky in high flows. A much younger forest and bigger U-shaped glacial valleys characterize the east side. Several campsites are conveniently spaced in the 10 miles from the pass to Toby Creek Trailhead. Don't slack off on hanging food to keep it away from bears.

With all of Canada at his beckoning, Earl Grey picked this area for a

Hamill Creek drainage from above Earl Grey Pass

summer vacation cabin that still stands near the east trailhead. With careful planning, two groups can start at opposite trailheads and exchange vehicle keys near the pass to avoid a long shuttle. Groups that end the trip on the west side can celebrate at Ainsworth Hot Springs Resort north of Nelson. East-side finishers can do likewise at Fairmont Hot Springs Resort south of Invermere or drive 11 miles east from Highway 95 toward White Swan Lake (the turnoff is 35.5 miles south of Invermere or 44.5 miles north of Cranbrook) and soak for free at Lussier Hot Springs. Guided treks on the Earl Grey Traverse might be available from outfitters based in Kaslo.

Options: You've come a long way baby, so go the extra mile for the best part of the trip. Scramble north on the ridge from Earl Grey Pass to a rocky point, then down and up again to 8,841-foot Shale Peak for one of best 360-degree views of big peaks and glaciers you can get without a helicopter.

99 | MONICA MEADOWS AND JUMBO PASS

Location: Purcell Mountains
Status: Unprotected
Distance: 4–5 miles round trip for each
Hiking time: 4–6 hours each or overnight
Difficulty: Easy to moderately difficult
Season: Mid-July through early October
Maps: Duncan Lake 82 K/7, or mapsheets 82 K/037 and 82 K/047
Information: Kootenay Lake Forest District, Nelson Office

A long, rough drive into the heart of the Purcell Mountains leads to a pair of trails—only a few miles apart—that will take your breath away. They are short, steep routes to the spine of this glaciated range, but the exertion isn't as breathtaking as the scenery. Either hike is worth its own overnight trip. Camp out or reserve a bunk in the hiker's hut at Jumbo Pass. Day hikers might like to go light and do both trails in a weekend or a long day in grizzly bear country. Call ahead for updates on the area's deteriorating roads and bridges.

From Kaslo, British Columbia, drive north on Highway 31, passing two good provincial park camping areas en route to Lardeau. Go 3.7 miles past tiny Lardeau, and turn right on Argenta Road. From the highway, go 0.8 mile, crossing Duncan River, and continue straight at the junction onto Duncan Forest Road. (Do not turn toward Argenta. See Hike 98.) At 7.4 miles, bear right onto Duncan-Glacier Creek Road. (A car-camping spot is just off the road.) Following are the directions to three stunning hiking areas from this point:

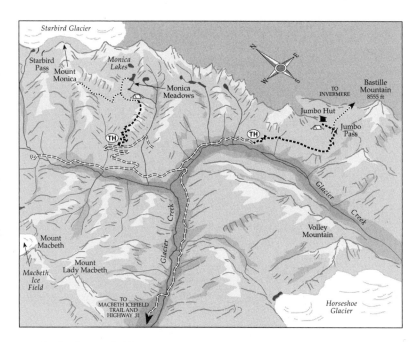

Macbeth Ice Fields: Drive about 6.5 miles (K-marker 20) and look for the steep, unreliably maintained logging road access to the ice-fields trail on the left just past Birnam Creek.

Jumbo Pass: Drive 14.7 miles and bear right at the junction onto Jumbo Road (K-marker 34). Drive 0.3 mile and bear right at the fork, then continue another 1.5 miles to the trailhead.

Monica Meadows: Drive 14.7 miles and bear left at the junction with Jumbo Road (K-marker 34). Go 1 mile and bear right onto Monica Meadows Road. A high clearance or possibly a four-wheel drive might be required to negotiate the ruts and waterbars in the last 2.4 miles to the trailhead. Given a clear day, the parking area, big enough for car camping, is among the most scenic trailheads you'll ever experience.

The hike to Monica Meadows starts just under elev. 6,000 feet and temporarily leaves the view of Horseshoe Glacier and Macbeth Ice Fields

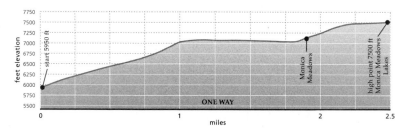

October at Monica Meadows, Purcell Mountains

and gets right to business. Seven fairly steep switchbacks gain about 1,000 feet in 1 mile before moderating and contouring around a ridge. Enjoy the raven's-eye view south across Glacier Creek to the Horseshoe Glacier, guarded by numerous sentinels between Emperor Peak to the west and Blockhead Mountain to the east. (Hat's off to whoever had the sense of humor to name nearby Squabble and Quibble Peaks along with Covenant, Truce, and Tranquility Mountains.) The trail drops toward a drainage and follows a creek up past the preferred camping area to an alpine plateau below a basin rimmed with jagged peaks. The Forest Service has discouraged backpackers from camping on the fragile plateau, where the trails become informal. Monica Meadows Lakes are to the right (east). A good trail switchbacks left uphill, past a tarn, to a bare ridge for better views of the peaks in every direction. Note the natural arch, rare in this region, on the east side of Monica Ridge. The short hiking season on this 7,000-foot plateau begins with riots of wildflowers and mosquitoes and closes in early October with the alpine larch ablaze in golden needles. Experienced off-trail hikers can spice this trip dramatically by skirting the rugged flanks of Mount Monica to Starbird Pass. (The easiest route to the pass, however, might be to bypass Monica Meadows Trailhead and continue driving up to the end of Glacier Creek Road and up logging spur roads, then bushwhacking up the creek that drains from Starbird Pass.)

Jumbo Pass: This trail begins at 5,200 feet with switchbacks heading steeply uphill. Then it gets even steeper before grading out a little into a fairly steady hump up a gully to the pass, elev. 7,500 feet, for a total elevation gain of 2,300 feet in 2.4 miles. Day hikers will require about 2 hours to reach the pass. Backpackers will need more time. From the pass, turn left along the scenic ridge gently uphill about 0.2 mile to the hut. Most hikers can be satisfied camping here, with an alpine tarn providing water and dazzling views provided by glacier-studded mountains, including Glacier Dome, The Lieutenants, Karnak, and Jumbo.

To stay at the hut, you must make reservations with the Columbia Valley Hut Society (see Appendix C). The provincial Forest Service, which coordinated hut maintenance and trail work, was taken out of the recreation business during a government shakeup in 2002. It wasn't clear which agency might pick up the recreational pieces.

From the alpine meadows, soak up the views of 10,000- to 11,000-foot peaks and be mindful that the scars from heavy-handed high-elevation logging are not likely to go away soon. On another issue, any Canadians you might meet here almost certainly will have an opinion about the jumbo-size ski resort planned for the valley below.

Options: Once at Jumbo Pass, find your own way in open terrain to countless views of alpine tarns and mountain valleys.

• Continue north from the hut as far as your skills allow.

• Continue east over the pass on the trail toward Invermere. (For access, see Hike 98.)

• Scramble up to one of the four summits of 8,555-foot Bastille Mountain, which looms above the southeast side of the pass.

• Turn this trip up Glacier Creek Road into a trilogy by capping visits to Monica Meadows and Jumbo Pass with a climb up to Macbeth Ice Fields. The 3.5-mile trek can be taxing, especially if trail maintenance has lagged. But after gaining 2,000 feet in elevation to an alpine lake and moraines near the ice fields, the effort will capture the mountaineer's soul. Check out Birnam Falls dropping into Graymalkin Lake and the 840-foot falls spilling out of the lake. Safe travel on the ice fields, however, requires special skill and gear.

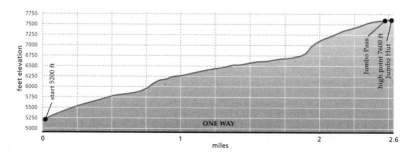

100 | MORTAR-PESTLE LAKES

Location: Purcell Mountains
Status: St. Mary's Alpine Provincial Park
Distance: 5.4 miles round trip
Hiking time: 4–6 hours or overnight
Difficulty: Moderately difficult
Season: Mid-July through early October
Map: Dewar Creek 82 F/16
Information: Kootenay Region Parks, Cranbrook Office

This little niche of wilderness is so far off the beaten track, it doesn't even have an official trail in its 22,650 acres. Hikers who visit St. Mary's Alpine Provincial Park can do it their way over the granite boulders and through the alpine larch, which ignite to brilliant gold in late September. This hike into two of the park's 30-some lakes is the gentlest possible introduction. Weak ankles? Be careful.

From Cranbook, British Columbia, take Highway 95A toward Kimberley. After passing through Marysville, go 0.3 mile and turn left (west) on St. Mary Lake Road. Continue on this road, passing St. Mary Lake, for a total of 24.5 miles and bear right at the Y onto Dewar Creek Road. Go 9.4 miles and bear right at the Y onto Road SP 3 at kilometer-marker 16. Head uphill about 13.5 miles, staying on the main road as it passes spur roads SP 3A, SP 3B, and SP 3C, to the Mortar and Pestle Lakes Trailhead. This was the landing for a logging operation, so there's a good chance you will have to seek out the trail to some degree. Extensions of the road have moved the trailhead farther up the slope. If logging continues, the road could go even higher, making the hike somewhat shorter. If logging ceases, the road could be gated lower and the hike extended.

The trail, such as it is, heads uphill, gaining 1,300 feet in about 1 mile, depending on where the access to the trailhead develops. Hikers have worked together in the past, hanging a little surveyor's tape or building a cairn when necessary. The trail tops out near a ridge, which is the park boundary. From here, it's easy to see why trails are not part of the management plan.

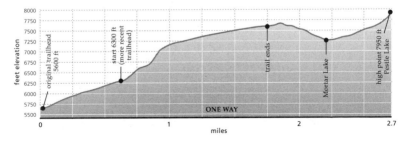

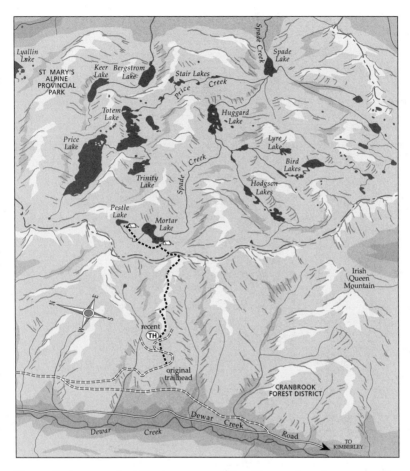

Dynamite is expensive! Contour around the ridge, and perhaps scramble up it for views of Mortar Lake and the surrounding area. Then pick a route angling down the rocks and ledges.

Routefinding in this area can be especially difficult in weather that renders poor visibility. A few inches of snow—a possibility even during summer—can slow your progress to a glacier's pace over the bouldered terrain.

The 1:50,000 scale topo map indicated above is adequate for the hike to Mortar and Pestle Lakes, but the ledges in the terrain call for more detailed maps if you plan to push routes farther into the wilderness. Adventurers need the 82 F/099 and 82 F/089 mining maps, and possibly others, available from the government agent in Cranbrook.

Camping is limited because even in the trees, the boulders leave little if any room for tents. Several sites can be found from Mortar up the slope to Pestle, but don't come here with a crowd looking for a group site.

Mortar Lake, St. Mary's Alpine Provincial Park

Options: Other accesses to the park include:

Westley Creek: Near the north end of Dewar Creek Road, this trail of sorts follows the north side of Westley Creek with access toward rewarding destinations at Nowitka Mountain and Lake in the northwest corner of the park. The terrain lends to a traverse south from Nowitka Lake to Larch Meadows, and Keer and Price Lakes before climbing a wall and skirting the north side of Trinity Lake, sidehilling around a ridge to Mortar. The hike could be done in either direction by leaving shuttle vehicles at the end of Dewar Creek Road and at the Mortar-Pestle Trailhead.

White Creek: A long, rough devil's-club-infested slog entering the park from the southeast. For masochists only.

Mount Manson Col: New logging makes this access to the south end of the park confusing. Roads can be very rough, but when bulldozers are unleashed as regularly as they are here, who knows what the future holds.

APPENDIX A

BONUS HIKES: UNSUNG FAVORITES

Some Inland Northwest trails are so convenient and commonly used that they're taken for granted. We fall back on these often uncelebrated routes for quick therapy from daily frustrations. We turn to them for extending the hiking season or for introducing novice hikers to the joy of walking or to follow the curiosity of a child. Hikers who want to explore these trails should buy the appropriate land management maps, but in most cases there's no particular need for the detailed descriptions given to the 100 featured hikes in this book. These are special hikes and highly recommended.

Hikes from Campgrounds

Easy to find and usually open earlier than high-country trails, these treks are choice leg-stretchers for hikers and families visiting some of the most popular campgrounds in the Inland Northwest.

LAKE ROOSEVELT NATIONAL RECREATION AREA

Hawk Creek: 3.6 miles round trip; moderate.

Hawk Creek Campground is west of Davenport, Washington, near Seven Bays on Lake Roosevelt. A lightly used trail, often hikable during winter, heads west from the primitive campground, past beaches, through sage, and loops up under basalt caves. Spring's the best time to view wildflowers and Hawk Creek Falls.

CHANNELED SCABLANDS

Fishtrap Lake: 4 miles or more round trip; easy.

A funky resort at Fishtrap Lake, west of Spokane and a few miles south of Interstate 90 from the "Fishtrap Exit," offers a shady car-camping spot on a good fishing lake and a base for a scenic trail above the west side of the lake on U.S. Bureau of Land Management land. Another trail heads north to Hog Lake and a nifty springtime waterfall. Get maps from BLM in Spokane. Avoid summer heat.

Palouse Falls: 3 miles round trip; moderate.

South of Washtucna, Washington, choose the larger campground at Lyons Ferry State Park on the Snake River or the tiny campground upstream at Palouse Falls Park, which is managed by Lyons Ferry staff. Informal trails lead up- and downstream from the Palouse Falls overlook, especially inspiring in spring when the swollen river gushes over the 198-foot cliff.

Kamiak Butte Loop: 3.5 miles round trip; moderate.

A well-groomed loop trail leads from the county campground and picnic areas to the 3,641-foot summit of this timbered ridge, rich with wild plants, standing like a sentinel from the Palouse wheatfields east of Colfax, Washington, and 12 miles north of Pullman. Check with Whitman County Parks in Colfax for possible late-summer closures because of fire danger.

Monumental Coulee: 3 miles round trip; moderate.

From Sun Lakes State Park Campground south of Coulee City, Washington, drive the Deep Lake–Dry Falls Lake Road 1.2 miles to the Camp Delany Trailhead (a gated road). Hike to Camp Delany, then go up the coulee through impressive basalt rock formations to Green Lake and a nearby overlook of Dry Falls, once the biggest waterfall on earth when all of this was created thousands of years ago by the great Ice Age floods.

CLEARWATER NATIONAL FOREST
NORTH FORK DISTRICT

Weitas Creek: Up to 30 miles one way; moderate.

Starting from Weitas Creek Campground at the confluence of Weitas Creek and the North Fork of the Clearwater River, Trail 20 follows a good cutthroat trout stream to its headwaters. Off-highway vehicles are making inroads here, but this trail and this stream are too special for hikers to abandon.

COLVILLE NATIONAL FOREST
THREE RIVERS DISTRICT

Meadow Lake Loop: 3.8 miles round trip; easy.

From Big Meadow Lake Campground, about 18 miles northeast of Colville, Washington, two trails combine to circumnavigate the lake and a meadow area. The lake is stocked with trout.

Springboard Loop: 2.5 miles round trip; easy.

From the Lake Gillette Campground east of Colville, Washington, this pleasant hike has interpretive information on seven points of interest. An overlook at elev. 3,600 feet offers a view of lakes Sherry, Gillette, and Thomas in the Little Pend Oreille River chain. The trail is named for the springboards that loggers used to lean against large trees so they could cut above the swollen base.

NEWPORT DISTRICT

South Skookum Lake Loop: 1.3 miles round trip; easy.

Skookum Lakes are 6.5 miles east of Usk, Washington, and the Pend Oreille River. A good trail starting at South Skookum Campground circumnavigates a lake planted with brook trout. The hike offers nice picnicking areas, fishing access, good views of the lake, and huckleberries.

REPUBLIC DISTRICT

Swan Lake Loop: 1.5 miles round trip; easy.

Swan Lake Campground south of Republic, Washington, a decent little mountain trout-fishing lake, is circumnavigated by this nifty trail, the perfect antidote for the guilt of too many s'mores. The trail starts near the community kitchen shelter, built by the Civilian Conservation Corps in 1933. Nearby Long Lake also has a trail.

Thirteenmile/Sanpoil River: Up to 16.5 miles one way; moderately difficult.

Ridge, cliffs, a short stretch of creek, and huge old-growth ponderosa pines greet hikers on this exceptional hike with a trailhead at Thirteenmile Campground on the Sanpoil River south of Republic, Washington, on the border of the Colville Indian Reservation. The hike has overnight possibilities. Consider ending a trip at the campground and shuttling vehicles to start more than 2,000 feet higher at Cougar or Bearpot Trailheads. In April and May, flowers bloom and eagles soar above cliffs over the Sanpoil River.

SULLIVAN LAKE DISTRICT

Sullivan Lake: 4 miles one way; easy.

Trail 504 runs from cool, shaded creek crossings to open scree slopes along the east shore of Sullivan Lake, which is 6 road miles east of Metaline Falls, Washington. The trail links Sullivan Lake Campground on the north end with Noisy Creek Campground to the south. The lake is a popular but reasonably uncrowded family camping destination with a swimming beach.

Sullivan Lake–Mill Pond Trails: 0.6-, 0.7-, and 2-mile loops; mostly easy.

Mill Pond Campground is a small and less-crowded facility between Metaline Falls and Sullivan Lake Campground. Two short trails loop around Mill Pond. The longer 2-mile loop on Elk Creek Trail 560 heads north of the paved Pend Oreille County Road 9345 uphill to a cool summer respite by a small waterfall before heading back downhill to the trailhead at Mill Pond.

IDAHO PANHANDLE NATIONAL FORESTS
PRIEST LAKE DISTRICT

Kalispell Island Loop: 2 miles round trip; easy.

A trail circumnavigating this large Priest Lake island links the several boat-in camping areas a short motor or paddle out of Luby Bay.

Lakeshore: 7.5 miles one way; easy.

From Beaver Creek Campground at the northwest end of Priest Lake, Trail 294 heads south along the lake, with bridge crossings over five creeks, to Granite Creek in Reeder Bay. Hikers could carry packs and camp at several beaches off this trail.

ST. JOE RIVER DISTRICT

St. Joe River: 17.2 miles one way; moderate.

From Spruce Tree Campground upstream from Avery, Idaho, near Red Ives, campers can hike as far as they want for a day or for several nights on this trail along the St. Joe River upstream to Heller Creek Campground. Spruce Tree is particularly popular with fly fishers who come to catch-and-release the St. Joe's cutthroat trout.

Marble Creek: Up to 5 miles one way; moderate.

About 35 miles up the St. Joe River from St. Maries, Idaho, turn south on Marble Creek Road 321 to Camp 3 Campground, a good base for exploring several interpretive trails featuring early 1900s logging camp history, complete with rusting steam donkeys and splash dams. The Marble Creek Trail itself has some of these features, plus fishing opportunities, campsites, and huckleberries.

ST. MARIES DISTRICT

White Pine: 3 miles round trip; easy.

From White Pine Campground, 15 miles north of Potlatch, Idaho, this enjoyable walk leads through some of the rare, ancient, and awesome white pines and cedars of northern Idaho. The giant white pine that was the trail's centerpiece— 6 feet in diameter and 200 feet tall—was felled in 1999 because it was rotting and in danger of falling. Much of the trunk was left on the site to compare with other giants that still stand.

COEUR D'ALENE RIVER DISTRICT

Mount Coeur d'Alene: 10 miles round trip; moderately difficult.

From Beauty Creek Campground in the Wolf Lodge Bay area of Lake Coeur d'Alene, Caribou Ridge Trail 79 gains 4,440 feet in 5 miles to the top of Mount Coeur d'Alene. The mountain was called Sticker Mountain in 1917 because of a forester's reference to the snags that fires had left sticking into the sky. Later, Coeur d'Alene citizens asked to change the name because it's in full view of the city.

U.S. BUREAU OF LAND MANAGEMENT, COEUR D'ALENE

Crystal Lake: 3 miles round trip; moderate.

From Interstate 90 at Cataldo, Idaho, take Exit 40 and head south 20 dusty miles, on LeTour Creek Road (becomes Forest Road 613) to Sheep Camp on the divide between the Coeur d'Alene and St. Joe River drainages. The campsite is used mostly by locals in summer and hunters in autumn. The trail starts east across the road from the campsite and drops down through talus slopes to timbered Crystal Lake. Trout, flowers, and huckleberries can be found here under 6,153-foot Reeds Baldy. Hardy hikers can make a loop, continuing up from Crystal Lake back to Road 613. From there, the easy way to finish the loop is by hiking the road back to the trailhead. Scramblers can take the higher, harder route on the spur trail that heads north to a lake overlook and then continuing cross-country on the rugged, rocky ridge that goes up and drops back down to the trailhead. Get the Idaho Panhandle National Forests Fernan area map.

KOOTENAI NATIONAL FOREST
TROY DISTRICT

Little Spar Lake: 7 miles round trip; moderately difficult.

From Spar Lake Campground west of Bull Lake, drive up Road 384 a short way to hike a steady grade up Trail 143, gaining 1,900 feet to Little Spar Lake. A few campsites are available at this cutthroat fishing lake snugged up against the Montana-Idaho border. The trail is usually clear of snow by July.

LOLO NATIONAL FOREST
SUPERIOR DISTRICT

Diamond Lake: 2.5 miles round trip; moderate.

Diamond Lake has a small, primitive campground with a pit toilet reached from Dry Creek Road, which is south of Interstate 90 between Superior and St. Regis, Montana. The trail goes to Cliff Lake, which has campsites in a cirque below the Montana-Idaho border, making it a destination for novice backpacking trips. From there, trails lead up to the Stateline Trail for good views and extended hiking.

OKANOGAN NATIONAL FOREST
TWISP DISTRICT

Tiffany Mountain: 4 miles minimum round trip; moderately difficult.

From Winthrop, Washington, drive north along the Chewuch River and take Forest Roads 37 and 39 northeast to Tiffany Spring Campground, a base for exploration on several excellent hiking and scrambling routes in a roadless area looming 1,000 feet or more above Tiffany Lake. Try heading east off of Road 39 on Trail 345 along Freezeout Ridge to Tiffany Mountain. From here, longer treks can be planned. Look for bighorn sheep, often south in Clark Peak area. Conservationists would like to see this area protected from any further road building.

NORTHERN IDAHO STATE PARKS
HEYBURN STATE PARK

Indian Cliffs: 3 miles round trip; moderate.

Heyburn State Park, 6 miles east of Plummer, Idaho, and then north on the shore of Lake Chatcolet, has a couple of nice trails. Indian Cliffs Trailhead is passed just after crossing railroad tracks before turning into park headquarters, where details can be obtained. The interpretive trail gains 520 feet in elevation to excellent views of the "river in a lake," where the St. Joe River separates Round and Chatcolet Lakes. Also check out the nearby trailhead for the Trail of the Coeur d'Alenes, a 72-mile paved rail trail.

ROUND LAKE STATE PARK

Round Lake: 3 miles round trip; easy.

Stewardship and Trapper Trails connect to circumnavigate Round Lake in this park, which is 2 miles west of U.S. Highway 95 and south of Sandpoint, Idaho. Park headquarters has brochures for this interpretive hike, just one of several features in a concentrated 142-acre state park package of camping, picnicking, swimming, and fishing.

FARRAGUT STATE PARK

High Point–Bernard Peak: 3 miles round trip; moderate.

Farragut is a sprawling park on a former military camp on the shores of Lake Pend Oreille east of U.S. Highway 95 and Athol, Idaho. The trailhead for this hike is just past park headquarters off South Road. Hike up through impressive rock formations for views of the lake. The trail and its spurs make several options for easier or extended hikes, including a link for a trek all the way up Bernard Peak.

THREE CHOICE CITY HIKES

Coeur d'Alene, Tubbs Hill: 3 miles round trip; mostly easy.

A gem of a trail circumnavigates Tubbs Hill just southeast of the Coeur d'Alene Resort, with two-thirds of the route overlooking Lake Coeur d'Alene and providing access to a few beaches. Trailheads are at the city boat-launch parking area or at a parking area near 10th Street and Mountain Avenue.

Post Falls, Q'emiln Riverside Park: 3 miles round trip; moderate.

From Interstate 90 at Post Falls, take Exit 5 and head south on Spokane Street, across the Spokane River, and right on Parkway to the trailhead at the end of the road. Enjoy the loop trails through this small preserve of native vegetation and rock outcroppings. Q'emiln (pronounced Kih-MEE-lin) was the name the Coeur d'Alene Indians gave to the village near the present site of Post Falls. The name means "Throat of the river." The village was vacated in 1878.

Spokane South Hill Bluff: miles of trails available; easy to moderate.

An evolving network of trails in Spokane graces the south-facing slope below High Drive and above Qualchan Golf Course and Hangman Creek. For a good introduction, walk south from the informal trailhead near 37th Avenue and High Drive, drop down off the bluff, and turn right on the first trail, which contours for a couple miles through eye-popping spring displays of arrowleaf balsamroot and serviceberries.

OUTSIDE COEUR D'ALENE

Marie Creek Loop: 12 miles round trip; moderate.

From Coeur d'Alene, Idaho, take the Harrison Exit at Wolf Lodge Bay and then turn north and follow Road 124 to the junction with Road 202. Follow 202 about 2 miles to the trailhead. Trail 241 follows Marie Creek about 3.5 miles, a nice hike in itself. To make the loop, continue up the trail out of Skipworth Creek, follow an old logging road for a few miles, then drop down a ridge back to the trailhead. No motorized vehicles are allowed (a rarity in this neck of the woods).

Graham Mountain: 11 miles round trip; moderate.

The trail to the 5,727-foot peak has long been enjoyed by day hikers visiting the Coeur d'Alene River Ranger District. From Interstate 90, drive north on Coeur d'Alene River Road 12.5 miles to the trailhead at Coal Creek campsite. Trail 41 follows the creek past abandoned mines and into an old cedar grove before climbing and eventually connecting with Graham Ridge Trail 17 to the summit, where there are remains of an old fire lookout.

APPENDIX B

EQUIPMENT LIST

Backpackers often list all the gear they might put in their packs and refer to it every time they assemble their equipment. Following is a sample list. Personalize it as needed. Subtract if possible. Be judicious in what is added. Additional ounces eventually add up to pounds you must carry on your back. The Ten Essentials are in **boldface**.

CLOTHING
- ❏ Fleece sweater
- ❏ Long-sleeve shirt
- ❏ Tee shirts
- ❏ Socks
- ❏ Underwear
- ❏ Shorts
- ❏ Long pants
- ❏ Long underwear
- ❏ Windbreaker
- ❏ Raingear (top and bottom)
- ❏ Gloves
- ❏ Visor cap for sun
- ❏ Stocking hat for cold
- ❏ Bandannas
- ❏ Boots or hiking shoes
- ❏ Camp or wading shoes
- ❏ **Extra clothing**

SHELTER
- ❏ Tent, poles, stakes
- ❏ Plastic tarp
- ❏ Sleeping bag and liner
- ❏ Sleeping pad
- ❏ Emergency space blanket

EATING
- ❏ Stove and fuel
- ❏ Water containers
- ❏ Pliers
- ❏ Pots, pans
- ❏ Cup, bowl
- ❏ Spoon
- ❏ Foil
- ❏ Pot scrubber
- ❏ Salt, pepper, sugar, spices
- ❏ Peanut butter
- ❏ Hot drinks
- ❏ Cold drinks
- ❏ Trail snacks
- ❏ Breakfasts
- ❏ Lunches
- ❏ Dinners
- ❏ Food hanging bag

PERSONALS
- ❏ Toilet paper
- ❏ Biodegradable soap
- ❏ Towel
- ❏ Toothbrush
- ❏ Floss
- ❏ Feminine hygiene
- ❏ Eyeglasses
- ❏ Medicines

IMPORTANT ITEMS
- ❏ **Map and compass**
- ❏ **Flashlight** (extra batteries, bulb)
- ❏ **Knife**
- ❏ **Matches in waterproof container**
- ❏ **Firestarter**
- ❏ **Extra food** and water
- ❏ **First-aid kit** (include blister treatment)
- ❏ Sun protection (**sunglasses**, sunscreen, lip balm)
- ❏ Hiking pole(s)
- ❏ Water purifier
- ❏ Nylon cord
- ❏ Insect repellent
- ❏ Candle
- ❏ Signaling devices (whistle, mirror)
- ❏ Reading material
- ❏ Pepper spray
- ❏ Licenses and permits
- ❏ Trailhead parking passes
- ❏ Repair kit (sewing, tape, etc.)
- ❏ Pack rain cover

LESS IMPORTANT STUFF
- ❏ GPS unit
- ❏ Notepad and pen
- ❏ Field guides to birds, etc.
- ❏ Zipper-type plastic bags
- ❏ Plastic garbage bag
- ❏ Camera and film
- ❏ Plastic trowel (for latrines)
- ❏ Fishing gear
- ❏ Thermometer
- ❏ Collapsible bucket
- ❏ Binoculars

APPENDIX C

ADMINISTRATION/INFORMATION SOURCES

GENERAL INFORMATION

Idaho Department of Lands, 4053 Cavanaugh Bay Road, Coolin, ID 83821-9704; telephone (208) 443-2516; *www2.state.id.us/lands.*

U.S. Bureau of Land Management/National Forest Information, 1103 North Fancher Road, Spokane, WA 99212-1275; telephone (509) 536-1200; *www.or.blm.gov/spokane.*

U.S. Forest Service, Northern Region, 200 East Broadway, P.O. Box 7669, Missoula, MT 59807; telephone (406) 329-3511; *www.fs.fed.us/r1.*

U.S. Forest Service, Pacific Northwest Region, P.O. Box 3623, Portland, OR 97208-3623; telephone (503) 808-2468; *www.fs.fed.us/r6.*

STATE PARKS

Idaho Department of Parks and Recreation, P.O. Box 83720, Boise, ID 83720-0065; telephone (208) 334-4199; *www.idahoparks.org.*
  • Farragut State Park, Athol, ID; (208) 683-2425.
  • Heyburn State Park, Plummer, ID; (208) 686-1308.
  • Priest Lake State Park, Coolin, ID; (208) 443-2200.
  • Round Lake State Park, Sagle, ID; (208) 263-3489.

Montana Department of Fish, Wildlife, and Parks, 1420 East 6th Avenue, P.O. Box 200701, Helena, MT 59620-0701; telephone (406) 444-2535; *fwp.state.mt.us.*

Oregon Department of Parks and Recreation, 1115 Commercial Street Northeast, Salem, OR 97301-1002; telephone (503) 378-5019; *www.prd.state.or.us.*
  • Wallowa Lake State Park, Joseph, OR; (541) 432-4185.

Washington Department of Parks and Recreation, 7150 Cleanwater Lane, P.O. Box 42650, Olympia, WA 98504-2650; telephone (360) 902-8500; *www.parks.wa.gov.*
  • Lyons Ferry/Palouse Falls State Park, Starbuck, WA; (509) 646-3252.
  • Mount Spokane State Park, Mead, WA; (509) 238-4258.
  • Riverside State Park, Spokane, WA; (509) 465-5064.
  • Steamboat Rock State Park, Electric City, WA; (509) 633-1304.
  • Sun Lakes State Park, Coulee City, WA; (509) 632-5583.

SPOKANE/COEUR D'ALENE AREA

Coeur d'Alene Parks and Recreation Department (for Tubbs Hill), 710 Mullan Avenue, Coeur d'Alene, ID 83814; telephone (208) 769-2250.

Dishman Hills Natural Area Association, 3415 South Lincoln Drive, Spokane, WA 99203; telephone (509) 747-8147; *www.sd81.k12.wa.us/ Regal/DishmanHills/56Dhill.htm.*

Mount Spokane State Park, 26107 North Mount Spokane Park Drive, Mead, WA 99021; telephone (509) 238-4258; *www.mtspokane.org.*

Post Falls Parks and Recreation Department (for Q'emiln Riverside Park), 408 Spokane Street, Post Falls, ID 83854; telephone (208) 773-0539.

Riverside State Park, 9711 West Charles Road, Ninemile Falls, WA 99026; telephone (509) 465-5064; *www.riversidestatepark.org.*

Spokane County Parks and Recreation Department, 404 North Havana Street, Spokane, WA 99202; telephone (509) 477-4730; *www.spokanecounty.org/parks/prhome.htm.*

U.S. Bureau of Land Management (for Mineral Ridge), 1808 North 3rd Street, Coeur d'Alene, ID 83814; telephone (208) 765-1511; *www.id.blm.gov/offices/coeurd'alene.*

CLEARWATER NATIONAL FOREST

Supervisor's Headquarters, 12730 U.S. Highway 12, Orofino, ID 83544; telephone (208) 476-4541; *www.fs.fed.us/r1/clearwater.*

Lochsa Ranger District, Kooskia Ranger Station, Route 1, Box 398, Kooskia, ID 83539; telephone (208) 926-4275.

North Fork Ranger District, 12730 U.S. Highway 12, Orofino, ID 83544; telephone (208) 476-4541.

Palouse Ranger District, 1700 Highway 6, Potlatch, ID 83855; telephone (208) 875-1131.

Powell Ranger District, Powell Ranger Station, Lolo, MT 59847; telephone (208) 942-3113.

COLVILLE NATIONAL FOREST

Supervisor's Headquarters, 765 South Main, Federal Building, Colville, WA 99114; telephone (509) 684-7000; *www.fs.fed.us/r6/colville.*

Newport Ranger District, 315 North Warren Avenue, Newport, WA 99156; telephone (509) 447-7300.

Republic Ranger District, 180 North Jefferson, Republic, WA 99166; telephone (509) 775-3305.

Sullivan Lake Ranger District, 12641 Sullivan Lake Road, Metaline Falls, WA 99153; telephone (509) 446-7500.

Three Rivers Ranger District, Colville Office, 755 South Main, Colville, WA 99114; telephone (509) 684-3711.

Three Rivers Ranger District, Kettle Falls Office, 255 West 11th, Kettle Falls, WA 99141; telephone (509) 738-6111.

IDAHO PANHANDLE NATIONAL FORESTS

Supervisor's Headquarters, 3815 Schreiber Way, Coeur d'Alene, ID 83815; telephone (208) 765-7223; *www.fs.fed.us/ipnf.*

Bonners Ferry Ranger District, Route 4, Box 4860, Bonners Ferry, ID 83805; telephone (208) 267-5561.

Coeur d'Alene River Ranger District, Fernan Office, 2502 East Sherman Avenue, Coeur d'Alene, ID 83814; telephone (208) 769-3000.

Coeur d'Alene River Ranger District, Wallace Office, P.O. Box 14, Silverton, ID 83867; telephone (208) 752-1221.

Priest Lake Ranger District, 32203 Highway 57, Priest River, ID 83856; telephone (208) 443-2512.

St. Joe Ranger District, Avery Office, H.C. Box 1, Avery, ID 83802; telephone (208) 245-4517.

St. Joe Ranger District, St. Maries Office, P.O. Box 407, St. Maries, ID 83861; telephone (208) 245-2531.

Sandpoint Ranger District, 1500 Highway 2, Suite 110, Sandpoint, ID 83864; telephone (208) 263-5111.

KOOTENAI NATIONAL FOREST

Supervisor's Headquarters, 1101 U.S. Highway 2 West, Libby, MT 59923; telephone (406) 293-6211; *www.fs.fed.us/r1/kootenai.*

Cabinet Ranger District, Cabinet Ranger Station, 2693 Highway 200, Trout Creek, MT 59874; telephone (406) 827-3533.

Fortine Ranger District, Murphy Lake Ranger Station, P.O. Box 116, Fortine, MT 59918; telephone (406) 882-4451.

Libby Ranger District, Canoe Gulch Ranger Station, 12557 Highway 37, Libby, MT 59923; telephone (406) 293-7773.

Rexford Ranger District, Eureka Ranger Station, 1299 U.S. Highway 93 North, Eureka, MT 59917; telephone (406) 296-2536.

Three Rivers Ranger District, Troy Ranger Station, 1437 North Highway 2, Troy, MT 59935; telephone (406) 295-4693.

LOLO NATIONAL FOREST

Supervisor's Headquarters, Building 24, Fort Missoula, MT 59804; telephone (406) 329-3750; *www.fs.fed.us/r1/lolo.*

Missoula Ranger District, Building 24, Fort Missoula, MT 59804; telephone (406) 329-3814.

Ninemile Ranger District, 20325 Remount Road, Huson, MT 59846; telephone (406) 626-5201.

Plains/Thompson Falls Ranger District, 408 Clayton Street, P.O. Box 429, Plains, MT 59859; telephone (406) 826-3821.

Seeley Lake Ranger District, HC 31, Box 3200, Seeley Lake, MT 59868; telephone (406) 677-2233.

Superior Ranger District, 209 West Riverside, Superior, MT 59872; telephone (406) 822-4233.

NEZ PERCE NATIONAL FOREST

Supervisor's Headquarters, Route 2, Box 475, Grangeville, ID 83530; telephone (208) 983-1950; *www.fs.fed.us/r1/nezperce.*

Moose Creek Ranger District/Fenn Ranger Station, HCR 75, Box 91, Kooskia, ID 83539; telephone (208) 926-4250.

OKANOGAN NATIONAL FOREST
Supervisor's Headquarters, 1240 South 2nd Avenue, Okanogan, WA 98840-9723; telephone (509) 826-3275; *www.fs.fed.us/r6/oka.*

UMATILLA NATIONAL FOREST
Supervisor's Headquarters, 2517 Southwest Hailey Avenue, Pendleton, OR 97801; telephone (541) 278-3716; *www.fs.fed.us/r6/uma.*
Pomeroy Ranger District, 71 West Main, Pomeroy, WA 99347; telephone (509) 843-1891.

WALLOWA-WHITMAN NATIONAL FOREST
Supervisor's Headquarters, P.O. Box 907, Baker City, OR 97814; telephone (541) 523-6391; *www.fs.fed.us/r6/w-w.*
Baker Ranger District, 3165 10th Street, Baker, OR 97814; telephone (541) 523-4476.
Wallowa Mountains Visitor Center (for Eagle Cap Ranger District, Wallowa Valley Ranger District and Hells Canyon National Recreation Area), 88401 Highway 82, Enterprise, OR 97828; telephone (541) 426-4978.

HELLS CANYON NATIONAL RECREATION AREA
Wallowa Mountains Visitor Center, 88401 Highway 82, Enterprise, OR 97828; telephone (541) 426-4978; *www.fs.fed.us/r6/w-w/hcnra.*
• Clarkston Office, P.O. Box 699, Clarkston, WA 99403; telephone (509) 758-0616.
• Riggins Office, P.O. Box 832, Riggins, ID 83549; telephone (208) 628-3916.

BRITISH COLUMBIA
B.C. Parks, East Kootenay District, Nelson Office, 401-333 Victoria Street, Nelson, British Columbia, Canada V1L 4K3; telephone (250) 354-6333; *wlapwww.gov.bc.ca/bcparks.*
B.C. Parks, West Kootenay District, 205 Industrial Road, Cranbrook, British Columbia, Canada V1C 7G5; telephone (250) 489-8540; *wlapwww.gov.bc.ca/bcparks.*
Kootenay Lake Forest District, 1907 Ridgewood Road, Nelson, British Columbia, Canada V1L 6K1; telephone (250) 825-1100; *www.for.gov.bc.ca/nelson/district/kootenay/rec/recsites/legend.htm* or *www.gov.bc.ca/srm.*
Invermere Forest District, 1902 Theatre Road, Cranbrook, British Columbia, Canada V1C 4H4; (250) 426-1700, (Invermere Office; 250-342-4200); *www.for.gov.bc.ca/nelson/district/kootenay/rec/recsites/legend.htm* or *www.gov.bc.ca/srm.*

Columbia Valley Hut Society (for Jumbo Pass Hut), Box 322, Invermere,
British Columbia, Canada V0A 1K0; telephone (250) 342-5005.

STATE AND PROVINCIAL WILDLIFE AGENCIES

Idaho Department of Fish and Game, 600 South Walnut, P.O. Box 25,
Boise, ID 83707; telephone (208) 334-3700; *www2.state.id.us/fishgame.*

Montana Department of Fish, Wildlife, and Parks, 1420 East 6th
Avenue, P.O. Box 200701, Helena, MT 59620-0701; telephone (406) 444-
2535; *fwp.state.mt.us.*

Oregon Department of Fish and Wildlife, 2501 Southwest 1st Avenue,
P.O. Box 59, Portland OR 97207; telephone (503) 872-5262;
www.dfw.state.or.us.

Washington Department of Fish and Wildlife, 600 Capitol Way North,
Olympia, WA 98501-1091; telephone (360) 902-2200; *www.wa.gov/wdfw.*

Ministry of Environment, Lands and Parks, Fish and Wildlife Division,
333 Victoria Street, Suite 401, Nelson, British Columbia, Canada VIL 4K3;
telephone (250) 354-6333.

Ministry of Water, Land and Air Protection, P.O. Box 9360, Stn. Prov.
Govt., Victoria, British Columbia, Canada V8W 9M2;
telephone (250) 387-9422; *www.bcfisheries.gov.bc.ca/rec/recreational.html/*
or *www.gov.bc.ca/srm* or *www.gov.bc.ca/wlap.*

APPENDIX D

Sources for Maps

FOREST SERVICE AND BUREAU OF LAND MANAGEMENT MAPS:
U.S. Bureau of Land Management/Forest Service Information Center,
1103 North Fancher Road, Spokane, WA 99212; telephone (509) 536-1251
(also sells access and parking passes for most Northwest forests that
require them).
ALL TYPES OF MAPS, U.S. AND CANADA:
Northwest Map and Travel Book Center, 525 West Sprague Avenue,
Spokane, WA 99204; telephone (509) 455-6981; *www.nwmaps.com.*
TOPOGRAPHIC MAPS:
U.S. Geological Survey Map Sales, P.O. Box 25286, Denver, CO 80225;
telephone (888) 275-8747 or (303) 202-4700; *www.usgs.gov.*
Natural Resources Canada, Centre for Topographic Information in
Ottawa; telephone (613) 995-0947; *NRCan.gc.ca.*
LandData BC, *www.landdata.gov.bc.ca.*

APPENDIX E

Hiking/Conservation Groups

The Backpacking Club, P.O. Box 9142, Spokane, WA 99209.
Boundary Backpackers, Route 1 Box 495, Bonners Ferry, ID 83805.
The Cascadians, P.O. Box 2201, Yakima, WA 98907; *cascadians.org.*
Hobnailers, Box 1256, Spokane, WA 99210.
Intermountain Alpine Club, P.O. Box 505, Richland, WA 99352;
www.imacnw.org.
Kettle Range Conservation Group, P.O. Box 150, Republic, WA 99166;
telephone (509) 775-2667; Spokane Office telephone (509) 747-1663;
www.kettlerange.org.
Kootenay Mountaineering Club, Box 3195, Castlegar, British Columbia,
Canada V1N 3H5; *www.kootenaymountaineering.bc.ca.*
The Lands Council, 921 West Sprague Avenue, Suite 205, Spokane, WA
99201; telephone (509) 838-4912; *www.landscouncil.org.*
Sierra Club, P.O. Box 413, Spokane, WA 99210.
Spokane Mountaineers, Inc., P.O. Box 1013, Spokane, WA 99210;
www.spokanemountaineers.org.

TRAIL COMPARISON CHART

Hike	Difficulty				Prime Season		Duration			Scrambling Options	Fishing	Old-growth	Grizzly Country	Family Friendly	Motor Vehicles Allowed	Rough Access Road
	Easy	Moderate	Mod-Difficult	Difficult	Spring & Fall	Summer & Fall	Day Hike	Overnight	Multi-Day							
Columbia River Basin																
1. Juniper Dunes Loop	•				•		•	•								•
2. Steamboat Rock Loop		•			•		•				•	•		•		
3. Northrup Canyon		•			•	•	•					•		•		
4. Odessa-Pacific Lake		•			•		•	•				•			•	
Colville National Forest																
5. Old Stage Road Midnight Ridge Loop		•				•	•	•	•				•			
6. Columbia Mtn. Loop (Kettle Crest North)		•				•	•	•	•					•		
7. Sherman Peak Loop (Kettle Crest South)		•				•	•	•	•	•				•		
8. Hoodoo Canyon			•			•	•	•						•		
9. Abercrombie Mtn.			•			•	•			•						
10. Sherlock Peak		•				•	•			•				•		
11. Hall Mountain	•					•	•							•		•
12. Grassy Top Mtn.		•				•	•						•			
13. Crowell Ridge			•			•	•	•	•	•			•			•
14. Shedroof Divide			•			•		•	•				•			
15. Salmo-Priest Loop			•			•		•	•	•	•	•	•			
Around Spokane/Coeur d'Alene																
16. Spokane River Loop	•	•			•	•	•					•		•		
17. Deep Creek Canyon Loop		•			•	•	•							•		
18. Little Spokane River		•			•	•	•							•		
19. Dishman Hills Loop		•			•	•	•							•		
20. Liberty Lake Loop	•	•	•		•	•	•							•		
21. Mount Spokane-Three Peaks Loop	•	•	•	•		•	•						•	•		
22. Mineral Ridge Loop	•				•	•	•							•		

Hike	Easy	Moderate	Mod-Difficult	Difficult	Spring & Fall	Summer & Fall	Day Hike	Overnight	Multi-Day	Scrambling Options	Fishing	Old-growth	Grizzly Country	Family Friendly	Motor Vehicles Allowed	Rough Access Road
Lolo National Forest																
23. Cube Iron Mtn. Loop		•				•	•	•			•			•		
24. Revett Lake	•					•	•	•			•			•		
25. Blossom Lakes	•					•	•	•			•			•		
26. Siamese Lakes Loop		•	•			•		•	•	•	•	•				
27. Heart Lake		•				•	•	•			•	•		•		
28. Hub Lake		•				•	•	•			•	•		•		
29. St. Regis Lakes		•				•	•	•			•	•		•	•	
Idaho Panhandle National Forests																
Coeur d'Alene River District																
30. Stevens Lakes		•				•	•	•		•	•			•		
31. Chilco Mtns.		•				•	•									•
32. Independence Creek		•				•	•	•			•			•		
33. Upper Coeur d'Alene River	•				•	•	•	•			•			•		
Priest Lake District																
34. Upper Priest River	•					•		•	•		•	•	•	•		
35. Upper Priest Lake-Navigation Trail	•					•	•	•			•			•	•	
36. Upper Priest Lake-Trapper Creek	•					•	•	•			•	•	•	•		
37. Lookout Mtn.			•			•	•	•		•				•		
38. Hunt Lake			•			•	•	•		•	•			•		
Bonners Ferry District																
39. Iron Mtn. Loop				•		•	•	•						•		
40. West Fork Lake		•				•	•	•		•	•			•	•	
41. Long Canyon Loop			•			•		•	•	•	•	•	•	•		
42. Fisher Peak			•			•	•						•	•		
43. Trout-Big Fisher Lakes		•				•	•	•		•	•			•	•	
44. Pyramid-Ball Lakes	•					•	•	•		•	•			•	•	
45. Myrtle Lake			•			•	•	•			•			•		
46. Two Mouth Lakes			•			•	•	•		•	•			•		
47. Bottleneck Lake-Snow Lakes			•			•	•	•		•	•			•		
48. Roman Nose Lakes	•					•	•	•		•	•			•	•	

Hike	Easy	Moderate	Mod-Difficult	Difficult	Spring & Fall	Summer & Fall	Day Hike	Overnight	Multi-Day	Scrambling Options	Fishing	Old-growth	Grizzly Country	Family Friendly	Motor Vehicles Allowed	Rough Access Road
Sandpoint District																
49. Harrison Lake		•				•	•	•		•	•		•	•		•
50. Beehive Lakes			•			•	•	•		•	•		•			•
51. Chimney Rock			•			•	•	•		•			•			•
52. Fault Lake		•				•	•	•		•	•		•			
53. Lake Darling-Mount Pend Oreille Loop		•				•	•	•			•			•		
54. Lake Estelle-Four Lakes	•					•	•	•	•		•			•		
55. Bee Top Ridge			•			•	•									
56. Scotchman Peak			•			•	•									
57. Green Monarch Ridge			•			•	•									
St. Joe District																
58. Grandfather Mountain		•				•	•	•					•			
59. Snow Peak			•			•	•	•								
60. Mallard-Larkins Loop				•		•		•	•		•	•				
61. Mallard-Fawn Lakes	•					•	•	•	•		•			•		
62. Bean-Bacon Loop				•		•	•	•			•					
63. St. Joe Lake	•					•	•	•	•	•	•			•		
64. Five Lakes Butte	•					•	•	•		•	•			•		
Clearwater National Forest																
65. Goose Lake-Stateline Trail	•					•	•	•	•	•	•			•		
66. Goat Lake-Rhodes Peak	•					•	•	•	•	•	•			•		
67. Cayuse Creek	•					•	•	•			•					
68. Kelly Creek	•					•	•		•	•	•				•	•
69. Pete Ott Lake-Cold Springs Peak	•					•	•	•		•	•			•	•	•
Nez Perce National Forest																
70. Selway Crags-Cove Lakes			•			•		•	•	•	•					•
Kootenai National Forest																
71. Ten Lakes Loop	•					•	•	•	•	•	•		•	•		
72. Cedar Lakes-Scenery Mountain		•				•		•	•	•	•		•			
73. Sky Lakes-Hanging Valley	•					•		•		•	•		•			
74. Granite Lake	•					•		•		•	•		•			
75. Leigh Lake	•					•	•	•		•	•		•	•		

Hike	Easy	Moderate	Mod-Difficult	Difficult	Spring & Fall	Summer & Fall	Day Hike	Overnight	Multi-Day	Scrambling Options	Fishing	Old-growth	Grizzly Country	Family Friendly	Motor Vehicles Allowed	Rough Access Road
	Difficulty				**Prime Season**		**Duration**									
76. Rock Lake		●				●	●	●		●	●		●	●		●
77. Wanless Lake			●			●		●	●	●	●		●			
78. Geiger Lakes-Cabinet Divide	●					●	●	●	●	●	●		●	●		
79. Chicago Peak-Cliff Lake	●					●	●	●			●		●	●		●
80. Engle Lake		●				●	●	●		●	●		●			
81. Bear-Baree Lakes Loop		●				●	●	●	●	●	●		●	●		
Umatilla National Forest																
82. Tucannon River-Diamond Peak Loop			●		●	●		●	●	●	●					
83. Oregon Butte	●				●	●	●	●						●		
84. Squaw Spring	●				●	●	●	●						●		
85. Twin Buttes-Wenaha River Loop			●		●	●			●	●		●	●			
86. Wenaha River				●	●	●	●	●	●		●			●		
Wallowa-Whitman National Forest																
87. Ice Lake			●			●		●	●	●						
88. Swamp Lake			●			●		●	●	●	●					
89. Mirror Lake		●				●		●	●	●	●			●		
90. Lakes Basin Loop			●			●			●	●	●					
91. Echo Lake				●		●	●	●	●	●	●					
Hells Canyon National Recreation Area																
92. Imnaha River Canyon	●				●	●	●	●	●	●	●			●	●	●
93. Snake River-Kirkwood Ranch		●			●	●	●	●	●	●	●			●		
British Columbia																
94. Gwillim Lakes			●			●	●	●	●	●			●	●		
95. Gimli Ridge-Mulvey Basin		●				●	●	●		●			●			●
96. Kokanee Glacier			●				●	●	●	●	●		●	●		
97. Silver Spray-Woodbury Basin			●	●		●	●	●	●	●	●		●			
98. Earl Grey Pass Traverse				●	●	●	●	●	●	●		●	●			
99. Monica Meadows & Jumbo Pass	●		●			●	●	●		●			●	●		●
100. Mortar-Pestle Lakes			●			●	●	●	●	●	●		●			●

INDEX

ABOUT THE AUTHOR

RICH LANDERS graduated with a degree in journalism from the University of Montana in 1975. After taking time off to ride his bicycle 5,000 miles across the United States, he worked in New York with *Field & Stream* magazine and in Montana with *Montana Outdoors* magazine. In 1977, he moved to Spokane to become the outdoor editor for *The Spokesman-*

Review. In that post he has won numerous writing awards and has been recognized as Conservation Writer of the Year by both the Idaho Conservation League and the Washington Environmental Council. Being a full-time outdoor writer, Rich spends much of his time in the field with notebook and camera and writes about both trends and issues in the Inland Northwest. He has been the Far West Regional editor for *Field & Stream* magazine and his work has been in other publications, including *Adventure Cyclist, American Forests, Canoe and Kayak, Outside, Runner's World,* and *The Washington Post.* He also coauthored *Paddle Routes of the Inland Northwest.* Rich was a trustee for the Spokane Mountaineers for six terms. He has hiked and paddled extensively in the western states, particularly with his wife, Meredith, and daughters, Brook and Hillary.

(Photo by Torsten Kjellstrand)

THE MOUNTAINEERS, founded in 1906, is a nonprofit outdoor activity and conservation club, whose mission is "to explore, study, preserve, and enjoy the natural beauty of the outdoors. . . . " Based in Seattle, Washington, the club is now the third-largest such organization in the United States, with 15,000 members and five branches throughout Washington State.

The Mountaineers sponsors both classes and year-round outdoor activities in the Pacific Northwest, which include hiking, mountain climbing, ski-touring, snowshoeing, bicycling, camping, kayaking and canoeing, nature study, sailing, and adventure travel. The club's conservation division supports environmental causes through educational activities, sponsoring legislation, and presenting informational programs. All club activities are led by skilled, experienced volunteers, who are dedicated to promoting safe and responsible enjoyment and preservation of the outdoors.

If you would like to participate in these organized outdoor activities or the club's programs, consider a membership in The Mountaineers. For information and an application, write or call The Mountaineers, Club Headquarters, 300 Third Avenue West, Seattle, WA 98119; 206-284-6310.

The Mountaineers Books, an active, nonprofit publishing program of the club, produces guidebooks, instructional texts, historical works, natural history guides, and works on environmental conservation. All books produced by The Mountaineers Books fulfill the club's mission.

Send or call for our catalog of more than 500 outdoor titles:

The Mountaineers Books
1001 SW Klickitat Way, Suite 201
Seattle, WA 98134
800-553-4453
mbooks@mountaineersbooks.org
www.mountaineersbooks.org

The Mountaineers Books is proud to be a corporate sponsor of Leave No Trace, whose mission is to promote and inspire responsible outdoor recreation through education, research, and partnerships. The Leave No Trace program is focused specifically on human-powered (nonmotorized) recreation.

Leave No Trace strives to educate visitors about the nature of their recreational impacts, as well as offer techniques to prevent and minimize such impacts. Leave No Trace is best understood as an educational and ethical program, not as a set of rules and regulations.

For more information, visit *www.LNT.org*, or call 800-332-4100.